MODERNISM AS A PHILOSOPHICAL PROBLEM

D1570718

For my mother,
Rita Doris Côté Pippin

Modernism as a Philosophical Problem

On the Dissatisfactions of European High Culture

Robert B. Pippin

Basil Blackwell

Copyright © Robert B. Pippin 1991

First published 1991

Basil Blackwell, Inc.
3 Cambridge Center
Cambridge, Massachusetts 02142, USA

Basil Blackwell Ltd
108 Cowley Road, Oxford, OX4 1JF, UK

Library of Congress Cataloging in Publication Data

Pippin, Robert B., 1948–
Modernism as a philosophical problem: on the dissatisfactions of European
high culture/Robert B. Pippin.
p.   cm.
Includes bibliographical references and index.
ISBN 0-631-17258-0   ISBN 0-631-17657-8 (pbk.)
1. Philosophy, Modern – 19th century.   2. Philosophy, Modern – 20th
century.   3. Civilization, Modern – 19th century.   4. Civilization, Modern –
20th century.   I. Title.
B803.P57   1991
190 – dc20

90–38302
CIP

British Library Cataloguing in Publication Data
A CIP catalogue record for this book is available from the British Library.

Typeset in 10.5 on 12 pt Baskerville
by Graphicraft Typesetters, Hong Kong
Printed in Great Britain by T.J. Press Ltd, Padstow, Cornwall

Contents

Acknowledgments

Much of the work on this project owes a great deal to several institutions: to the University of California, San Diego, for a sabbatical and other forms of research assistance; to the University of California for a "President's Research Fellowship in the Humanities," which made possible a year of reading and writing free from administrative and teaching responsibilities; and to the Earhart Foundation of Ann Arbor, Michigan, for a very generous Research Fellowship.

I am also much indebted to several individuals, especially to Stephan Chambers, my editor at Basil Blackwell. Conversations with Mr Chambers were instrumental in conceiving the general form of the book, and I much appreciate his support and encouragement. My thanks too to Ms Annita Christie at Basil Blackwell for much patience and efficiency in the last couple of years. For their kind support of various fellowship and grant applications, I am grateful to Alan Wood, H.S. Harris, Henry Allison, Fred Olafson, Stanley Rosen, Richard Kennington, Jerry Weinberger, Charles Griswold, and Drew Hyland. I have benefited a great deal from correspondence with Stanley Rosen about the issues discussed below, and from comments on individual chapters by Charles Griswold and Drew Hyland. I owe a very substantial debt to several people who generously read and commented on earlier versions of the entire manuscript. These include Jay Bernstein and an anonymous reader, both of whom made several suggestions that led to quite substantial revisions in the last three chapters, and Andrew Feenberg, with whom I have often discussed these topics during very pleasant lunches in La Jolla (where, overlooking the Pacific, entertaining the idea of a "crisis" in modernity requires intense and sustained concentration).

Special thanks too, to my son, Andrew Pippin, who kindly agreed to various domestic arrangements that made my work day much easier, and to my wife, Joan, without whose support and understanding this work, and much else, would have been impossible.

And worse I may be yet. The worst is not,
So long as we can say, "This is the worst."

Shakespeare, *King Lear*

1

Introduction: The Modernity Problem

1 Sensing the End

This book presents an interpretation and assessment of the current controversy within the Western academy about the status and fate of modernity, particularly the dispute about such extreme issues as the end or completion or the very "legitimacy" of modernity. Although the problem of the nature or even the existence of a modern epoch is a very old one, this elusive topic has recently attracted renewed attention in a wide variety of academic disciplines and has come to involve very different issues in literary theory, art, architecture and music criticism, social history, political theory, sociology, and philosophy. Specialists in such disciplines have always been used to categorizing historical epochs ("the Classical Age," "the Dark Ages," "the Enlightenment," "neoclassicism," "romanticism," etc.) and it has recently come to seem to many an important fact (to be "reported" to government bureaucracies)[1] that contemporary Western civilization might no longer be continuous with what had been categorized, vaguely if commonly, as modernity. The current age is better understood as a radical break with such a tradition; perhaps its distinct character is simply and exclusively this negative relationship to the failed promises of its past, as in the popular, wholly negative designation, "postmodernity."[2]

This claim that modernity could be coming to a kind of end, in much the same way that classical Greek civilization ended, or the feudal world ended, is both intriguing and extraordinarily ambitious. What is most intriguing is that those interested in such claims about modernity are usually interested in far more than an account of an historical event, as in the political and military demise of the Greek empire, or the visible signs of the weakening influence of the Catholic

Church in late medieval Europe. The general idea is roughly that the end of such forms of civilized life involved a variety of internal intellectual and moral crises, that many of the fundamental ideals officially pursued in such epochs began to lose their public authority under the weight of effective criticism, or that the general view of the good life shared in such communities came to seem inappropriate in a changing historical setting, often prompting revolutionary intellectual and social activity. The same kinds of doubts about the legitimacy and authority of many modern presuppositions about humanism, consciousness, rationality, subjectivity, national identity, the Western European canon of great texts, gender, or even being itself, are often involved in contemporary questions about the "end of modernity."

Adding to the complexity, many participants in the current postmodernity discussion understand themselves to be raising issues and pursuing options in a way far more radical than, or at least very different from, the first mid- to late nineteenth-century discussion of a purported modernity crisis. Within the arts at least, and among some philosophers, it is, after all, not news that what some regard as the great achievements of European modernity, such things as an urban, cosmopolitan civilization, material prosperity, a methodologically secure, rationally grounded science, individual liberty, might also reflect a dangerously naive optimism, merely class-based interests, might represent or presuppose disguised forms of repression, or might contribute to a stultifying, boring, even a pointless life. One now hears, however, that such intense dissatisfaction with the characteristic optimism of bourgeois civilization, so prominent in literary and artistic "modernism," was still too indebted to modern ideas of subjectivity, or rationality, or the "metaphysics of presence." According to such commentators, the great nineteenth- and early twentieth-century experience of the "death of God," or its skepticism about any universal or objective values, and its disillusionment with the modern notion of progress, simply led either to a sense of absence (a "nihilism" still tied to traditional expectations) or a new "divination" of man and human power (as in modernism's celebration of aesthetic experience and the ominous rhetoric of the likes of Spengler and Jünger). Postmodernism would then be understood as the "death of *man*" or of such humanism and its faith in human power and transcendence, as well as of God; the end of all attempts to discover ultimate "origins," or a certain method, or to revolutionize human consciousness.[3]

My main interest will be in this first, nineteenth-century experience, the "romanticism to modernism" cycle in literature, art, and, predominantly, in philosophy, the cycle in which the "modernity ideal" first began to lose its hold on the European imagination.[4] Later in the book, I discuss the relation between such early, "anti-bourgeois" dissatisfactions, and the contemporary issue of "post-modernism," at least as the issue has come to be understood in philosophy.

As I shall try to make clear in this chapter, there is, roughly, a common, basic issue at stake in many such discussions, one I shall designate simply as the problem of "autonomy," or of genuine self-determination or self-rule. This issue in many different forms stretches over the historical problem of modernity as itself a category – whether an origination, or new self-grounding in history is possible – and includes the familiar issues of social and political self-determination, the possibility of genuine, rational enlightenment, and the appeal of romantic expressivism. It is also central to many of the earliest European doubts, in the arts as well as in philosophy, about modernity; suspicions, one might say, about the failure of attempts at true autonomy. As I shall try to show, this complex of problems should lead us back to a number of philosophical issues – problems about the very possibility of autonomy, critical self-reflection, and self-rule – most at home in the German Idealist tradition and its aftermath, a tradition, I shall claim, not yet accorded the attention it deserves in the current discussion.[5] Simply put, in the account I give, so many come to be so dissatisfied because modernity seemed to promise what it finally could not deliver – an individually and collectively self-determining life – or because they lost faith that they knew what that would mean, or because some came to believe that it was not such a wise thing to have promised in the first place. Such dissatisfactions, I shall claim, all involve a variety of philosophical issues best addressed in the works of Kant, Hegel, Nietzsche, and Heidegger.

Before we attempt to specify such a philosophical version of the modernity problem, however, a number of preliminary remarks are required. First, we need to admit that all such discussions, contemporary and *fin de siècle*, are almost unmanageably abstract and ambitious because they presuppose so much. In particular, they often first presuppose some (occasionally rather potted) account of the nature of the modern enterprise itself, and some more detailed reading of its recent history and especially of recent manifestations of a purported "crisis."

The first question, the question of just what is supposed to be ending, is a book-length topic in itself. In the first chapter below I shall rashly attempt a survey of the various issues involved. However, initially the character of the "modernity" in question is relatively uncontroversial. At such a level, what can be said is that there is something that can be identified as the modern social and intellectual tradition. (Even though the term "the Enlightenment" is often used to refer only to an eighteenth-century French movement, for reasons I hope will become clear in what follows, I shall use the terms "the Enlightenment," "modernity," "the modern sensibility," etc., interchangeably.)[6] Moreover, it is pretty clear that this enterprise includes such things as: the emergence of the "nation state," a political unit constituted by a common language and tradition, with an authority transcending local feudal fealty and based on some explicit common representative, even, eventually, on some self-understanding or "principle"; more and more ambitious claims for the supreme authority of "reason" in human affairs, contra the claims of tradition, the ancestors, and, especially, the Church (the public status of reason, it was hoped, could provide the social integration and cultural stability long a function of tradition and religion); claims for the authority of natural science (modelled basically on mathematical physics) in the investigation of nature (including human nature); the corresponding "demystification" of life, especially natural phenomena; an insistence on the natural rights of all individuals, above all else the right to freedom, the maximum expression of an individual's self-determination; the domination of social life by a free market economy, with its attendant phenomena of wage labor, urbanization, and the "private ownership of the means of production"; a belief in, if not the perfectibility, then at least the improvability of mankind, and a commitment (at least within the "official culture") to a variety of virtues that originate in Christian humanism: tolerance, sympathy, prudence, charity, and so on. In the aesthetic domain, modern forms of artistic expression eventually came to be understood as not bound to the imitation of classical models, to be distinct, and even, in the famous *Quarrelle*, to be superior to such models. Above all else, modernity is characterized by the view that human life after the political and intellectual revolutions of the seventeenth and eighteenth centuries is fundamentally better than before, and most likely will, thanks to such revolutions, be better still.

For many the philosophical "issue" or problem of modernity (as opposed to its historical, social, or economic dimensions) is simply whether there are or are not "good arguments" for the claims made by Descartes, or Leibniz, or Hobbes, or Rousseau in behalf of the new way of ideas, or the new approach to political life. For many others, however, such discussions often simply already reflect a number of modern presuppositions about what will count as a good argument, and we need a broader and more inclusive view of modernity as a whole before we can begin any philosophical assessment, or even know what to argue about.

And there are various forms of now well known, more summary, more inclusive characterizations of such an epochal self-consciousness. Modernity is sometimes understood as most importantly a rejection of antiquity. (We would probably now call modernity "the post-classical".) The end or *telos* of human life for many classical authors was the peaceful contemplation of the order of the cosmos, and the place of human being within such a cosmos. This was understood to be a desirable end even though its achievement as a way of life was highly unlikely and there was no art or science that could serve effectively as a means to such an end. Given our inescapable finitude, the occurrence of such a life of pure contemplation was wholly a matter of chance. For many modern authors, starting roughly with Machiavelli, this notion was rejected in favor of a different conception of the end of human life – "lower," but given the right *techne*, achievable – the satisfaction of the passions. Nature was to be mastered, not contemplated; the distinction between theory and *techne* was collapsed and modern humanism, as a kind of technological self-assertion, was born. The ancients had been dreamers, orienting their reflection from a utopian view of what ought to be. The moderns have awakened from such slumbers; "light" has dawned, and our reflection will henceforth securely, even certainly, be oriented from the way things are.

To be sure, such distinctly modern claims emerged in a complex context, one in which a great many religious, traditional, and classical notions still had great authority, and were still invoked, often with confusing effects, in many early modern manifestos.[7] Sometimes what appears startlingly modern, even impious, rhetoric, such as Descartes's call to "master nature" and "enjoy the fruits of the earth without toil" appears within what at least seems to be a relatively conventional scholastic, theological framework. (Sometimes too, the modern reader is so struck by such passages about the purposes of modern science, that one can forget that it took well over two centuries before the steam engine, electricity, and other "fruits" from the "tree of knowledge" finally made something like Descartes's picture a plausible one, and longer still for the science he hoped would provide the most obvious benefit, medicine.)

Complexities aside for the moment, though, it was this standard, recognizable, intensely philosophical Enlightenment self-under-standing which, sometime around the latter half of the nineteenth century in continental Europe, began to be radically called into question (as first in an indirect, non-philosophical way by poets, novelists and painters) thereby inaugurating an accelerating and more theoretical series of ideology critiques, genealogies, psychologic-al unmaskings, "death of God" theologies, aesthetic experimentation, and assorted dismantlings and revolutions still with us today.[8] The idea of a "crisis" in modernity's self-confidence became more and more popular in the high culture of European art, literature, and philosophy, although the expression of this idea took many different forms.

As we shall see, many such reactions involved a renewed attention to the problem of human finitude, an emphasis on the limitations of human self-determination and self-understanding (or an emphasis on the "ideological" pretensions of the modern assertion of human power), although there was little emerging consensus about the nature of such limits or the proper consequences to draw from the realization. In many ways the question of human finitude, or of our natural or biological or ecological or historical or ontological "boundaries," became one of the central *aporiai* of modern and post-modern self-consciousness. The idea that the achievement of greater scientific mastery and some success in achieving economic and political self-determination had all been made far too much of, that, in many important areas of human life, such achievements were irrelevant and tended to create a dangerous and superficial optimism, began to take hold. But from its first appearance, it was very unclear how to state or formulate this sense of limitations or finitude. Those who did were immediately accused of an atavistic premodernism, religious piety, nostalgia for antiquity and its strict (racist, sexist) hierarchies of rank, and so on. Contemporary attempts to state the same suspicions about modernity by reference to the hiddenness of Being, the ever present play of human power, the all-determining language of the unconscious, or the failure of reflection (the omni-presence of text) have merely reformulated this familiar dialectic.[9]

Many other such nineteenth-century reactions, starting roughly with Baudelaire's essays, began to insist that the basic problem with the "official" or Enlightenment, bourgeois notion of modernity was just the sense of limitations or finitude it presupposed. Modernity's great problem, as envisioned by a line of thinkers from Baudelaire to Nietzsche, was that it had not been "modern" enough, that the restless, perpetually self-transforming, anomic, transient spirit of modernism had to be affirmed much more honestly and consistently, and not qualified by the residual Christian moralism of Kant or the insistence on sobriety, calculation, and prudence typical of thinkers like Smith or Locke, or even by the typically modern hope for the public authority of philosophy and science in culture as a whole. For many of these writers, an "aestheticization" of the modern spirit, an emphasis on originality, constant novelty, the ceaseless creation of new forms of life, and so forth, would fulfill its promise.[10]

Finally, for still others, stretching from Max Weber (and to some extent Freud) to the Herbert Marcuse of *One-Dimensional Man* and the Saul Bellow of *Mr Sammler's Planet*, modernity is a spiritual disaster, a demeaning routinization of human life, but a kind of necessary fate, so successful in its transformation of life and human desire as to be itself untransformable. In Weber's famous words, the "whole cosmos of the modern economic order" is an "iron cage," producing its "specialists without spirit, sensualists without heart," and its "delusion" that "this nullity . . . has achieved a level of development never before attained by mankind."[11]

And, as just noted, such doubts about modernity, now long-standing and much discussed, have become especially prominent again in our own age, although for a number of reasons. For one thing, the great self-confidence and progressivism characteristic of the modern enterprise and especially what seemed its nineteenth-century fruition, all looked even more difficult to accept after the historical horrors of the twentieth century. The fact that "art, intellectual pursuits, the development of the natural sciences, many branches of scholarship flourished in close spatial, temporal proximity to massacre and the death camps"[12] has raised for many doubts about not only modernity's self-assurances, but about all of Western culture, has raised the issue "Why did humanistic traditions and models of conduct prove so fragile a barrier against political bestiality?"[13]

For another, the contemporary problem of modernity has assumed an intensely political, even geo-political form. Many contemporary discussions of social "modernization" have become simultaneously intense and charged debates about "Westernization." Some developing nations have discovered, often to their chagrin, that the introduction of such things as efficient, differentiated systems of management, an emphasis on science and technology in school curricula, and the encouragement of individual initiative and a critical spirit in society, all bring along a variety of unanticipated expectations and often have profound consequences for the traditional authority of what had been the dominant religion or political ideology.[14] A modern society, at least as it has come to be understood in the West, seems to have a dynamic all its own, introducing rationalization and productive efficiency, promoting a sense of individual responsibility, but also threatening tradition and social integration, and promoting anomie, consumerism, alienation, disaffection; even, perhaps, a commercial-ized culture of kitsch.[15]

For another, in Western Europe since the 1960s, the political and especially the ecological implications of a general allegiance to mod-ernity have become objects of a great deal of scrutiny, and have given the modernity debate its current highly rhetorical character. In the endless struggle of the intellectual Left to find ways to puncture the smugness and blind self-satisfaction of official bourgeois culture, the latest and perhaps last field of battle has become the question of modernity itself, of the very possibility of what some consider the essentially bourgeois modern revolution, the confident movement that destroyed in a few generations what had seemed unassailable for millennia, and that promised a future of security, empowerment, peace, and contentment.

2 German Homesickness

For the most part in what follows, I shall be interested in presenting an interpretation and assessment of how the issue of modernity originally came to be not so much a cultural or social or political but a philosophical problem. By posing the issue this way, I mean to try to identify presuppositions about the human subject, self-consciousness, freedom, and human sociality unavoidably involved at the core of the modern project, and to explore the attempts by various thinkers to think through and to attempt to justify or re-formulate or, finally, attack such presuppositions. This will mean, of course, a great narrowing of focus (especially a concentration on the philosophical dimensions of the "autonomy" problem) and will push to the margin some of the social concerns that have animated writers from Carlyle to Marx to Adorno and "culture critics" from Baudelaire to Simmel to Enzensberger and Eagleton. By doing so I do not mean to imply any large-scale claim about the centrality of philosophy, or that things have ended up as they are because of what philosophers published. To put it in a relatively tame way, issues in philosophy often simply express most economically and dramatically a variety of issues that pervade the social and cultural fabric, and philosophical language, if nothing else, can be an economical way of discussing a number of these issues.

To be sure, this immediately introduces a much larger controversy which, for reasons of space, I must avoid, or at least postpone. Many commentators on the modern experience have argued that the problems addressed in what follows simply cannot be understood without a deeper analysis of the social and historical context within which a distinctly modern philosophy, as well as modern art and literature, arose. Modernity, they argue, is essentially a bourgeois experience; its self-understanding reflects the self-understanding required in that historical epoch dominated by the middle class, with its private property, market economy, and liberal democratic institutions. This complex claim promises some sort of explanatory connection between the growing dissatisfactions, dilemmas or "contradictions" faced by "bourgeois philosophy" and the social organization of production in capitalist societies, that the modernity crisis in the late nineteenth century reflects the inability of capitalist societies to reproduce and legitimate themselves.[16]

There is still a rich and controversial debate about what such a claim for a connection might mean, and whether such an account of modernity as "ideology" can be given. Here I need only note that whatever is eventually decided about those two issues, we shall not be able to proceed very far in understanding such a connection if we do not have a clear, sensitive picture of the actual internal dynamic of European philosophy's growing dissatisfaction with the principles and promises of Enlightenment claims about reason and subjectivity. My own view is that there is a great deal to be learned about the sufficiency of modernity itself, in its social and economic as well as cultural dimensions, from thinking through the philosophical fate of the notion of Enlightenment modernity, but I propose no general defense of that claim here, and concentrate on the details. Along the way, I shall try at least to suggest how these philosophic issues are connected with more familiar "dissatisfactions."

In the interpretation I shall present, the most successful and comprehensive formulation and assessment of the nature and legitimacy of modernity began in the German Idealist tradition, particularly, first, in the work of Kant and Hegel, and then in two thinkers greatly influenced by if highly critical of that tradition, Friedrich Nietzsche and Martin Heidegger. That orientation will, I realize, provoke a good deal of disagreement with those who prefer other focal points for an assessment of modernity. After all, the Idealist tradition, and almost all of the "culture of dissatisfaction" I shall be considering, could be seen as continuous with the indisputably first document of such dissatisfaction, Rousseau's *Second Discourse*, and there is much to be learned from prolonged attention to Rousseau.[17] And, as already noted, there are many who think who think of philosophical formulations as mere symptoms, that the origin and current fate of the idea of modernity has much more to do with quite contingent social and historical events than with philosophic programs. So the rather "German" approach I am suggesting needs a bit of an introduction.

My proposal proceeds from the two premises asserted above: that those thinkers most successful in identifying, justifying and eventually doubting the deepest assumption in modernity's self-understanding (the assertion of autonomy) were those in the post-Kantian German tradition, and that this story of the initial attractiveness of such a philosophic self-understanding and eventual doubts about it, is central to any successful narrative of the social authority of many modern institutions.[18]

Indeed one of the things that distinguishes this tradition (let us say the "Kant to Heidegger" cycle), especially when compared with the French and British, is its intense preoccupation with the very possibility of a truly modern epoch, and the various hesitations, doubts, qualifications and, in general, dissatisfactions, which emerged in considerations of this question. For some historians, this should all be explained by reference to a romantic, or religious or even mystical strain in German culture generally. I present here no view about the cultural or religious origins of the oddly problematic fate of the idea of modernity in German culture, or about its social consequences in twentieth-century history. And I am ignoring figures like Lessing or Mendelssohn or Heine or the neo-Kantians. My point is to try to explain, sympathetically, what bothered so many German philosophers about modernity, and to show that what bothered them is of great relevance for thinking about and assessing many other late modern phenomena in European high culture.[19]

That so many were both greatly enthused and greatly bothered by the idea of modernity points to a number of issues straight away. Modernity, as the name suggests, implies a decisive break in an intellectual tradition, an inability to rely on assumptions and practices taken for granted in the past. Indeed one of, if not the deepest issue at stake in both the very earliest formulations, and the late nineteenth- and late twentieth-century discussions of modernity, is the problem of historical discontinuity, a "revolution" in human thought responsible for either a great "discovery" about method, or later a great "unmasking" about power, text or being. If the assumption of such a break is to make sense, we shall need to be able to defend some view of the determinate insufficiencies of premodern (or perhaps modern) institutions. What, the question becomes, could possibly have been so originally wrong-headed as to require a "revolution," (both Copernican and political) an "instauration," a "founding of the sciences," a radically new beginning?

This point immediately leads to another much more complex issue. It is already obvious that the whole question of what modernity claims for itself, and what philosophic issues are raised by such claims, presupposes a kind of historical narrative not traditionally (until Hegel) treated as itself a philosophic issue. Originally, the conventional view was that there was no distinctive philosophical problem raised by reliance on such a reading of history, because the substance of the narrative was simple: everybody pre-modern had been wrong, confused by religious prejudices, a naive science, and bad arguments. And we no longer are. This began to change with Leibniz's more "reconciliationist" approach to philosophical history, and eventually became a much more complicated issue when many modernists began to suspect themselves (and their own tendentious narratives) of reliance on the same sort of contingent, ungrounded conventions, even prejudices, as pre-modern thinkers. As we shall see, the problem of the "legitimacy" or the "failure" of modernity was soon deeply entangled in the issue of how to interpret the historical origin and fate of modernity.

It will take a while for us the see the emergence of such problems, particularly in the thought of Nietzsche and Heidegger. At the outset, the issues were more straightforward. I want to focus attention especially on the way in which Kant and the language of "critical philosophy," his attack on "dogmatism" in all its forms, first dominated the German discussion of this issue. Such a view of pre-modern thought (as dogmatic, insufficiently self-conscious, unable to explain or account for its own possibility) provided the framework for the first attempt to think through Kant's achievement in these "epochal" terms, to make modernity ("the achievement of full self-consciousness") itself a philosophical problem, G.W.F. Hegel's idealism.

Kant, more simply put, was the first thoroughgoing "philosophical modernist" and so also first manifests some of the deepest *aporiai* in modernity. He rejects the very possibility of what had been the foundation of pre-modern and early modern thought – rationalist and theological metaphysics, on the one hand, and empiricism on the other – and insists on a thorough critical or self-determining reflection. Reason can now completely determine for itself what is to count as nature itself; but (and here the beginning of the *aporia*) in some sense cannot be satisfied with the result, must be dissatisfied with its "ignorance of things in themselves." Or, pure reason can be practical; we can determine the will on the basis of a strictly universalizable maxim; however, there is little chance that we could ever actually overcome our self-interest sufficiently for this to be very likely. We must settle for "legality," not morality. Later, as I shall try to show, the issues created by Kant's hesitant revolution and its Hegelian reception were to cast a long shadow over the work of the two later thinkers most identified with European doubts about modernity, Nietzsche and Heidegger.

Moreover, it is at least initially plausible to suggest that this philosophical context is not irrelevant to the swarm of aesthetic and social issues mentioned above. It is widely accepted that much of what distinguishes modern social and political life is its appeal to distinctly philosophical (and distinctly modern) notions of rationality, right, and justification, and much of what is distinctive about modern art is the intense philosophical self-consciousness of the likes of Manet, Flaubert, Baudelaire, Wagner, Eliot, Pound, and so many others, their sense of art as the pursuit of some self-consciously held aesthetic idea, and their sense of the dependence of that idea on the fate of modernity, on what kind of "new" art was needed "now." Of course not many of these figures were much concerned with the modernity issue in German Idealism and the Nietzschean and Heideggerean reaction to that tradition (although some were), but, again, I hope to show the value of that tradition and that reaction for thinking through and assessing the insistent claims made on us by modernist art and criticism, claims about a modern crisis and an aesthetic redemption.[20]

This is especially true of one issue in particular, already suggested by the above remarks on Kant. The Kantian name for that issue, the great, single modernity problem in the German tradition, is "autonomy." Most generally construed, such an ideal simply expresses the oldest classical philosophical ideal: the possibility that human beings can regulate and evaluate their beliefs by rational self-reflection, that they can free themselves from interest, passion, tradition, prejudice and autonomously "rule" their own thoughts, and that they can determine their actions as a result of self-reflection and rational evaluation, an evaluation the conclusions of which ought to bind any rational agent.

But the classical idea that ignorance is a kind of slavery and knowledge the only true liberation, while continuous with much of the Enlightenment self-understanding, also assumed an ideal that was at odds with emerging modern thought. The assumption that the cosmos was an ordered and purposive whole, and that an individual could be said to be free (truly "who he was") only when functioning purposively in such a whole, began to look like an indefensible anachronism within the modern (non-teleological) view of nature. To be sure, some aspects of the classical ideal survived this transformation in the understanding of nature. Within modern "naturalism" a recognition of our wholly natural status was a precondition of an enlightened (an presumably better) life, a realization that freedom could only be a freedom from external constraints in the satisfaction of wants, and that autonomy was the power to satisfy these wants efficiently, that reason was the "slave of the passions." It survived also in the romantic qualification of such views, in the view that one could be "estranged" from or foreign to one's own wants, that many did not reflect one's essential or true self. To be free in this sense would be to be true to one's real, not merely apparent nature, to be able to "express" and realize one's individual nature.

But with Kant especially a more radical (and I shall claim, more consistently modern) view of such an ideal emerged, one no longer tied to any view of the realization of some natural end or passion or essential self. What distinguishes the post-Kantian expression of this ideal is the invocation of what Hegel called "absolute freedom," true "self-determination," in explaining this ideal.

In Kant's practical philosophy, for example, autonomy does not require the power to satisfy one's wants, or a kind of personal authenticity. True autonomy requires that I will only those actions (adopt as my maxim only those maxims) which can be consistently willed by all other rational agents. I "rule" myself by not allowing my contingently formed desires to be the "determining ground of the will." And Kant's general insistence on autonomy is even much broader than this theme in his practical philosophy.

Reason itself, in all its manifestations, does not, in Kant, discover the human place within Nature or serve some natural end or passion; it "legislates to Nature"; it does not discover the good life, it pre- scribes the rules for human activity, be Nature as it may. Such a "spontaneous subjectivity," completely determining for itself what to accept as evidence about the nature of things, and legislating to itself its proper course of action, is, if nothing else, the appropriate image of modernity's understanding of itself as revolutionary and "self-grounding," and so an invaluable forcus for raising a number of questions. The general "German" idea of self-determination or a self-grounding is, Hegel says, the principle of modernity, as funda- mental in that tradition to the modern authority of natural science as it is to modern claims for liberal-democratic institutions. And it is the principle that has generated the most suspicion among those con- vinced that this is what would have to be defended if modernity were to be defended, but who remain dubious about such prospects.

Thus on the reading I propose, the possibility of a "self-reassurance"[21] of modernity does not finally depend on any technol- ogical success or failure, on "Cartesian foundationalism," or on the achievement of any unified, scientific or naturalistic world view. Kant was, to a large and decisive degree, right about the limitations of all such proposals, and right that being modern demands instead being radically critical, that the modern subject can rely only "on it- self," its own spontaneous self-legislation, in determining the agenda of an age freed from dogmatic dependence. Whatever ends up being the historically decisive result of the modern revolution – that, for example, we end up regarding ourselves and our capacities in essent- ially "neurophysiological" language, or on some sort of analogy with "texts" – it will, from this Kantian perspective, still be a self- determined result, one we shall end up imposing on ourselves, rather than simply discovering.[22] And this means that such a proposal or historical event will simply re-open the central modern philo- sophical question: by what criterion should such a collective self- determination occur, a criterion we cannot simply be said to "share" by being human, or to "find" inscribed in Platonic heaven?

This means the appropriate question at issue (asked many, many times after Kant) becomes whether such a subject can be so radically independent or self-determining, and especially whether such self- legislation can be said to be rational, whether its results can be said to apply universally to any agent attempting such critical freedom, all because the results are what such an agent "would himself deter- mine." On the account I present, Hegel best realizes such a project, or most successfully rejects Kant's inconsistent qualifications on such an enterprise, and attempts to think it through to its conclusion, and Nietzsche represents, in effect, Hegel's most problematic opponent, the thinker who best raises the question of the whole possibility and even desirability of such a "self-reassurance," a self-conscious justification. The issues raised by this confrontation, I shall suggest, are not in any significant way resolved or transcended in later attempts at a "re-thinking" of the whole modern project (or a suspicion of the whole autonomy ideal), and I focus on Heidegger's Nietzsche lectures to make this point, or at least to suggest why it might be so. The picture I present thus depends on a rather non-standard reading of Kant and Hegel and so raises the philosophic issue of modernity in a way not currently represented by those with some hope for a partial revival of a pre-modern perspective (Arendt or Strauss or MacIntyre), contemporary, often very non-traditional, and highly qualified defenders of modernity (Habermas, Rorty, Toulmin, Taylor), or those convinced that a postmodern age is either upon us or ought to be hastened or resisted (Heidegger, Lyotard, Vattimo, Jameson, and many, many others).

My intention was to write a small and manageable book about such issues, to present a readable exposition of the philosophical problems at stake, to offer a plausible narrative about the development of the problem and to try to suggest the importance and relevance of the philosophical context for various non-philosophical manifestations of the "modernity problem." I have therefore tried to keep scholarly issues confined to footnotes, and, for the most part, to avoid the details of textual and interpretive controversy (although, admittedly, much of what is said in the following could be challenged on those grounds). To facilitate references, I have tried to make use of standard English translations, although I have made emendations where necessary, and to refer in the majority of cases to the English language secondary literature or translations of important secondary sources. Along the way in the account, I have raised several questions about the general notion of a modernity crisis that I hope will be of interest to literature and art critics, sociologists and political theorists, or anyone interested in what Nietzsche reported to be the "afterglow of European civilization", even, perhaps, "the age of the last men."

2

Modernity and Modernism

1 Modernity as a Historical Category

Common philosophic claims characteristic of the founders of early modernity are no easier to identify than common philosophic dissatisfactions in what appears to be the ever-weakening hold of the idea of modernity on the nineteenth-century European imagination. When we raise questions about the origin and the decline of the modern sensibility, we enter a much explored, tangled maze of difficult questions. Is it even possible to identify a common modern sensibility? When and for what reasons did it come to seem important to Christian Europeans to think of themselves as modern? What is the connection, if any, between the notion of modernity and the Christian European experience? When and for what reasons did it come to seem to post-Christian Europeans not so important to characterize their tradition this way, to think of modernity as a "belated" or secularized Christian phenomenon, or a "myth", or a piece of bourgeois ideology, or as having failed or even ended?

This is not a historical study but it is important to begin with some sense, however brief, of the philosophical problems immediately raised by invoking the historical category of modernity, especially if we are to discuss eventually the sweeping, quite various nineteenth-century European disaffections with the whole notion. As I have suggested, there is both a common modern ethos and some sort of common, emerging dissatisfaction with that ethos, and although any summary will run a number of risks, we can't orient ourselves without at least a brief attempt at one. In this chapter, I shall try to provide a rather high-altitude survey of the major issues involved in the identification of a modern epoch and an equally general summary of the growing European doubts about the official promises of such a new beginning, many most visible in the beginnings of aesthetic "modernism." These historical and cultural issues will, I hope, introduce us to the underlying philosophical controversies.

The very idea of the modern, if we begin there, is, it is safe to say, very much a product of the Western European, Christian tradition, perhaps its most representative or typical product, even though the term itself is literally of Roman origin and predates by some time the sixteenth- and seventeenth-century formulations of an explicit, revolutionary project. It is widely conceded that the term came into existence sometime in the late fifth or early sixth century (derived from the adverb *modo*, "recently" or "of this time") and that a significant, even problematic distinction between *moderni* and *antiqui* can first be noted in the speculations of the Roman historian Cassiodorus about the virtues and practices of the "old" Rome in this "new" time, so much under the influence of the East and the Germans.[1] In that context, the original problem was not, as it was to become, a kind of opposition between ancients and moderns, but a way of "translating" ancient wisdom and practices into a new context.

This, though, was only the beginning of what would later be a very long history of the notion of the modern in Christian Europe. Basically, the story is one of the gradual emergence of modernity as far more than a chronological category, a simple way of marking "now" versus "then." This began to occur when the "now" came to be understood as something other than a continuation or transformation, even a radical transformation, of the ancient ways, and instead as marking an age of genuine novelty, an era with assumptions about the highest or fundamental things incompatible with past assumptions. It was this notion of a new beginning, or of an instauration or founding, that would generate so many philosophical problems and many factors helped prepare the way for its emergence.[2]

As is often pointed out, Judaism and especially Christianity, by their very nature, helped promote such a general historical or "epochal," revolutionary consciousness, and this by virtue of their very unGreek notions of eschatological time, a God beyond or outside of nature, involved in the history of a people or mankind, and especially by virtue of the Christian notion of the Incarnation, a decisive, revolutionary moment in time, before and after which all was different.[3] Such a general view of things was bound to make it easier to think in an epochal or revolutionary way, to foster some general sense of the unacceptable or unredeemed nature of the present, of the need for salvation and a hope for the future's redemption of the present, and to create the intellectual problem of what to say about the period and peoples who lived before this decisive event; especially, for Christians, about the Jews and pagan antiquity.[4]

In early Christianity this problem was secondary to an attention to the historical future, since the temporary status of the secular or fallen world was much emphasized, and belief in an immanent Second Coming was widespread. When it became more and more unlikely that one's chief historical stance should simply be a preparation for the apocalypse, the problem of temporality became more complex and numerous issues involving the proper Christian reconciliation with the actual world, human historical institutions, and the past, became much more prominent. So Christianity, it is said, with its linear, eschatological, progressive and revolutionary concept of time, prepared the ground for a later, much different sort of revolution and *eschaton*.

The different and more complex question of how much of modernity's historical and revolutionary self-consciousness ought to be viewed as a "secularization" of such Christian themes has recently become quite controversial and I shall return to the issue shortly. We ought also to not first some of the other major stages along the way in the development of a distinctive and philosophically charged notion of modernity.

In part, that story is the story of images. Sometime around the twelfth century, representatives of Christian European civilization came to be sufficiently convinced of the achievements of such a cultural project that the question arose of how to state properly the nature of the relation between modern and ancient civilizations, even to state, however tentatively, the superiority not just of the Christian religion, but of the Christian world. The famous image associated with the "School of Chartres" expresses these initial, still tentative affirmations. John of Salisbury writes in his *Metalogicon* (1159),

> We frequently know more, not because we have moved ahead by our own natural ability, but because we are supported by the mental strength of others, and possess riches that we have inherited from our forefathers. Bernard of Chartres used to compare us to puny dwarfs perched on the shoulders of giants. He pointed out that we see more and farther than our predecessors, not because we have keener vision or greater height, but because we are lifted up and borne aloft on their gigantic stature.[5]

Of course, this reconciliation issue also arises in a different way for St Thomas in his attempt to read the Philosopher, Aristotle, as having anticipated Christian metaphysics and ethics. Thomas thus might be said to have pioneered the art of "historical reconstruction" so prominent in much contemporary philosophy of science. According to such views earlier figures in science or philosophy, while wrong in their theories, were as right as they could have been in their time. Thus the ancients can be read and profitably studied, since they reveal both how much of what would turn out to be Christian metaphysics can be known by unaided reason, and yet still how little can be known without divine revelation and grace. The deeper tensions, however, in the ancient and the emerging modern world view were soon to become more prominent, and the notion of helpful giants or brilliant anticipations would give way to more polemical contrasts.

This shift begins to be visible in the idea of a new beginning or a rebirth prominent in the Renaissance. It is to the early Renaissance that we owe the familiar periodization of history into antiquity, the Middle Ages, and Modernity, and to thinkers like Petrarch in the fourteenth century that we owe the notion of modernity as a kind of awakening from a long, "dark" sleep. Of course this illumination was explained as a rediscovery of antiquity, but, and this is the significant fact, it was not understood simply as a conservative or nostalgic reaction, an insistence that we return to the old ways because, as in many future reactionary moments, the modern or contemporary world had created chaos or confusion. Paradoxically, the return to the old was viewed as birth, *rinascita*. It was the living, contemporary world that had become old, dark, dead, and it wasn't long before the novelty and distinctness of the new humanism, the new celebration of human power, or the recreation in a new way of ancient glory, was the chief emphasis.(6)

There were, of course, immediate expressions of caution about such a heady sense of power and novelty. Montaigne, especially, began to express doubts about the danger of novel social changes and potential political upheavals, and Pascal, while a partisan of much of the new science, defended the superiority of the ancients in "matters of the heart," in areas where "research" was impossible. But by the end of the seventeenth century modernity could more and more be understood as fundamentally incompatible with and superior to antiquity, and there was, to say the least, a growing unease about the possibility and desirability of a truly "modern" Christianity.[7]

This was particular clear in the famous late seventeenth, early eighteenth-century *Quarrelle des anciens et des modernes*, the dispute (known in England as the Battle of the Books) about the relative superiority of ancient and modern literature, and especially about the suitability of the ancients as models of literary practice. The proponents of modernity, the likes of Perrault and Fontenelle, did not mount what we would now regard as a deep or convincing case. In fact, the whole dispute now seems simply petty to modern readers. Homer is imprecise and unscientific because he says Odysseus was recognized by his dog after twenty years, and we know that dogs cannot live that long. (Oh, replies Boileau, what about that famous dog of our own king who lived for twenty-two years!) Homer has no "taste," is a primitive writer, because he allows a hero, Achilles, to say such things as "dog-face." We must be superior because we simply have more rules to follow. And we must have a superior moral sensibility, something we should expect to be reflected in our art, because of our Christianity. And so on.

Again, what is important about this dispute is the evidence it provides for the growing credibility of the idea of the modern as incompatible with antiquity, or even the early Christian age, and so for the beginning of the great philosophical problem this conviction would create. In this case the issues are matters of taste, and do not permit a very wide field for discussion. The problem emerging becomes much clearer when we consider the wide variety of themes modernity was now beginning to claim as, distinctly, its alone. I've no decisive list of these modern assumptions, but I mean the kind of now very well known, typical claims that explicitly emerged in Bacon and Descartes, the original heroes of the later, eighteenth-century French Enlightenment project, and in the works of participants in that movement itself, in d'Alembert, Condorcet, Diderot and others, such things as: a view of nature as to be mastered, not contemplated; a "mathematizable" and materialistic view of nature; a rejection of final causes in explanation; compared with antiquity, a much more "realistic" view of the ends to be achieved by knowledge, ends such as health, pleasure, freedom from pain, and not, say, "wisdom"; an expectation of great social benefits from the free and unimpeded pursuit of scientific knowledge, and a corresponding assumption that the fundamental cause of human injustice was scarcity, that this problem could be corrected; and a general belief in the progressive and politically ever more enlightened course of human history.

It was the recognition of the deep incompatibility of these claims with virtually all of the traditional assumptions about science, art, religion, and life itself that raised to such prominence the question of a justification or legitimation, a "founding" of modernity. If, that is, the moderns were not doing better, were not finally accomplishing what had long been attempted by human civilization, but, basically, were doing something else, were just "changing the subject," then how could they argue that they were doing what ought to be done? They might argue that the modern project fulfilled the desires of what any "enlightened" human being would want to see satisfied, or could not "naturally" help but want satisfied save for the confusions created by superstition and religion. Or they might argue that the modern project fulfilled what "any rational agent" would choose as the major institutions and practices of society. But such claims obviously trade heavily on notions of enlightenment, self-knowledge, or reason that, potentially, beg the questions at issue. If, in sum, modernity does represent such a discontinuous shift, an adoption of new agenda, then the "question" of modernity, of its worth or significance, seems to be more a question of will, or self-affirmation, rather than reason or a new discovery, and this fact opens the door for a whole host of classical responses.

That is, broadly speaking, from the ancient point of view (expressed as well as anyone by Swift in his account of the floating island of Laputa) much of the modern project is, somewhat paradoxically, both vulgar and excessively utopian. It is vulgar in its systematic pursuit of the lower or ignoble objects of desire (it ignores the hierarchy of human desire), and utopian in its mistaken belief in the power of human *techne* to satisfy these desires, as well as in its mistaken belief that such a satisfaction will resolve the fundamental problem of human justice, or simply, in any sense, will be satisfying. On Swift's devastating, prescient account, the invitation to be modern is simply an invitation to blind oneself to "human concerns," as they are experienced by humans; instead, to impose, willfully, a mathematical order on everything, resulting in a "floating," sterile world, whose inhabitants are incapable of understanding such things as the ignobility of adultery, and whose political and social authority stems exclusively from their power to produce the best weapons (the floating island itself).

From his point of view, the modern project can be best assessed by attention to its historical consequences, by asking whether it can fulfill its extravagant promises. Not only, such an assessment often goes, is its "self-grounding" a mere self-assertion, an act of massive hubristic will, but its implications, presumably more and more visible in modern life, are ultimately disastrous, even nihilistic. The rejection of antiquity means a willful rejection of any rational assessment of a hierarchy of human ends, of the purposes to which the great modern technique is to be applied. On this view, modernity looks to be

thoughtlessly committed both to extending mere biological life inde-
finitely and purposelessly, and to a constant, anxious, preparation
for the obliteration of life. In social terms, modernity promised
us a culture of unintimidated, curious, rational, self-reliant individuals, and it produced, so went the later charge, a herd society, a
race of anxious, timid, conformist "sheep," and a culture of utter
banality.[8]

2 The Legitimacy Problem

Such problems, however, are only the beginning of a very involved
story. The claims made for a kind of "historical autonomy" by the
early modern thinkers and by the official promoters of the Enlightenment were so extreme that they immediately invited compelling
counter-charges: that such proponents had either absurdly over-
estimated the power of unaided human reason and reason-aided
observation and experimentation to discover "what must be known"
in order to live a coherent and satisfying collective life, or had begged
the basic question by simply asserting (or willing) that a coherent
and satisfying collective life was a life based on what a methodologically regulated reason and experiment could determine; or more
simply that the claim for autochthony, or historical independence,
was exaggerated, that, in ways sketched earlier, the self-
understanding of modernity was as much inherited as created, and
even that the modern ideas of a political salvation and of progress
should be understood as "secularizations" of essentially Christian, or
pre-modern ideas.

So, the Great Debate about Modernity was under way, a debate
correctly characterized by Hans Blumenberg as fundamentally about
the "legitimacy" of modernity.[9] This is the question that naturally
arises when the various dimensions of the modern project are well
enough advanced for it to seem to some that a different epoch had
arisen in human history, ruled by different principles, after different
ends;[10] that a discovery had been made, not just about facts, but
about a new way of life. For others, of course, it wasn't all that
different, but a relatively self-deceived repetition and for others still,
it was different only by being so foolish, hubristic, and dangerous. As
we shall see, many of these claims and objections would be repeated
in debates still going on today.

There is no way such an extraordinarily complex issue can be assessed here, <u>but we can at least note that, on both sides of the issue,</u> for those who <u>insisted on the radical novelty of modernity, and for</u> <u>those more reconciliationist, or just dubious,</u> there were plenty of problems. Let us consider the "radical break" proponents first. A kind of dilemma emerges from that way of looking at the implications of the idea of a modern epoch, a "damned if you do, damned if you don't" problem most visible in Descartes. Modernity's early philo-sophic self-understanding has always been captured most concretely by Descartes's famous radical doubt, an extreme rejection of every-thing accepted on trust, authority, tradition, common sense; a suspension of our inclination to accept, and to begin reflection from, the immediate "looks" of things. Given what Descartes himself was discovering about optics, what astronomy had discovered about the apparent motions of heavenly bodies, what the new physics was telling us about matter and motion, and the great sense of natural contingency created by late Medieval notions of divine omni-potence,[11] the common-sense, trusted world of appearances might indeed be thought of as a kind of dream, perhaps a show staged by an evil genius. Things, it was turning out, were not at all as they seemed, indeed as they had seemed, comfortably, for countless generations.

Descartes, that is, should not be understood as a brilliant philo-sophical puzzler, an individual genius manufacturing "how do I know that I am not dreaming" brain-teasers. The palpable philo-sophical paranoia in Descartes is an expression of the historical mood understandably created by the mounting evidence that the "world" of sensible forms, sensible images imprinted on souls, teleological explanation, souls as principles of motion, and earth-centered universes, was a kind of long dream, from which, it appeared, we were now awakening, although the long powerful suc-cess of this show or dream suggested that we might only be beginning another dream.[12]

But Descartes's bold decision, in the face of this historically pro-voked distrust, to treat as false whatever is conceivably dubitable, created the first horn of the dilemma. Once so much is put in doubt (once the world is "lost") on what basis can the human subject "re-establish" a connection with the actual world? On what basis or foundation can a true "science" of reality be built?

Descartes's famous answer to this question simply created *the* mod-ern problem in philosophy. For Descartes's answer is, in a word: method. If we can discover the right method, if we can construct a procedure whose "rules" can in general be argued to produce safe or even "certain" results, repeatable in other experiments, at other times and places, we will have the weapon we need to master the elusive, deceptive nature.[13] In an argument of momentous historical consequences, Descartes argued that the thinking subject's certainty of his own existence, his existence as a thinking or mental being, was the foundation of this method. Whatever may be dubitable, the subject cannot be deceived that he is thinking what he is thinking. This self-certainty became the "measure" of the method. If certain contents of consciousness, ideas, could be said to have internal characteristics or properties identical with the cogito's extraordinary, original self-certainty, then those ideas would count as methodologically certified and thereby as "true."

Descartes called these internal features "clarity and distinctness" and his method was to allow us to begin with the contents of our mental lives alone, all that was left after the doubt had been invoked, and to proceed "outwards" again, to identify which of our ideas could be counted on to represent truthfully, to be more than mere ideas. Clear and distinct ideas possessed this mark, and what this meant, when all the metaphysical smoke about two substances and immortality and the creation of eternal truths had cleared, was that what could be mathematizable in the sensible world (extended matter moving uniformly in space) ended up counting as "what there really is," as substance.

This whole enterprise, while full of terms and strategies peculiar to Descartes, is often rightly treated as thoroughly paradigmatic of the self-consciousness of philosophic modernity. All that we had inherited had been rejected as a dream. We would start again, and not be deceived this time. We would find a method, a "new way of ideas," and especially we would begin by relying only on ourselves. This rejection and attempt at a new beginning does initially leave us only with the ungrounded "seemings" of our mental lives, but by a rigorous attention to the internal characteristics of such ideational content, we can securely re-establish a connection with reality, a connection successful enough to suggest the (wholly impious) end of "mastering nature and enjoying the fruits of the earth without toil."

But it also conjures up the demon of modern philosophy, scepticism. Nothing, as Descartes himself seemed to realize, in the methodological identification of these internal features, in clarity and distinctness, of itself justified any metaphysical result. Being, or substance as Descartes ended up understanding it, was only the result of the application of the method, and there was no convincing reason to

*D. and the
3rd of
skepticism*

think that what satisfies our self-certifying criteria for what there is, what is least susceptible to certain kinds of doubt, still gets us where wanted to go, "back" to the world we suspended in the moment of doubt. Descartes's feeble attempts at arguing for a benevolent God who insures that clear and distinct ideas are true never convinced anyone, and the general modern dilemma was fixed. Given the self-understanding of an extreme break in the tradition, of a need for a new beginning not indebted to old assumptions, and so wholly self-grounding, the modern philosophic enterprise appears locked in a kind of self-created vacuum, determining by argument or reason a method for making claims about the world, but unable to argue convincingly that what results is anything other than what the method tells us about the world, be the "real" world as it may.

Now, perhaps, contrary to appearances, Descartes is really not interested in metaphysical results. Perhaps the prediction and control of natural events, not truth as traditionally understood, is what justifies his own or any putative method. Perhaps the idea of a methodologically "best confirmed result" (once we have a more sophisticated notion of confirmation, or "falsification," than Descartes) is all we can expect in our cognitive lives. But such qualifications would ultimately just re-raise in a different way the question of, say, the "value" (and other "costs") of such technical control, when compared with other possible ends in human life; or the justification for accepting only methodologically confirmable results in contexts where such results tell us very little of what we need to know, and where such procedures simply don't seem appropriate. On the assumption of modernity's self-defined legitimacy, in other words, the suspicion of a merely self-defined assertion of will, in more traditional terms, a sceptical suspicion, will always be looming on the horizon.

If the legitimacy of the ends, epistemological criteria, and major institutions typical of modernity cannot be very well understood as a kind of sudden "discovery" of the truth, or as a wholly original, rationally conceived inauguration or founding, perhaps, goes the other side of the dilemma mentioned above, our perspective in understanding this origin ought to be broader. Perhaps we ought to see modernity as in some way much more deeply connected with the complex ancient and scholastic traditions. Perhaps the whole modern historical sense is a myth; perhaps modernity is a kind of repetition of Christian, or even Platonic themes.[14]

Readings which reject modern claims of novelty and a reliance on reason and method alone have become quite characteristic of discussions of modernity since the nineteenth century, and we shall consider a number of them in accounts below of Hegel, Nietzsche, Heidegger and others (all three deny in different ways the "radical break" claim). But, apart from the very large issues raised by these thinkers, there are more immediate and manageable problems involved in the general denial of the modern as *autochthon*. The most straightforward have to do with controversies about the secularization thesis mentioned several times now, and they introduce us to the other side of the dilemma mentioned above.

The clearest example of the position in question is Karl Löwith's in his 1948 book, *Meaning in History*. Löwith, surveying figures from Voltaire to Marx, tried to show that central to all of them was a very typical modern notion of progress, that this belief could not, as in modernity's myth about itself, be said to be due to reason, but was prior to, and an important condition of, the meaningful exercise of reason, and so that the notion must be a secularized version of a Christian view of time. The modern idea of progress is a "secularization of the eschatological pattern of Christian progress."[15] Since assumptions about progress are quite important to modernity's sense of its own legitimacy, Löwith believes that his analysis can thus be said to contribute to a "de-legitimation" of modernity, of its claims to be superior to the Christian and ancient worlds, since based wholly on reason, not faith or tradition.

Such a relatively unphilosophical and general sense of secularization can be observed popping up frequently in discussions of distinctly modern phenomena, in Weber's account of the spirit of capitalism, in summary accounts of Marx's chiliastic view of history, replacing the Last Judgment with the classless society, or in some accounts of the modern psychology of anxiety and guilt. But, for all its pervasiveness, the notion is not all that useful for this general issue – how to "qualify," let us say, modernity's exaggerated sense of its historical autonomy. This sort of secularization thesis simply goes too far in the other direction. For one thing, there are enough disanalogies between the modern notion of progress and Christian eschatology to make appealing to Christianity in order to explain the modern notion highly dubious. For another, many modern authors were well aware of the similarities between their own views and traditional Christian ones. They were not unknowingly secularizing, but explicitly borrowing for their own purposes, often with quite unchristian ends in mind.

What would be more interesting would be a position that was not committed to any notion of a radical modern self-creation, but which also avoided any mere "repetition" thesis as well. The best known contemporary attempt at such a position is Hans Blumenberg's *The*

Legitimacy of the Modern Age, and his arguments reveal nicely the
problems created by such a qualified and historicist view of modernity's legitimacy.

Blumenberg advances, in effect, the odd-sounding view that the
moderns should be understood as participants in a debate about the
most powerful Christian heresy, Gnosticism, that "the modern age is
the second overcoming of Gnosticism."[16] What this roughly means
is that the Christian theological tradition, in its long attempt at a
successful theodicy, its attempt to reconcile the existence of a benevolent, omnipotent God with the existence of a finite, "fallen" world,
reached an *aporia* that could only be solved by what Blumenberg calls
the modern "self-assertion," or could only be resolved by an essentially non-Christian project, the "liberation of theoretical curiosity"
and the attempt to "master nature." He tries to show this by showing
how the only consistent Christian position on divine omnipotence so
affirmed the utter, incomprehensible power of God that it destroyed
the possibility of arguing for any secure, visible divine order in the
world, and so created the sense of an alien, unpredictable, wholly
contingent nature. Or, "The Middle Ages came to an end when
within their spiritual system creation as 'providence' ceased to be
credible to man and the burden of self-assertion was laid upon
him."[17] This occurred when, "The destruction of trust in the world
made him for the first time a creatively active being, freed him from a
disastrous lulling of his activity."[18]

This sort of account raises a number of scholarly and theoretical
problems. It is not at all clear in some famous cases that the anti-
contemplative, practical goal of the mastery of nature is so decisively
linked to the paradoxes of late medieval voluntarism. That problem
does not seem to bother Bacon very much, and Descartes's positon,
rather than attempting to solve the issue, seems to make it worse by
assuming that God can suspend the law of non-contradiction.[19] But
the theoretical issue is what is of interest here.

Blumenberg is defending a historicist theory, what he calls a theory
of "sufficient rationality," according to which the legitimacy of modernity cannot be measured by any abstract or atemporal account.
What makes the modern ideas of method, technical control, utility,
and so forth, "legitimate" is (and is only) their success in resolving
problems that the tradition out of which they originated could not
solve. "In the perfection of Scholasticism, the potential for destruction is already latent"[20] and the "self-assertion" of the moderns
simply represented a more successful response to that destruction
than anything permitted within the resources of late Scholasticism.

The problem this creates is: what else we have to be able to say in order to claim that such a successful response to *those* problems ought to be understood as indeed a legitimation of modernity. If the issue comes down to a resolution of Scholastic problems, even in a non-Scholastic way, then we shall need to be able to say something about the original significance of these problems themselves, in order for their resolution to be significant. There is nothing about the sufficiency of the modern response that makes it legitimate or even, all things considered, rational. Why, to go back to an earlier point, would it not have been just as rational simply to reject the original assumptions on which the Christian problems were built, to make use of pre-Christian or pagan notions of nature and philosophy? Were modern thinkers necessarily bound to these Christian assumptions and their implications? Why? Should the early modern, mechanistic notion of nature as extended substance be interpreted as somehow essentially tied to the paradoxes of extreme voluntarism?[21]

The point of such questions returns us to the dilemma mentioned before. On the one hand, the self-understanding of early modernity suggests a degree of historical independence and a notion of a "self-grounding" or presuppositionless beginning which (i) looks an easy target for a revisionist historian, (ii) which threatens to beg the important "legitimacy" question, and (iii) to create an unsolvable scepticism problem. On the other hand, more "dialogic" theories of "sufficient rationality," at least Blumenberg's, ones that reasonably try to measure the legitimacy and justification of modernity against the concrete theoretical options available at the time, threaten a historicism that undermines the whole issue of legitimacy in favor of the merely "historically appropriate." It does, that is, unless we know something more about the legitimacy of the Christian tradition (something, for example, only Hegel really attempted)[22] and something more about modern legitimacy itself, something more than that the moderns solved various Scholastic problems. One very standard view, then, of the modern instauration asks much too much of it; and one very sophisticated counter-view asks much too little.

And, with issues such as these, we are close to the fundamental issue. For at bottom, this sort of a dispute about the foundation of modernity's claim for intellectual or philosophical legitimacy, with one side simply attempting such a foundation, and another side assuming the *naïveté* of such an approach and addressing the issue in mostly historical terms, clearly calls for a thorough discussion of the general possibility of a self-grounding, or of a critique by reason of itself, an account of the very "possibility" of knowledge. Does Kant's new "instauration" (announced by his using a quotation from Bacon's *Instauratio Magna* as the epigraph for the *Critique of Pure Reason*) create or at least suggest a different and successful way of resolving these issues, or, as claimed by later philosophical critics, are he and his Idealist colleagues simply the clearest representatives of the modern intellectual failure?

3 The "Culture of Rupture"

Just as it would be misleading to try to understand the origin and the initial appeal of the idea of a modern epoch without attending to such things as developments in modern science, *aporiai* in important theological debates (and, with sufficient space, social and economic changes, religious wars, inventions, explorations and discoveries, etc.),[23] it would be equally impossible to understand the emergence of the idea of a "crisis" in the philosophical claims of modernity without at least a brief attempt at a sketch of the larger context within which the European dissatisfaction with the modern project developed. In the following chapter we shall return to the philosophical issues suggested by the above discussion – the problem of what Kant called reason's "self-legislation" – but since I shall argue that that whole discussion is of great relevance for thinking clearly about the fate of the modern project in general, we should look ahead a bit first at the general shape of that "crisis" mentality.

In this case, however, the most visible and dramatic phenomena are social and, especially, aesthetic, rather than scientific and theological. These phenomena are sometimes loosely grouped together under the primarily aesthetic label "modernism," itself a complex and ambiguous designation, since it often denotes both a heightened and affirmative modern self-consciousness (a final attempt to be "truly" modern, to create in a radical and unprecedented way a form of life, indeed a sensibility, finally consistent with the full implications of the modern revolution), as well as an intense dissatisfaction with the sterile, exploitative, commercialized, or simply ugly forms of life apparently characteristic of social modernization (or "bourgeois" forms of modernization).[24]

Of all the many things denoted by the term, modernism has also been understood to propose (or to threaten) a great shift in European high culture, or at least an implicit insistence on a shift in authority,

from philosophy primarily, but also from science and religion, to art
as the leading or "legislating" force in a genuinely modern culture.[25]
The poet (and the novelist and painter) will become the "antennae of
the race," especially the "unacknowledged legislator" for mankind,
and this shift has, for its proponents, become necessary because
of the altered historical circumstances of modernity, because, in
Virginia Woolf's stunning and somewhat silly claim, "On or about
December 1910, human nature changed."

That is, this insistence on such a transfer of authority is not
comprehensible unless it is viewed, first, against the background
of an emerging, widely shared consensus in European high culture
that the early modern hopes for a genuinely new, progressive,
fundamentally better epoch had proven false.[26] This sense of dashed
hopes had its origins both in historical observation and in theoretical
claims, claims that took many forms, from a belief (most famously
associated with Freud) in an underlying, ahistorical, irrational element in human life, unreachable by humanistic reform, to a historical
claim that modernity was itself still too premodern, too committed in
its official project to Christian and moral ideals inconsistent with
its own secularism (a view, for now, we can label with the name
"Nietzsche").

Secondly, in trying to understand this emerging sense that the
original Enlightenment project had proven impossible or self-
deceived, that it had terminated in what George Steiner calls "the
great ennui" of the nineteenth century, and so a new "nostalgia for
disaster,"[27] we also need to pay attention to the fate of the central
defining issue of the modern self-understanding. That is the modern
attempt at a genuine self-determination, in both a sweeping historical
and an individual sense. The question is what this came to mean by
the mid-nineteenth century, why its social manifestations came to be
perceived as so objectionable, and why it seemed to so many that
only one form of such self-determination, a radical act of imagination,
or a complete, aesthetic self-definition, would fully realize the otherwise discredited notion of a "free life."[28]

However, while there is such a general convergence of themes,
ideas, sensibility, and so forth characteristic of aesthetic modernism,
it is a difficult issue to discuss briefly. There is no philosophic
manifesto for any movement, and what critical essays exist, by, say,
Baudelaire, Nietzsche, James, or Eliot, often address different issues
in radically different terms. A novel or a poem or a painting obviously need of itself carry no heavy philosophical baggage; it might be

directed only at an isolated phenomenon of modern life, and have nothing of interest to say about "modernity"; and so in trying to determine what philosophical claims might be at stake simply in an art work being presented this way rather than that, or structuring the experience it presents this way rather than that, there is always a danger of speculative over-kill, of making the work do or say more than it can or should.

And there are other difficulties in discussing in such a sweeping way such a non-movement. There are historical gaps in developments in different art forms and genres, and there are different assumptions at work in different national literatures and national art traditions. Literary modernism begins early, emerging eventually from late eighteenth- and early nineteenth-century romanticism, and initially addresses somewhat different issues in the poetry, say, of Baudelaire, and the novel of Flaubert. Modernism in painting, while clearly a technical classification relevant, at least stylistically, to the likes of Goya or Turner, develops somewhat later, perhaps first with Manet, and then in a different and more radical way with the post-impressionists, typically, say, with Cézanne. Modernism in music is later still, a late nineteenth-century or "Wagnerian" phenomenon, the implications of which were not fully clear until the more radical experimentations of the twentieth century. And architectural modernism is, for the most part, a distinctly twentieth-century phenomenon in some ways in tension with the romantic origins of much of the literary modernist sensibility.[29] And then there are all the divergent movements, hard to bring together under one umbrella: symbolism, naturalism, futurism, dadaism, surrealism, *art trouvé*, etc.

However, for all the differences and ambiguities, I shall assume in the following that there are sufficiently clear convergences about modernity, impossible to ignore, evident in many seminal works. One doesn't have to be a card-carrying Hegelian to believe that the sudden emphasis on such things as dramatic aesthetic experimentation, novelty or a radical escape from tradition, artistic autonomy and an *épatez la bourgeoisie* sentiment, across so many genres and traditions, in so short a span of time, evinces something of general significance about the historical legacy of the original dream of modernity, a dream in effect, dreamed up by philosophers and condemned as a nightmare by poets, novelists, and painters. I shall try to spell out these convergences below and suggest a way of considering their philosophical importance.

In the simplest terms, modernism in the arts, again a descendant of the romantic movement,[30] eventually came to reflect bourgeois culture's growing dissatisfaction with itself, a sense that modernity's official self-understanding – Enlightened, liberal, progressive, humanistic – had been a misunderstanding, a far too smug and unwarranted self-satisfaction, a subject matter naturally suited for irony and satire. In contrast with romanticism however (itself still an essentially redemptive, Christian phenomenon) the modernist sensibility does not rely on a contrast between the dullness and drudgery or anomie of daily life, and the "true world" of nature or a spiritualized inner realm, to be "expressed" in poetic activity.[31] The artistic imagination is no longer viewed as a vehicle or medium; it is, in modernism, *sui generis*, and by being *sui generis*, or difficult, opaque, strange, elitist, uncommercial, self-defining, and so on, artistic activity alone demonstrates a kind of integrity and autonomy foreclosed in bourgeois life. That life, modern life, had become so routinized and blind to itself that a wholly new creative activity was "called for" now. This new form, by being outrageous or obscure, would be resistant to commercialization and mass culture, and would be the only genuine art now possible, an intensely self-consciousness, historical, even philosophical art, however purely "aesthetic" its goals, deeply motivated by an idea of what modernity had become, and by a demand for a finally modern "honesty," a recognition of the contingency and mutability of human ideals.

In Baudelaire's essays, especially "The Salon of 1846," (with his famous discussion there of "The Heroism of Modern Life") and the later "The Painter of Modern Life," this self-consciousness and tension in modernity become much more apparent. The early Enlightenment conception of the modern, as we saw, is formed by means of a contrast and a conflict between the emerging modern sensibility and the ancient and the scholastic. Baudelaire now insists on a very general contrast between "the modern," understood simply as the momentary, the temporal, the contingent, even the ephemeral, and any appeal to stability, the classic, or the eternal, or, for philosophers, the universal. "Almost all our originality comes from the stamp that time imprints upon our feelings."[32] And "Absolute and eternal beauty does not exist, or rather it is only an abstraction skimmed off the surface of a variety of beauties. The characteristic of each form of beauty comes from the passions, and since we have our particular passions, we have our own beauty."[33]

This proposal leads Baudelaire to assert a primacy for the artistic imagination that would become quite typical in modernism. The poet or artist is obliged to find the "heroism" and beauty of modern life, to see it where it is not visible to the ordinary beholder, but he does so by projecting and imaginatively transforming modern images, and thereby by redeeming modern life. Where there had seemed to be urban ugliness and vacuity, even "evil," the artist and the artist alone can create beautiful aesthetic detail, can celebrate the mobility and freedom of daily life, its intensity of passion, even its "flowers of evil."

Baudelaire's aestheticism, his emphasis on artifice and creation, takes the general modern idea of a self-making to a kind of extreme, most apparent in Baudelaire's famous rejection of nature and his celebration of the dandy. So, the fact that much in modernity is a mere self-assertion, a kind of vain celebration of human power, is no longer perceived as a problem, but as a solution. (At least so it seems in these essays. Baudelaire, especially from the late 1850s on, was well aware of the darker sides of modernization, its social costs and aesthetic impact.)[34] The modern posture is not illegitimate; if it is honestly embraced, it is beautiful, interesting, at least (and for many at most) of aesthetic value.[35]

Of course, it is not all interesting or beautiful in any traditional sense. What makes it interesting is, and is only, the artist's creative power, something that becomes even more prominent and self-celebratory in Flaubert. In Flaubert's *Madame Bovary*, what turns out to be of great transcendent value in the story of Emma is Flaubert's story itself, the virtuosity demonstrated by the author in telling a tawdry story of provincial infidelity with such great style and cool irony. The story is "redeemed," rendered worthy of interest, important, only by its telling, not by the discovery of an "internal" point or purpose to the suffering and misery of the characters (all of which counting as an implicit assertion that there is no such point or purpose). Emma herself is portrayed in part as pathetic because she believes in "literature," or the romantic novels she takes for literature or "art." She expects it to be about something, to have a moral, to lead somewhere. (She is also partly heroic because her refusal to live "literally," her faith in the redemptive power of the imagination, her intuitive realization that romantic sexuality will principally define the modern possibility of adventure and self-assertion, all intimate Flaubert's own aesthetic.)[36] Flaubert manages to affirm with a kind of divine hauteur that it is indeed the literary act, the work of imagination, that is supremely important in the modern world, but this because there is nothing in the world of Charles Bovary and Leon and especially the prototypical Homais, that is of any competing, intrinsic importance, and it is the transforming act of imagination that is of importance completely of itself, and not for any moral or romantic reasons.[37]

And the substance of the book brilliantly introduces us both to many of the concrete social dimensions of the modernism problem, and to the important link between this emerging sense of the disastrous social consequences of modernity, and the new aesthetic, with all its philosophical baggage, implicit in the work of so many modernists. All the characters (in this and many other modern novels) believe in the great modern myth, whether expressed romantically by Emma, or in the petty bourgeois attitudes of Homais, the pharmacist and shopkeeper; they believe in what René Girard has called the "spontaneity" of their desire; they believe they are modern individuals, self-determining and free. They believe that they pursue the objects of their desire because they have determined that these objects are worth pursuing, because and only because, the objects are of worth to them. And they are all, it turns out, wrong; their desires are everywhere dependent on "mediators," on others who certify or make worthy their desires, others whom, given the extreme importance of the desirer's self-image as independent, they eventually come to hate and compete with. Almost all desire in the modern novel is an imitation of desire, a desire for an object or a state of being, or a goal, which is routed through another's or many others' desires.

In Girard's striking picture of the dynamic of social modernization, it is, apparently, the collapse of religion, of an "external," stable, or unapprochable religious mediator bestowing a supreme worth on various ends, that signals the beginning of the difficulty.[38] Girard's account seems to presuppose a kind of theoretical, original indeterminacy in human desire. We begin with simply a multitude of wants, unsure about which desires to pursue, or how to begin evaluating which to pursue. In a narrative that resonates with Nietzschean as well as Hegelian themes, Girard argues that modern individuals, left without "external," divinely secure reassurances about what is "truly desirable," flounder, and turn to each other for support, to "internal" mediators, or other individuals.[39] The more unapproachable or idealized such mediators are in this "triangular desire," the more stable the desire. If what you want has been deemed desirable by a god, or the dead sacred ancestors, or even "aristocrats," those who know *to ariston*, the best, the desire can be securely and confidently pursued. But the accelerating insistence on the equality of individuals, or the attack on the legitimacy of religion or distinctions of rank, transforms mediators into wholly individual or contingent "others", and so also rivals and obstacles, as one imitates a mediator even as one questions, then despises his power and prestige, as one strives to supplant him or her and become the object of imitation oneself. Modern desire itself is thus linked inevitably with jealousy, vanity, snobbery, or in a Nietzschean word, *ressentiment*.[40] And all of this is, for Girard, the great narrative of all modern novels, and the central experience of later modernity.[41]

By contrast with such a literary narration of the dynamic of modernity, many modern philosophers, such as Machiavelli, Hobbes, and Hume, in one way or another (to speak somewhat sweepingly) retained a faith that some sort of "objective" account could be given of human desire, or they retained a belief in, say, the primacy of the body, that the body produced, according to some law, basic, even universal, natural, species-specific desires, passions, and especially fears which pushed and pulled human agents. There were therefore "naturally" desirable or fearful objects and states.

As we shall soon see in detail, Girard's account of the modern novel portrays the problem of desire, and especially the historical and social contingency of desire, in a way much more compatible with later European philosophers like Hegel and Nietzsche. In that context, such a faith in "nature" is gone, gone largely, as we shall see, because of the modern insistence on spontaneity and self-determination, on the unavailability of any direct appeal to nature. (Here begins the deep connection between idealism and the modernity problem itself.) Given the right setting, the right kind of social reflection and self-consciousness, anything is desirable or fearful. The modern novel reflects as little faith in a hierarchical, ordered nature, as in a mechanistic natural origin. Human life has become, in a collective sense, completely self-determining, but (and here are the intimations of the crisis mentality) in a way that is thereby completely contingent. Without old forms, old authorities, old criteria, what looks to some like liberation and the beginning of autonomy looks to others like the emergence of a new, contingent, mutable, unstable social authority, the great subject of the novel form.

It is in this sense that, in Girard's terms, the central "metaphysical" issue in accounts of modern desire is "the setting," the new power of a fluid, unpredictable social dynamic in modernity, a claim implicit in the very existence of the novel as a genre. No one, in the modern novel (i.e., once the *naïveté* of romantic notions of autonomy and integrity are rejected) simply knows or even feels what ought to be desired or pursued. We can see, in reading the novel, the way in which a character's view of herself is self-deceived, or inadequately reflects the influence of the past or others. So, we can appreciate, in a way the character often cannot, the way in which his or her pursuits and avoidances must be understood to arise through the mediation of others. Emma wants what she thinks her romantic aristocrats would want; Marcel wants what the mysterious Guermantes seem to want. In Kafka's *The Trial*, K., pathetically, wants to do what the authorities, the Court, want him to do, but, in a typical later modernist extension of this theme, he cannot, literally, find such authorities. There is no one available even to imitate, and hence his typically affectless, banal, confusing life. He has lost his "mediators."

So, at the heart of the substance of many modern novels, there is some evidence about what I am calling the philosophical issues involved in the modernist revolt. What is most important appears to be a link between the dawning sense of a failure in the social promise of modernization – individual autonomy and collective rationality – and the appeal of a radically autonomous, self-defining "cult" of art. A look at one or two novels won't settle the issue, but it is striking that many of the same social themes, and many of the same aesthetic or formal issues that seem linked to those themes, are visible elsewhere in the culture of modernism.

Consider one brief example from the beginnings of modernism in painting, Manet's *scandale, Olympia* (1863). Several aspects of the painting, and "Impressionism" in general, evoke the connections between idealism, contingency, and modernism sketched above. The technique employed creates the sense that what we are seeing is not (cannot be) "the person," a nude reclining on a couch, as much as it is a momentary flash of vision itself; an instant or impression is itself painted. The flatness of the color, the broad, quickly applied brush strokes, the starkness of the contrasting areas of color, with little or no half-tones or shading, capture a brief, wholly contingent moment in perceived time (even, ironically, as the mythological overtones and the great stillness and seriousness of the painting evoke and parody the classical idea of eternal significance). The object is itself a representation, a "view," one that, immediately if implicitly, suggests a philosophical as well as "painterly" issue. That the painting is painted as it is, in such a radically new style, inaugurates not merely the famous impressionist concern with "how the eye actually sees," but a modern metaphysical issue, an implicit assertion of the wholly transient, fragmented and perspectival nature of the real, a reality accessible only in contingent, individual "moments" of representation.

This assertion of the complete particularity of Olympia is reinforced by the ironic, anti-allegorical tone of the work, its mocking reference to the universalist pretensions of very similar poses in Giorgione or Titian, as if to insist that there is no "Sensuality" or "Love" or "Faithfulness" or even "Beauty." There is only this woman; perhaps, given the almost gross materiality of the woman, the grey, corpse-like color, the vaguely unclean hands and linens, only this material thing, this body, here, now, as suddenly viewed. One can thus already detect in Manet's choice of subject matter a fascination in modernism and ultimately in postmodern discussions with the radical particularity of existence, and so, in the general terms introduced above, a denial of the "dependence" of the intelligibility of objects or persons or moments on the universal categories or descriptions of science or philosophy or even language itself as originally understood. The implicit claim is that this ineffable, original, "independent" matter of existence, can be properly captured in some form of radical experience, ranging from the apparently trivial, momentary scenes captured by impressionists, through the attack on traditional notions of coherence or order mounted by the cubists, to found-object or Pop art and the chance transformations of Cage. (And the various problems in such a radical nominalism are already suggested, in the almost "dead" materiality of the object, and the ever accelerating insistence that "the object" is only a moment of vision, dabs of paint, sequences of noises.)[42]

The sense or meaning of this momentary representation is clearly also at issue in the direct, unashamed gaze of the woman at the viewer. Nothing captures better the tone of modernism than this look. It seems to ask the bourgeois viewer (or purchaser): And what, exactly, are you looking for? What did you expect, those pink idealizations of classic paintings? This, this body and, at the same time, in a clearly related claim, these dabs of paint, are all there is. The gaze immediately raises the issue of how the painting is now, in this new context, to be evaluated, all in a way connected with how modern forms of life are to be evaluated, are to be "seen" or represented. The aesthetic issue is to be raised because the old "mediators," the classic canons and ideals, are rejected, leaving, Manet already suggests, only the unredeemable particularity of modern existence and the sheer materiality of the painting itself.

The social issues suggested by the painting are, as T.J. Clark has shown, just as complex, and are related to the aesthetic experimentation. For, on the plausible if not certain assumption that we are looking at a prostitute,[43] the social issue of the consequences of

modern nominalism and materialism are also immediately raised.
Stripping away the religious and moral "frame" by which the body
had been viewed, implicitly accusing such a framing of hypocrisy,
sentimentality, falsification, does just leave us with this body and the
question challengingly captured in the gaze: how she is to be viewed
in this new "frameless" setting. Such a novel situation suggests, all at
once, an air of liberation, a self-congratulatory sense of honesty. The
woman seems modern, free, autonomous, unhampered by traditional
assumptions, starkly naked and direct. She seems, that is, as free and
potentially self-defining as the painting itself. Yet at the same time,
the subject matter hints at what force, now wholly secular, will
inevitably re-frame the issue: money, or "exchange relations" unre-
stricted by traditional constraints, a matter simply of "free" contract
between individuals, or of "naked" power.[44] (An issue even more
dramatically suggested by another look, that on the face of the
barmaid in *Un Bar aux Folies-Bergère*, tired and almost despairing
amidst the "gaiety" and new bourgeois "freedom" surrounding her,
the kind celebrated less ambiguously by Renoir, Degas, and
others.)[45]

Given the obvious new audience, or better, new market, for paintings, the bourgeoisie, the challenge and questions raised by those
looks are obviously also of relevance for the paintings themselves. As
we have now learned, there is almost no assertion of aesthetic independence, no outrage or profanity or obscurity, which is not in some
way immediately rendered "dependent," an object whose meaning
now emerges only when viewed or mediated by others, especially as a
commodity.

This complex connection between a growing, highly pessimistic
sense of "what modernity had become," the aesthetic experimentation inspired or provoked by that view, and the philosophic issue of
autonomy raised by those experiments, was already noted as central
to modernist literature. As is typical in Flaubert, the modern emphasis on form, technique, aesthetic theory, is both an implicit denial
of the success of modern claims for social autonomy and self-
determination in daily life, and an expression of a continued allegiance to this idea in art. Of course, the philosophical problem all
this raises is obvious and must be addressed shortly. It is, simply,
how to understand genuine "independence" or autonomy, whether it
involves a radicalization of the classical ideal of freedom through
knowledge (even the knowledge of necessity), the self-imposing of a
moral law, political equality, a poetics of originality and creation, or

a kind of thoroughgoing ironicism, a constantly tentative, qualified posing or discursive play.

4 Paradoxes and Problems

So, at issue in much of the modernist sensibility is the way we have come to understand the worth of the most characteristic features of modern social life and how the growing dissatisfaction with such features is linked with the larger philosophical problems immediately raised by general claims for a modern epoch. Thematically, within the modern novel, what we have already identified as the heart of this philosophical issue is, as just noted, much in evidence. Let us baptize the issue officially, borrowing the Hegelian formulation that will be central to the rest of this study, the dialectic of "independence" and "dependence." To be a modern individual is to demand independence; on the one hand, historical and intellectual "maturity," as Kant put it, a freedom from a dependence on historical tradition and the power to rule one's own beliefs; on the other, social or existential self-direction and autonomy. To some extent, novels like those of Flaubert, or Stendhal, or Proust begin to imply a great doubt about the pretensions of such social independence, when it is understood within the official self-understanding of the Enlightenment, and that doubt will be reflected in Nietzsche's characterization of almost all the major institutions of modernity as functions of *ressentiment*, or "herd society," all expressions of "failed independence."

Moreover, the claims about failure are not merely moralistic, a residue of a romantic hope in true independence, given a stronger will, or a more resolute refusal to participate in bourgeois conformism. Girard is right to call this modernist treatment of desire "metaphysical," since Flaubert, for example, is not moralizing about Emma's weakness, Dostoyevsky not hectoring us about the failures of the singular Underground Man, Proust not having some fun at the expense of these snobs. The novels all take a profound historical perspective; the fate of their characters is in some way portrayed as a necessary fate. There is no language within modern self-understanding for simply accepting the enormity of their dependence on the utterly contingent mediation of their desires by others. They must deceive themselves about it, promote their own false independence, and so live lives of envy, self-hatred, and disillusion. What independence there is, the independence of the artistic imagination, is often achieved at the price of a very costly social "refusal," as in the modernist obsession with gamblers, outlaws, con men (all figures of the ever alienated artist) those who try to act out or confirm their independence from the mediation of others; or more typically, at the price of great loneliness and isolation, in a way, at the price of the cessation of human desire, as in the later Marcel, in his cork-lined room, Henry James's artist characters (e.g., Ralph Touchett), or Thomas Mann's paradigmatic artist-figures, sick or even dying.

There are, I think, two preliminary things to conclude from this rapid survey of the emerging modernist sensibility. First, to start with the obvious, modernism in art already announces a complex crisis mentality, a deep concern with the effects of social modernization. It is important to note that we do not find in typical modernist work simply the usual satire and sarcasm of the comic sensibility, the wit and sometimes the contempt of Aristophanes, or Molière, or Shakespeare, directed at the usual human foibles. Homais is not the standard, sly, self-serving buffoon. He is made to mouth the rhetoric of the Revolution as if he represents the Revolution and not its perversion; he identifies himself as "modern"; he even wins the Legion of Honor, and is at least as much a social force as an individual. T.S. Eliot is not describing this particular "Waste Land," London, as if it just happens that this place is a "heap of broken images." At the heart of Conrad's *Heart of Darkness* is not a universal truth about "unbridled" or "uncivilized" man as he is in himself, despite the way the novel is commonly read. At the "Heart of Darkness" Marlowe finds an outpost of modern European commerce and the most efficient ivory-trading company employee in history, a completely consistent and so mad representative of "all Europe."[46]

Secondly, to a large degree in reaction to this experience of dissatisfaction and even revulsion, the modernist aesthetic itself arose, a new sense of the nature and significance of art-making. Of the many issues involved in such a topic, I have focused on the problem of the autonomy of art, one of the central canons of modernism, but in itself ambiguous and hard to characterize properly. Roughly, I have been suggesting that the most important general philosophical issue in all of modernity's self-consciousness involves the problem of autonomy, and independent self-legislating. This concerns first, the "epochality" of modernity itself, the idea of a historical revolution, or a self-grounding epoch. This problem emerges again at the moment when, for artists at least, the social crises of industrial democracies begin to appear. Again there is a lot of talk, not about reform or forcing the Enlightenment project to live up to its own ideals, but about wholesale negation, revolution, another new sensibility, now self-affirming or self-creating, rather than a universalist or rational self-legitimation.[47] This in turn suggests a tremendously heightened role for the artist, the figure whose imagination supposedly creates or shapes the sensibilities of civilization.

Both issues, at the beginning of modernism *per se*, already suggest their own disintegration, already suggest a variety of internal tensions and paradoxical ideals. For one thing, this celebration of modern aesthetic values – creativity, anti-traditionalism, integrity, historical self-consciousness, a willingness to explore all the dimensions of human life, without moral or religious constraint – is, as the historical case of Flaubert also makes clear, not easy to affirm within the larger context of modern social life, a context that, one might argue, paradoxically makes possible the private explorations of self, or the formal experimentation so characteristic of modernism. This is the bourgeois context of scientific sobriety, economic self-interest, prudence, health, safety, calculation, etc. The artist claims to celebrate what is truly modern in modernity, the tolerance for radical change, novelty, the unusual, and so forth, but he finds himself vilified, or worse, ignored (or worse still, embraced, lionized) by the public representatives of bourgeois modernity.

Or, to state a similar point more polemically, the idea that modern art can maintain an independent, critical, "negative" perspective on modern social existence (the kind of thing Adorno tried to promote as a defense of modern art) may turn out to be a grotesquely self-serving illusion. Modernist art may be simply the deepest expression of the modern crisis, understood either as paradigmatically "bourgeois art," or ultimately as nihilistic, self-consuming and as much a historical dead-end as bourgeois civilization itself. For many so-called post-modernists, modernism represents the last game played by Western bourgeois high culture, an elitist code designed only to preserve and celebrate the "subjectivist" point of view of an exhausted but still immensely powerful upper middle class.

For another, the modernist aesthetic is itself unstable. The extreme insistence emerging in Baudelaire and quite prominent in Flaubert and later modernists on both the autonomy and the profound significance of aesthetic values insists that if the great paradigm of artistic production is no longer imitation, if the particularity of individual vision and/or the absence of inherent value in the natural or meta-physical world undercuts the possibility of such a mimetic ideal, then the great issue becomes the relative worth of different sorts of produc-tion or creation (or even what makes creation, or any act, "art"). This problem, as we shall see, will create an aesthetic crisis within modernism itself very similar to the epistemological problems of philosophic modernity. Proponents of aesthetic modernism will be led to affirm its significance by a kind of aestheticization of all perceptual or cognitive issues (so that artistic activity best or most honestly expresses all human activity) through a long period of ironic experimentation (wherein the potential contingency or arbitrariness of expression is much in view) to a full-blown crisis, and "end of art" art, or an anti-novel novel, etc.[48] The central issue is, again, the problem of independence, or in many cases, individuality, the (poten-tially impossible) demand for an autochthony of the individual consistent with that claimed for modernity itself, an autochthony supposedly possible for the great artist.

To make this last point, let me conclude by using Proust again as a typical, final example of the philosophic issue raised by the implicit claims of modernist art. For many readers of Proust, particularly those whose philosophical programs share much with the sensibility of modernism (recently, readers like Alexander Nehamas and, with quite a different agenda, Richard Rorty), the above suggestion that there is a profoundly typical, unresolved modern tension in Proust, that Proust still embodies the *aporiai* that result from the modern demand for a revolutionary form of independence, misses Proust's achievement, his finally coming to terms with the contingency of human self creation. On such a reading, Proust is a completely consistent modern aesthete, an "ironist" who refuses to theorize about his irony, who only weaves together his "network of small, interanimating contingencies."[49] Proust gives up the idea "that there is a privileged perspective from which he, or anyone else, is to be described," and manages "to debunk authority without setting him-self up as authority." His activity itself suggests a displacement of philosophy by literature and he is therefore in many ways the hero of Rorty's recent book, the chief proponent of the valued Rortyean post-philosophical activity, "re-description," a genius at creating a pattern of his past life, and a perspective on authors that would lead to him, to the author writing the novel, as if with necessity, even though created wholly out of authorial imagination.

X   This view seems to me much too unhistorical and so misses the great pathos of Proust's novel, and therewith the pathos, or internal tension, of modernist high culture in general. The dissolution of the Guermantes's authority for Marcel is, first of all, portrayed on a larger canvas than one limited to Marcel's individual aesthetic experimentation. As with Kurz, "all of Europe" is at stake, the old Europe about to dissolve in the decisive events of the First World War. Their collapse into outright venality and money-grubbing (or their exposure as, all along, vain poseurs), figures for Marcel, finally, the absence of all "mediators" or authorities in the world that would result from the War. The kingdom of taste was all that had been left from the old world, and taste is unmasked in the novel rather than celebrated.

And all of this is treated as a condition of Marcel's own final aesthetic retreat. He "historicizes" his own aesthetic credo in a way that depends on the later Marcel's self-consciousness or reflection (his claim to "authority") a clearly philosophic and historical self-consciousness that makes possible or helps to justify his aesthetic construction. His "reading" of the disastrous fate of French high society, in other words, is not just an element in his private narrative. The reason he comes to value his isolated, aesthetic life depends essentially on the truth of such a reading. It can't all be "inside" his imaginative onstructions without our losing any sense of the significance of those constructions.[50]

Given this historical view about modern culture, and the consequences the later Marcel draws from the two great events of the novel – the deterioration of a social authority based on taste or aesthetic sensibility, and his disappointment about the possibility of love, or even friendship – it would be a misreading to view these events as merely the way Marcel, or Proust, "comes to see things." The events are portrayed as a historical loss, a great disillusionment of "world historical" not private significance, only very partially "redeemed" by Marcel's final aestheticism.[51]

Further, Marcel himself had, earlier, tried to "live out" his poeticizing social psychology, to view himself and others aesthetically, with Albertine, and it had been a disaster, as much a disaster as the prefigured affair of Swann and Odette. In those passages, with everyone else writing their own narratives, struggling for independence, or control of the script, a great and excruciatingly painful uncertainty and conflict is created. This conflict emerges often because so litttle "fits" the narrative Marcel gamely keeps trying to create and so suggests a kind of finitude and dependence not resolved until the events have occurred and he is no longer involved, when he is in effect, dead to the world, indicates that his aesthetic independence is considerably more complicated and ambiguous that the aesthete reading allows.[52]

The significance of this interpretive issue involves more than a hermeneutical problem. Several very general issues are involved. First, it is often said that the rise of aesthetic modernism to some extent inaugurates a kind of renewal of the old quarrel between philosophy and poetry. As noted earlier, looked at this way the Enlightenment is simply a radicalization of philosophy itself, a demand for universality and necessity on one's criteria of description and assessment. So, for example, if the principles appealed to in political life are to be justified, they mut be justified as much more than the way we go about things; the principles must be binding "for any rational agent." The very existence of poetry or the arts, particularly in modernity, implies a claim that the irreducible individuality and contingency of many of the most significant aspects of human life cannot be accounted for by the universalist and abstract language of philosophy and science.

This is all true, but it also needs to be looked at historically. What initially emerges from this summary is how much of both the modern and modernist sensibility depends quite concretely on a kind of "reading" of their respective predecessors, a collective sense of what philosophic options had become at a certain point in time. And these are often highly controversial, even tendentious readings.

The "philosophy-poetry" contrast sketched above, for example, simply accepts a version of the basic alternatives originally set out by Plato and radicalized by the Englightenment. The problem of modernism can then be understood as framed by a sense of alternatives ultimately derived from Enlightenment and romantic philosophy: either there is a truth out there to get at, or a truth in the self to express, or there are just experimental, ironic re-descriptions, attempts to create a kind of discourse future generations might find useful in getting about and securing what they want (what Plato called sophistry). Such a sense of the alternatives might be wrong, a misreading, and it might being by making assumptions already quite controversial.

Artists, poets, novelists and philosophers, that is, do not just begin experimental, ironic attempts at radical "re-description"; they do so in response to a common view of their historical inheritance and with a clear view of what has "now" come to be understood about that legacy and, presumably, its pretensions. And it is one thing to note, as a literary historian or critic, what such a common view might actually have been (that lots of people believed it), and another to assess that reading, to ask if a whole cultural agenda is being set on the basis of a potted or ideologically distorted or simply narrow historical narrative. The rise and fall of modernism does not, in other words, simply tell us something about what we have become. It does, in a way, but it also tells us how we have come to understand or interpret ourselves, and so it introduces a question as well as a historical event. The question conerns the potential fragility or distortion of the narratives that generate these "grand categories."

The more particular question it raises, or at least the one issue I want to pursue is, again, how to understand the modern demand for autonomy, and how to assess its historical and social implications. It would not be an exaggeration to say that all significant European philosophy after Kant defines itself by some sort of opposition to the official Enlightenment understanding of historical revolution and individual self-determination, and it is certainly true of the "modernity theories" of those thinkers we shall examine next, Hegel, Nietzsche, and Heidegger. The question is, do any of them successfully identify and successfully criticize, or reformulate, or dialectically complete, or discard for powerful reasons, the assumptions at the origin of the "crisis" so much at issue in literary and aesthetic modernism?

3

Idealism and Modernity

1 The Kantian Enlightenment

Kant's major work is called *The Critique of Pure Reason*, and its principal targets appear to be Descartes, Leibniz, and Spinoza on one flank, and Locke and Hume on the other, or virtually all the major early modern philosophers. It is therefore not at all surprising that contemporary German academic conservatives, Jacobi et al., the anti-Enlightenment crowd, upon hearing the book's title, the objects of its attack, and its intention to show once and for all the limits of human reason and the unknowability of things in themselves, would have anticipated an important ally. Superficially, a book called *The Critique of Pure Reason* looks to be the opening salvo in the European counter-Enlightenment.[1]

These religious and romantic conservatives, however, were to be sorely disappointed. For, even though the work does have such intentions, and does execute them brilliantly, it does so, paradoxically, by an ambitious radicalization of the modern principles of enlightenment or self-examination. Even though Kant claims to be "limiting" knowledge to "make room for faith," his arguments for such limitations never presuppose the standpoint of faith, and instead present an internal critique by reason of itself, simultaneously asserting the absolute authority of rationality, and demonstrating, somewhat paradoxically, what the first pronouncement of such a supreme ruler would have to be: a restriction of knowledge, of itself, to "possible experience" (understood as sensory experience, or the phenomenal) and its "conditions," a denial that unaided human reason can discern the nature of reality.

As Kant explains his own position, he makes it quite clear that he considers himself to be moving beyond the (as he saw it) half-hearted attempts at providing a foundation for modern science in the likes of Descartes and Leibniz and Spinoza and Hume, attempts still tied to unwarranted metaphysical and theological commitments, and/or un-justified, inconsistent views about human psychology. Moreover, he also insists, contrary to many views of his project then and now, that he is not doing so by re-working standard (and ultimately dead-end) modern positions, by arguing that objects are "really" mental con-structions, or that his own enterprise is either a metaphysical account of the mind's inner nature of a psychological inventory of the faculties at work in experience. The issue he virtually invented, the "con-ditions of the possibility of experience," is, he insists, a radically new formulation of philosophy's task, and so provides for the first time the appropriate way of thinking about the deepest philosophic issues in the modern revolution. The self-grounding required for modernity to be modernity can now be accomplished without empiricist founda-tionalism or metaphysical fancies. The modern subject will determine for itself, completely and unconditionally, what to accept as evidence about the nature of things and, ultimately, what to regard as an appropriate evaluation of action. It will be completely self-determining, not bound to the "given" as foundation, not committed to the dogmatic belief that "the order of thought and the order of things are one," and insistent that only if "pur reason can be prac-tical," can indeed be the exclusive object of the will, can human beings be said to be free.

Kant's idealism, then, his replacing the great classical and early modern theme of "nature" (the discovery of which originally made philosophy possible) with a new issue, a self-legislating or "spon-taneous subject," determining for itself "critically" what is to count as an objective claim about nature or a binding claim on other agents, marks the emergence of a wholly modern philosophical project.[2] This topic will require a good deal of comment below, but by emphasizing Kant's modernism, I mean to suggest that his project is more consistent than any other with modernity's general self-understanding as an origination in history, a beginning not bounded or conditioned by tradition or religious authority, finally free and independent, and so fully self-conscious about its own possibility. By rejecting as uncritical both the rationalist presumption that concep-tual truths tell us anything about things in themselves, and the empiricist attempt to find an immediate datum of experience on which knowledge claims could be built, Kant finally inaugurates in a radical and consistent way the modern idea of a new, self-determining beginning.

And he was largely successful, at least historically, in arguing that such a critical enterprise, focused in a new way on the human subject and the "forms" of its cognitive, practical and aesthetic activity, is what would have to be defended if the deepest philosophic dimensions of the modern enterprise were to be defended. Put most directly then, after Kant, philosophical modernism in the German tradition came to mean the rejection of all forms of metaphysics (understood as the a priori knowledge of substance), a conviction that the "British" problems with empiricism and scepticism had been overcome, and the inauguration of a new problem, that of the nature of a self-determining or spontaneous subjectivity. The obvious question quickly became whether this claim for a radical philosophic independence was possible, or whether there were hidden commitments, historical or metaphysical presuppositions, or other forms of uncritical dependence that insured Kant's failure and so ultimately the failure of philosophical modernity.[3]

Moreover, the fact that Kant reformulated the modern principle of account-giving or reasoning in general as fundamentally a critical and not a metaphysical or psychological enterprise, while it best captures what Foucault has called, in an essay on Kant, "the attitude of modernity,"[4] raises a number of further questions. Specifically it raises the issue of Kant's ability not merely to point out the uncritically held assumptions of his predecessors and colleagues, but to promote in his own voice this critical attitude. How, exactly, does one justify such an "attitude," a point of view, or, quoting Foucault's essay again, an "ethos,"[5] in this case an ethos of absolute criticism or complete self-consciousness?

After all, from the classical or Socratic point of view, such a critical attitude begs the question from the start. The completion of philosophical desire is, or ought to be, wisdom, not autonomy; one is from the outset of one's reflections already naturally "placed" or situated within the cosmos, with all the inheritance and dependence that entails. Intimations of this "place" and its implications can be gleaned only as one occupies such a place, not from any "transcendental" or "absolute" perspective from "without." For a variety of reasons, this ultimately meant for Socrates a great scepticism about what we now call methodology and a reliance on an ambiguous, never ending, "dialogue" with others. If, by contrast, the modern philosophical orientation is not to be understood as a simple decision to adhere to a methodology or a set of beliefs, but originates as an attitude or spirit, a refusal to be "dependent," or to tolerate such Socratic ambiguity, and so a search for genuine "independence" or "maturity," the question that naturally arises about this critical spirit is not just its possibility, but how to understand both its historical and intrinsic authority. Why, at this time, or at any time, be "critical," insist on independence, and in what sense?

Kant's briefest and most revealing answer to this question is given in the well known 1784 essay "What is Enlightenment?" Actually there appear to be three tacks in the essay. First Kant relies simply on the rhetoric of shame, "daring" his readers to think for themselves, pointing out the "laziness" or "immaturity" of dependence on authority or tradition. Immaturity is wholly "self-incurred" according to Kant and therefore a matter of shame, not apparently a matter of historical or political opportunity. (This is already a revealing mix of natural and artificial images. Strictly speaking, or biologically, immaturity is a state that happens to one; one "leaves" it by outgrowing it.) On this view, enlightenment is therefore a matter of "courage." Second, he suggests that, given a certain initial condition (the emergence of some freedom of thought), then general public enlightenment is "inevitable," as if enlightenment is a result of a kind of social dynamic, a dynamic that itself motivates the will of otherwise lazy and immature citizens, and is not the direct result of their will. (This is all a view roughly equivalent to some of what he says in his essays on history, and more consistent with the biological image of maturation.) Third, he also suggests, in discussing restrictions on enlightenment, that enlightenment itself is a "sacred right of mankind," and that there is therefore a corresponding duty to promote enlightenment.

A case could be made that all of these finally amount to an essentially rhetorical exhortation to "be modern," since the latter two possibilities rest on an account of freedom that itself leads us back, apparently, to non-theoretical issues. That is, Kant, unlike say d'Alembert, does not identify the Enlightenment with the "liberation of theoretical curiosity," the advancement of natural science, or even with the achievement of a critical attitude. He is too much a partisan of Rousseau for that. All these accomplishments are held to be essential features of modernity, but they all depend on the central Kantian "principle of modernity," freedom, especially the freedom of thought. The latter accomplishments would not have been possible or even defensible, save for the appeal and legitimacy of this original imperative.

This principle of course has a political dimension, the claim that scientists and intellectuals, as "learned individuals" (*Gelehrte*), speaking only in a public voice, ought to be free to advance and criticize ideas. But the notion also and more fundamentally refers to a speculative and moral principle, an extremely general *"critical"* attitude about adherence to beliefs or the evaluation of actions. In that sense, since such an attitude is viewed by Kant as independent of and even a condition for modern theoretical and scientific achievements, it cannot, on such an account, itself be seen as the result of a theoretical discovery. The inauguration of modernity cannot then be understood as the "discovery" that human beings are self-determining and not naturally or theologically dependent or finite in ways previously thought.[6] And this is the beginning of an extremely complex claim in Kant: that his own assertions about human freedom are not matters of fact, or substantial, metaphysical claims. A self-determining freedom is a "condition" for making any claims about the world or our own action.[7]

Moreover, for a variety of technical reasons, Kant believed (or finally came to believe in the mid 1780s) that there ultimately was no "theory" of freedom, that we were in all senses ignorant of the world of things in themselves and coult not claim to know that we were free or could be wholly self-determining, either in evaluating our own beliefs or in directing and assessing our actions. However, neither his general Rousseauean allegiances nor his technical claims about noumenal ignorance are the end of the story, or ought to send us back to factors such as historical resoluteness, or rhetoric, to explain Kant's central adherence to the principle of a free or self-determining thought. Although he is certainly interested in advancing a certain attitude of independence and self-reliance, in both theoretical and political contexts, his main strategy in defending such an attitude rests on formulating a new kind of account in philosophy, something he calls a "transcendental philosophy." This account does not attempt, as in the popular essays, simply to encourage us to reject dependence and assert independence. Rather, Kant attempts to show that in all empirical experience, or representation of objects, and in all intentional activity, there simply are, necessarily, spontaneously self-legislated rules or conditions, that human awareness and action is spontaneously self-determining, whether recognized as such or not. On this reading, the Kantian "revolution" is not, at least not originally or primarily, something we join or reject as a practical matter; and so the problem of Enlightenment does not involve (again at least not originally) getting the unenlightened to start doing something or acting differently. The first step is to realize what has been involved all along in thinking, judging and acting. It is by realizing how much of the shape of our experience and action is "up to us," not "determined" by what we find in the world or by the passions or human nature, that the modern insistence on autonomy can be most effectively defended. In a way reminiscent of Rousseau, this fundamental strategy is thus negative or critical; it is by seeing that there is, or better, can be, nothing in experience and action to depend on but our own self-legislating activity that we can best be called on to acknowledge and realize this self-determination, best be prevented from false appeals to authority, metaphysics, or even religion.

And, we can already note, for all of their many differences, this strategy in defending a demand for autonomy (an insistence that we simply are "constructing" in claims to know or to act well, and can only deny that necessity in *naïveté* or willful ignorance) does not change much in Hegel, Nietzsche, Heidegger, Foucault, Habermas and many other descendants of Kant. From now on, avoiding the modern imperative – *sapere aude* – in one way or another shall henceforth mean: being "dogmatic."

In Kant's case, then, the basic defense of the modern principle of autonomy occurs in the actual details of his various *Critiques*, in the account of what is "necessarily" presupposed in any self-conscious experience, or the undeniable "fact of reason" in all action, or the universal if "subjective basis" for the claims of aesthetic judgment on all rational agents. These details defend an everywhere presupposed rule-governed "spontaneity" in thought and action and judgment and that is the case that must be examined if we want to understand how Kant promotes his Enlightenment program. Indeed, as Foucault has pointed out, Kant seemed to realize that only by linking the spontaneity of the subject with the very possibility of experience or action could such spontaneity be self-limiting, not arbitrary or ungrounded, and so a safe, prudent aspect of modernity to insist on.

2 The Limits of Transcendental Idealism

Kant's manner of making his case for the central famous claims of the first *Critique* makes clear the radicality of this modernism. Those claims, summarized very briefly, are, first, that knowledge is only possible by means of empirical experience of spatio-temporal objects. Insofar as we can be said to know anything, we know it by means of observation and inference, and by means of scientific laws ultimately connected to the possibility of experience. However, more famously,

Kant also argued that, even so, a form of a priori knowledge other than mathematics, a philosophical knowledge not justified by appeal to direct experience, was available. For, he claimed, all experience itself is possible only by means of what we originally require of experience for it to be possible at all, our "subjective" conditions, what he called the forms of intuition (space and time) and the categories (concepts such as substance or causality).

Kant tried to show why it could not be the case that the origin of all synthetic connection in experience, the basis of judgment or predication, our thinking together this bit of experience with that, was experience itself, as if simply noticing the regularities in repeated experiences ("association") could be said to be responsible for all the concepts regulating such synthesis or connecting. Essentially, he tried to show why, on such a model of a wholly learned or empirically produced unity, we would not be able to account for the continued identity of the subject of experience, for what he called (in a phrase Hegel called an "ugly monster") the "transcendental unity of apperception." In an argument we fortunately do not need to review here, he tried to show why such a subject, identical through time, aware of and, in a certain sense, independent of, its own experiences, required a form of receptivity "already lying in the mind," and principles of unification and discrimination that could not be derived from experience. Both conditions were' thus said to legislate unity to experience, all as a "condition for the possibility" of such experience for a unified, continuous subject.

So a genuinely a priori knowledge of these "subjective conditions" and a proof of their "objective validity" was indeed possible. It also turned out though, as a result of this argument, that all knowledge could be said to be only of objects as they are subject to these epistemic conditions of ours, or only of "phenomena," and not of "things as they are in themselves," or things considered independently of these conditions. Nevertheless a genuine form of non-empirical knowledge about the forms of human cognition, or a form of philosophy, was possible.

Kant's project was, at least in terms of historical effectiveness, a death blow to both the classical and modern metaphysical tradition, the attempt to know a priori the nature of things, what philosophers came to term "substance." In effect, Kant succeeded (again in historical terms) in arguing that what was knowable was exclusively knowable by the empirical procedures and systematic theorizing of modern natural science. However, he also argued (with more ambiguous historical results) that this all did not mean the displacement of philosophy by science, for no science could account "for its own possibility," could, as a science, justify a claim that following some method, or conforming to methodological constraints on theory formation, translation, confirmation, testing and so forth, could be said to produce knowledge. No science, in general, could explain whether and if so how, knowledge, in the simplest sense, a veridical representation of an object, was originally possible.

Kant argued that his critical philosophy could show such a possibility, and his general case that philosophy's new task was to demonstrate and assess the "conditions of the possibility" of various activities, moral and aesthetic experience, as well as cognition, was among the most influential intellectual achievements in history. As noted, for one thing, it gave philosophy what seemed like important and indispensable work to do, after its centuries-long inquiry into the hierarchy of natural forms, the ends or natural purposes of species, the connections between souls and bodies, the properties of God, and so forth ceased to have much historical authority. Kant's enterprise thus inaugurated the most important philosophic moment in the modern revolution, the end of traditional metaphysics, the attempt by philosophers to show that, if "by reason" we could show a thing must be thought to be, or could not be thought to be, such and such, then the thing simply must be or could not be such and such. It was this assumption that was at work in everything from Parmenides' claim that, no matter the appearances, if change, or difference, or creation, was *alogos*, or contrary to reason, then there could not be change or difference or creation, to Descartes's claim that, if the mind could be known clearly and distinctly without knowledge of the body, then mind must be independent of body, and it was the assumption Kant challenged most successfully. And his challenge also inaugurated a very different sort of philosophical inquiry from that familiar to the empiricist tradition, a "formal" conception of philosophy's task, no longer about the "nature of things," but about the "conditions" for finding out the nature of things (or later, the condition for a language about things, or the "structure" of discourse or action, etc.).[8]

As might be expected, this "Copernican turn" also inaugurated a new and vexing set of problems, problems, we shall soon see, deeply connected with the general modern problems of "self-grounding" and autonomy. First, with respect to Descartes's great scepticism issue, Kant seems to want to have it both ways. As we noted in the previous chapter, Descartes's attempt at a radical inauguration of a new method raised the modern "subject-object" scepticism problem,

or the issue of how we could certify that the methodological procedures possessing the greatest subjective certainty, built from the least
challengeable premises, committed to the fewest assumptions, based
only on clear and distinct ideas, could be said to represent the world
accurately, no matter even how safe or reliable predictions based
on such a method turned out to be. Kant's claim is to have avoided
such a problem. For him, the idea of beginning with the experience
of mental states, and then working "outwards," trying to discover
which states possess the internal marks that render them reliable
representations of objects in themselves, misses the nature of the
"subject-object" relation on several counts. In the first place, it is an
error to think of "subject" and "object" as originally independent or
distinct. In experience, a manifold of sensory impressions can count
as a discriminated object only by being already subject to general
principles of unification and discrimination, principles whose origin
lies in the subject, or which are non-derived. If we can determine
these necessary conditions (i.e., can prove they are necessary), there
will no scepticism problem or "relation to objects" problem, since we
will have discovered the rules for what can count as an object.

For another thing, Kant rejects the whole Cartesian (and empiricist) picture of beginning with incorrigible mental states, the minimum datum of experience. In a claim that was to have far-reaching
consequences for the rest of the German tradition, he insisted that
simply being "in" a mental state could not count as an experience at
all, much less a foundational one. An object of consciousness, even a
moment in the flow of my mental life, can count as a determinate
moment or object, only if I construe it, or take it to be such a
moment. The basic question does not involve trying to determine the
original "content" of the state; the prior question concerns the "rule"
by means of which a subject could take this state to be such and such
a state. The mind is not a passive receptacle or a mirror (even of
itself) but, in Kant's language, a "spontaneity." This means that it is
a self-determining activity, not originally determined by a "given,"
because already determining for itself what is to count as a given.[9]

This though, creates the "having it both ways" problem. For, even
though Kant appears to be contemptuous of the legacy of sceptical
problems in modern philosophy, he clearly lands himself in a new
version of the issue. Even though he claims we do have knowledge
of experienceable, external, spatio-temporal objects, his account of the
"possibility" of such knowledge means that we have such knowledge only as subject to "our" conditions, conditions valid only for
experiencers like us, with spatio-temporal forms of receptivity and

discursive intellects. This means we cannot be said to have know-ledge of "things in themselves," and has seemed to many to give to the sceptic with the other hand what was taken away with the first.

This problem is connected with another. If empirical knowledge depends on conditions that cannot be accounted for by an empirical or as we now say "naturalist" investigation of "what happens when we come to know something" (the "illustrious Locke" tried that and ended up begging the question) nor by a metaphysics of the human subject, a new kind of account of what the mind really is in itself (Descartes's failure), then what in the world is "transcendental phi-losophy?" Is it, in Beck's nice phrase, "supported by nothing on earth and suspended from nothing in heaven?"[10]

These large issues are connected to Kant's role in the modernity problem, to which we should now return. In Kant's general view of the matter, to be "premodern," or in any sense less enlightened than one should be, is to be "uncritical." In the obvious sense of that term, this just means claiming to know something, or to make a claim on others, without being able to justify such a claim against objectors. Stated so generally, such a formulation is as applicable to Socrates' inquiries in the Platonic dialogues as it is to Kant's epistemology, and Kant clearly means to use the term in a somewhat more technic-al sense. That sense involves his radical notion of the spontaneity of the human intellect, its complete autonomy in attempting to justify or criticize some claim to know. This can mean a number of different things in Kant's work, but it has as a consequence the extraordinary claim that in philosophic inquiry especially, "reason is occupied with nothing but itself" (B708/A680) or that reason somehow does not ultimately rely on some privileged or indubitable or intuited piece of evidence, but completely determines for itself what to accept *as* evidence about objects or what to regard as appropriate in determin-ing action. Moreover, adding to the difficulty, while Kant regards reason as a purposive activity, such purposes, he claims, cannot be regarded as naturally fixed, or simply characteristic of the species. If there are purposes regulating the rationality of some systematic or practical activity, they too must be determined to be purposes by reason. Nothing "is" a purpose (or a motive for action) unless taken to be so, spontaneously, by reason.

This then means that in attempting to be truly "critical" about our cognitive claims, we can never hope to resolve one epistemological problem by reliance on any other epistemic claim about an object or state of affairs or end. The problem of our knowledge of the external world cannot be resolved by some supposedly higher order claim about the nature of the mind or the existence of a benevolent deity; the problem of regularity and uniformity in experience cannot be resolved by reliance on a claim about the nature of sense impressions and the laws of association. There are no minds or impressions or deities or laws to be inspected or apprehended by the mind. The task is to avoid rigorously any uncritical or dogmatic reliance on any further claim to know.

This turns out to mean, first, that the activities of the "understanding," presented by Kant as the faculty originally occupied with the discrimination, synthesis, and classification of the directly apprehended sensory manifold, must be understood to be spontaneous (defined at B75/A51 as "the mind's power of producing representations from itself"), that the mind's capacity for receiving impressions cannot be said to be solely responsible for the production of genuine representations of objects. We produce the representations in a way that must be partially independent of any given material of sensation, and so in some sense self-determined, although certainly not arbitrary. Secondly it means that the faculty Kant calls "reason," the faculty responsible for the large-scale integration of discriminated or synthesized experiences into some interconnected system, a genuine science, is equally "spontaneous," or undetermined by the given or by any object in the formulation of that system. Reason, Kant frequently says, "commands" nature and does not "beg," it "legislates," it even frames "for itself with perfect spontaneity an order of its own according to ideas, to which it adapts the empirical conditions" (B576/A548). Since the spontaneous, legislating reason is also the heart of Kant's idea of moral autonomy, he summarizes his general position in the 1785 *Groundwork* with the claim,

> Man now finds in himself a faculty be means of which he differentiates himself from all other things, indeed even from himself in so far as he is affected by objects, and that faculty is reason. This, as pure self-activity, is elevated even above the understanding ... with respect to ideas, reason shows itself to be such a pure spontaneity that it far transcends anything which sensibility can provide it...[11]

All of which means that the Kantian principle of modernity is not Cartesian certainty but a principle that rensonates with political implications, the achievement of autonomy, reason's complete self-legislation, or its declaration of radical independence and self-sufficiency. Kant clearly believes that he can determine what any human subject must "legislate to experience" in order for there to be minimum distinctions in experience, distinctions required for there to be a self-conscious, identical subject of experience (distinctions like that between the subjective succession of representations, and the objective representation of succession). And he believes he can determine what general systematic principles are required in order for there to be a systematic unity of experience, general scientific systems that in some, often confusing, sense, he also claims are required for any concept formation and so for any first-order empirical discrimination. These sorts of claims do not depend on discovering the "nature" of anything (although of course, they seem to depend on discovering something like the nature of the mind), but concern only the rules or principles by means of which a judgment about the nature of anything could be justifiably made (whatever the nature of the mind). Reason thus grounds itself by reference only to its own requirements, and the "transcendental scepticism" that Kant admits results from this (we do not know things in themselves, but only things that are subject to these requirements) is, he clearly believes, no great threat to the power and authority of modern natural science or the achievements of critical philosophy.

Aside from the scepticism problem, though, there is a more obvious, and historically more dramatic problem in view at this point, a problem that will soon send us into, it is fair to say, the ever more extreme "reactions" of post-Kantian, German philosophy. As we have noted from the outset, Kant defined his project in opposition to rationalist and empirical formulations of the modern philosophical enterprise. This opposition alone suggests the problem now at hand. There is, after all, something philosophically comforting in being able somehow to "tie down" or "anchor," to check or to test our speculations about substance or being or even the good life. Early attempts to do natural philosophy or metaphysics or ethics in an ever more independent way, free from ecclesiastical or traditional or political authority, inspired an understandable concern about such self-regulation in many early modern philosophers (focused, often, on the great scepticism bugbear), prompting the well known concerns with an ultimate court of appeal in empirical experience, or a reliance on updated, classical doctrines of intuition, certainty, or self-evident axioms and geometric method in the rationalist tradition. But Kant has argued that there are no immediately accessible experiences to serve as a foundation for "thoughts," and that no metaphysical implications follow from conceptual or, as he saw it, purely "logical or methodological necessities.

Such critical arguments raise the stakes considerably for his own positive account, his attempt to discover indispensable subjective conditions necessarily presupposed in all experience. If experience in some fundamental way underdetermines the basic conceptual classifications with which experience is finally discriminated, and if "pure reason" cannot determine "objectively," independently of experience, such conceptual constraints, is Kant not on the verge of replacing reason with the imagination, of, *de facto*, poeticizing the origin of our most fundamental classifications, or rendering them "groundless" rather than "self-grounded?"

Of course, there are many volumes of controversy about such issues, but for our purposes we can simply note and briefly examine the historical effects of Kant's attempt to meet this challenge. In general terms that effect is easy to state. Roughly, for his immediate successors in the Idealist tradition, Kant was perceived to have succeeded decisively in his negative task, in undermining "dogmatism" in prior philosophy, and in blocking straightforward appeals to eudaimonism, moral sense, and perfectionism in ethics (that is, he succeeded in elevating freedom or self-determination to the supreme philosophic principle of modernity). But he was thought to have failed to account for any truly self-legislated constraints on experience or action. Instead, it was alleged, he reverted to some form of dogmatism himself, appealing to "characteristics" of the human species, the "nature" of our pure forms of intuition, a non-derived, supposedly complete "table of concepts," metaphysical claims about the twin "ends" of human life, a requirement for "postulates" of practical reason, and so forth, which could not be critically defended.

This then, roughly, is the philosophical version of the modernity issue in the German tradition: how to be radically "critical," and so to escape "dogmatism." And it wasn't long before Kant's powerful critical spirit was invoked against the Master himself. Fichte was the first to suggest that even the Kantian appeal to reason or to philosophy might be viewed as dogmatic or ungrounded unless we could show how such a commitment could be viewed as the "product" of a subject's purely self-determining, or absolutely free activity.[12] Contrary to someone like Kierkegaard later, who, under the influence of the late Schelling's attacks on Hegel, made a roughly similar point, the early Fichte tried to remain a "transcendental" philosopher and actually deduce the relation between such a pure self-determination and its necessary products. He himself came to regard the attempt as a failure and adopted what, for want of a better term, could be called a religious or non-idealist position.

And with this question, an extraordinarily complex set of "reflex-

ive" or self-referential logical issues were raised in Jena and Nürn-
berg and Heidelberg and Berlin, issues that, for many readers then
and now, quickly spun out of control, generating endless neologisms
and hermetic, self-generated "systems."

For Schiller and the young Hegel, the more obvious and accessible
focus for these concerns was Kant's moral philosophy. There the
initial problem concerned Kant's claim that only an action motivated
by pure practical reason, or done for the sake of the morally right,
could be considered a truly free and morally worthy action. Among
many other concerns, Schiller and Hegel wanted to know how Kant
could distinguish between simply recognizing the principle under
which "a purely rational agent" would act, and being motivated
oneself to act that way.[13] Kant's strict dualism between autonomy
and heteronomy seemed to end up meaning that I am only truly free
and self-determining when I am not motivated, or not primarily
motivated, by the things I really care about.[14] So again, in the terms
we have begun to use, the issue was how one could be said, now in
some hyper-original sense, to determine oneself to make the moral
law a motive for action. Any answer that reverted to a claim that we
are rationally obliged to act that way would clearly beg the question
they were interested in.

But, it now appears, any answer at all, any appeal to principle or
reason or passion or unconscious motive or structure, will look like
simply an invitation to raise the raise the critical question again, to
ask why such a principle or ground would itself have originally been
taken by a subject to be a principle or ground justifying this action or
judgment. In Fichte's language, the "I" must everywhere "posit"
itself and the "not-I" in order for either to be determinate objects of a
subject's experience. Yet, in Schelling's attack on Fichte, the "I"
originally presupposes the division between "I" and "not-I" and
cannot be shown to originate it. The clash between those who accuse
a radical transcendental idealism of a groundless, potentially "nihilistic" self-originating subjectivism,[15] and the idealist charge that their
opponents had retreated into uncritical dogmatism, an indefensible
reliance on something – Nature, or Being, or the *Indifferenzpunkt*, –
"outside" of and determining subjectivity, had begun, and would
reappear in Heidegger's "confrontation" with Nietzsche, in Derrida's
with Husserl, in the post-Sartrean, structuralist attack on phenomenology in general, and in many, many other contexts.[16]

In all such discussions, very large, almost unmanageably abstract
issues are at stake, and complicated hermeneutical problems arise
everywhere. Yet, I want to claim, it is always possible to see the

relevance of these issues for the (even larger) problem of how to assess the promises of Enlightenment modernity. As we have seen in many different ways now, that problem emerges with a claim for the inauguration of a new, fully reflective form of account-giving, and the establishment of new ends or purposes for such account-giving, that we have been deceived and short-sighted, and won't be henceforth. As we have also seen, in historical terms this raised questions both about the actual historical roots of the modern desire for autonomy and mastery, and about the very possibility of a revolutionary notion of reason itself. Of the many ways we could discuss such issues, I suggested we begin with Kant's actual attempt at a fully critical, or wholly self-conscious and so independent version of reason. It was this attempt that, first, gave the fullest philosophical expression to a claim that struck deep at modernity's own early optimism: that reason could not know, represent, imitate, or use as an ideal, Nature, substance, being as it is in itself. Kant in other words, both insisted on and tried to complete the modern ideal of a full maturity or self-reliance (a self-grounding of reason) even as he insisted on the restrictive and problematic consequences of this project. It is in that sense that one can say that the full dimensions of the philosophic problem of modernity came to full, if unresolved expression.

Thus, it can also be said, while the line between Kant's idealism and many of the aesthetic issues discussed earlier, such as the self-referentiality, even the self-absorption, of modernist art and literature (their attention to their own way of conditioning or even constructing an experience of the real) is not a direct line of historical influence, it is an extremely important thematic link, one which allows some of the unexpressed presuppositions of the latter to be examined and assessed. This is especially true since, as we have very briefly seen, it was Kant's revolution that created the ever more complex and finally, I think, unmanageable problems of "self-grounding" or reflexivity we shall see re-appearing in artists and modern novelists, as well as other thinkers concerned with the foundations of philosophical modernity.

That is, there is a general analogy to be drawn between the accelerating dynamic of German philosophical modernism on this question (the Kant to Nietzsche connection especially) and the dynamic visible in modernist art, where the rejection of natural models and representational ideals, the insistence on painterly autonomy, became an ever more experimental, abstract, self-defining project, until finally the very notion of a "dependence" on the idea of "art" and its tradition, was viewed as dogmatic.[17]

Thus the dimensions of this issue should not be confined to problems in "idealist logic" (the logic of a self-determining of self-grounding thought) and its rejection by Nietzsche and Heidegger. At issue again is the modern possibility of independence and autonomy, or a genuine self-rule, and the tensions and paradoxes created by that notion reappear in social and aesthetic contexts as well. Doubts about the possibility of such vaunted autonomy are, we already noted, everywhere present in modern novels, suggesting both the question of how we are to accommodate ourselves as moderns to some notion of dependence, whether on history, others, class, or "text," (all without a reintroduction of dogmatism) and the emergence of the counter-ideal of artistic, rather than philosophical or rational, autonomy.

But these latter issues are barely on the horizon and will be easier to discuss in the context of Nietzsche and Heidegger's use of art, especially as a foil for the modern, even the entire, philosophical tradition. For the moment, the next state in the narrative I want to present involves the way in which Hegel sought to "complete" the Kantian revolution in philosophy, and by doing so, to complete (or "sublate") the *aporiai* of modernity itself.

3 Hegel's Experiment

The Kantian insistence on autonomy is multi-faceted and raises a number of complex, theoretical issues. It also occupies a very special place in any picture of the historical emergency of the modern notion of autonomy in general. In order to introduce Hegel's reformulations of Kant (reformulations which, I shall argue, are really radicalizations), we should keep that larger context in mind. To do so, I shall risk a brief side trip at the outset of this discussion of Hegel.

By most standard accounts, the distinguishing feature of most modern notions of autonomy is individualism, a claim that true self-determination must involve some sort of search within for one's basic desires, needs, or interests, or for one's true or authentic self, and then the ability to realize such a content by an individual. Being self-determined primarily involves not being determined by others to want what they want, and not being prevented by them or by circumstances from attaining what I want. Such an individual is free if in possession of such a content, and unconstrained by others or by institutions in their pursuit, and is rational if the satisfaction of such ends is efficient, successful.

More explicitly, one classic modern model for such individual autonomy is simply the efficient satisfaction of one's interests. While it can sometimes seem that on this model, one is free simply if the passions one finds oneself motivated by are efficiently satisfied, traditionally much of the value or worth ascribed to this "efficient satisfaction" theory of freedom still involves some valorization of individual power in managing such satisfaction. There is, in other words, nothing worthwhile in "being free," if all that amounts to is being unconstrained and successful in the satisfaction of one's strongest passions. If benevolent aliens were to insure such immediate and efficient gratification, one would not, on this model, be in any satisfying or worthwhile sense, free. I, perhaps in concert with others, must arrange or effect this satisfaction for it to be of any worth.[18]

Another, more romantic ideal still much with us in mass culture, holds that individual self-determination requires more than an endless satisfaction of wants, that one's true, unique, authentic "self" must be discovered and realized, and that without such a discovery one is not free, but enslaved to whatever wants one simply finds oneself having. Indeed, it is likely that in such a situation one is enslaved to others, to those who created such wants (as in Rousseau's famous account). Such a notion of an individual nature within everyone, "who you really are," was often, in early romanticism, associated with a view of nature as a whole. Identifying this true, underlying, creative, spontaneous self, also meant you were identifying that part of you that was itself a part of emanation of the energy or life or world-soul of nature as a whole.

These individualist notions of freedom are often viewed as a response to a collapse in the authority of the classical or pre-modern view of freedom as the true realization of one's identity or nature. Such a view did not require a search within for an individual nature of self; just the opposite. Realizing one's true nature, and so being fully free, instead required finding one's place or role in something "outside" oneself, first in the *polis* or social community, and ultimately in nature or the whole. By understanding that one could only be oneself by realizing this function within the whole (rather than, as sometimes interpreted, sacrificing oneself for the sake of the whole), one could achieve a satisfying and finally free life. The widespread collapse of the metaphysical support for such a view of an ordered, hierarchical cosmos or Divine Order is what, on many accounts, provoked the modern assertion of freedom as a radically individual self-determination (particularly in Charles Taylor's recent work).[19] Since there were, it seemed, only individuals, having to rely primarily on themselves in deciding what to do, the primary task of modern civilization looked to be finding a way of allowing each to realize effectively the results of such self-determination.

Kant's position also involves a rejection of such a classical ideal and an assertion of an individualist model of freedom. But Kant claimed that I, as an individual agent, could only truly be said to be "directing" my action, to be determining for myself what I should do, when I did not act primarily on the basis of any sensible motive, or desire for happiness, or contingent interest. This was "hetero-nomy," not autonomy. In a reformulation of Rousseau's romantic notion, Kant claimed that I could only be free as a practically rational agent, something that now meant much more than power or efficiency in achieving ends, as in the empiricist model of agency. Such views, for Kant, accepted the ends of action as given, as not themselves self-legislated, and so accepted a kind of unfreedom. My end in action must be to be rational (in Kant's compressed terms, the will must "will itself," or its own freedom); my end must be to act for the sake of my rationality and therewith according to a principle valid for all other rational agents. I am free when I act for the sake of reason itself, when the maxim, or motive for my action could be "universalized," or when I assure myself that all other agents could also act consistently on such a maxim.

In the context we have been developing, the details of Kant's moral theory are not as important as the critical spirit that requires it. That is, Kant's views are not motivated simply by some sense of the *historical* "failure" of the classical appeal to nature or the whole, or God's will, in perfectionist or teleological models of self-fullfillment and freedom. Any such appeal is not, on Kant's view, simply suspect or dubious. It is "transcendentally" impossible, a reversion to dog-matism, or to claims whose objectivity cannot withstand the critical investigation of the possibility of objective claims. This of course also means that any attempt to claim a general knowledge of human nature or the passions or even my own individual basic interests, are all subject to the same critical doubts. For Kant, much of the En-lightenment attempt to naturalize, or render more scientific, our view of human nature is, if asserted in a practical context, just as dogmatic as classical metaphysical views. While we might be able to identify the strongest or most prevalent human passions, there is no critically defensible warrant for the claim that, therefore, the satisfaction of such passions ought to be a human end, or must thereby count as a motive for action. A passion, for Kant, is a motive for action not simply by occurring, but by being taken by me to be motive (all in a way analogous to his claim that no occurrence of a mental state is a determinate experience unless I construe it as such a state).

We might note too that, in very recent times, while many intellectuals and philosophers have become quite suspicious of modern doctrines of self-determination, and while classical models of finitude, tragedy, the priority of community or tradition, and of virtue, have become more popular, the novels of Bellow, and the work of Gadamer, or MacIntyre or Taylor, have all just set in motion the dialectic described above, prompting pointed "critical" questions about the "whole" within which virtues are to be understood, or the "metaphysical" status of this supposedly "prior" community, or mere sighs about philosophical exhaustion and a "retreat" into religious faith or tragic resignation.

It is that critical animus that inspired Kant's successors. And to make a long story very short, it also set up the problem Hegel saw himself as inheriting. As we have already seen, the kinds of questions Kant asked his predecessors were quickly asked of him. Theoretically, the question was: how has it come to be that we require experience to be categorized in various, ineliminable ways, in just *these* ways? No one in this tradition was content with Kant's reliance on some innate "logical form" in human judgment as an answer. Practically, the parallel question was: if freedom requires a radical self-determination, in what sense would a subject come to determine itself as a strictly rational being, as always subjecting its maxims to a "test," rendering them universally consistent with the possible actions of other agents? In the language that began to develop, why would a subject "identify" with such an end? Similarly, few in this tradition were content with an answer like: we simply find ourselves subject to the law. If Kant is right, we don't find ourselves subject to anything, but determine ourselves to be subject to it. And if that is so, though, then free self-determination appears to be prior to, rather that equivalent to, rationality, and Fichte's early challenge (his claim for the absolute priority of freedom) is correct.

Kant tried to argue that there was a kind of "fact" of reason in moral experience, an unavoidable realization of our rational natures that led to a kind of feeling of "respect" for ourselves as rational, and that this feeling could be said to motivate our "interest" in the moral law and a life conditioned everywhere by it. But such appeals to the language of "fact" and "feeling" were dogmatic red flags to the young Fichte, or Schiller, or Schelling, or Hegel. They were indications that the critical philosophy was still dogmatic and the logic of full self-determination had not been sufficiently explored.[20]

For the young Hegel, the term of art for such a failure of critical self-determination was "positivity." This term was originally much used in Hegel's early essays on religion (e.g., the 1795 "Positivity of the Christian Religion") and referred to an allegiance based on command or authority alone, a moral doctrine experienced as imposed from the "outside," merely "posited," rather than self-determined, viewed as the product of one's own will. Hegel, inspired by the harmony and immediacy of Greek folk religions, and originally at least, by the Kantian ideal of moral autonomy, evoked in his early essays past models of such non-alienated religion, and searched for modern institutions that might provide an integrated and collective experience without sacrificing such an ideal of self-determination. Even in these essays, however, his language was often infused with the very general critical terminology of Kant. In the "Positivity" essay, for example, in explaining the notion, he says, "The result of this [the becoming more positive of early Christianity] was to make *reason* a purely *receptive* faculty, instead of a *legislative* one, to make whatever could be proved to be a teaching of Jesus ... an object of reverence purely and simply because it was a teaching of Jesus or God's will [my emphasis]"[21]

Later, in essays from his Jena period, the use of the term "positivity" and all that it implied, became broader, and significantly, for our purposes, was used to characterize Enlightenment modernity itself. In his 1802 essay, *Belief and Knowledge*, he writes that "Enlightened Reason won a glorious victory over what it believed, in its limited conception of religion, to be faith as opposed to Reason. Yet seen in a clear light, the victory comes to no more than this: the positive element with which Reason busied itself to do battle, is no longer religion, and victorious Reason is no longer Reason."[22] By claiming that Reason is no longer Reason, Hegel means to claim that the results of the otherwise very different philosophies of Kant, Jacobi, and Fichte, has been to render Critical Reason, insistent on a complete justification of any claim to know, incapable of accounting for its own possibility, and so of limiting its own power in a way that insures a new form of positivity, or a worship of what Hegel calls the "positive knowledge of the finite and empirical."[23] The Enlightenment thus becomes a "hubbub of vanity without a firm core,"[24] a purely negative or critical enterprise, unable to articulate to itself its own possibility.

Hegel's response to this situation is to reaffirm what he considers the principle of modernity, called without qualification "absolute freedom." In the 1801 *Difference* essay, he states explicity the extraordinary principle he wants to defend: "That the world is the product of the freedom of intelligence is the determinate and express principle of idealism."[25] Showing this would, somehow, establish reason as completely self-legislating, not at all "receptive," and so not reliant on any positive or dogmatic premise, nor, in an ultimately inconsistent way, merely negative or sceptical. And, as the word "product" indicates, Hegel promises to do all this without ending up with any "aliented" subject, legislating to an external, indifferent, or hostile nature. An absolute reconciliation is possible.

All of which introduces us to one of the most hermetic philosophic projects in existence. For most commentators, there is only one way in which Hegel can achieve such an infinite (or in no way finitely determined) "Absolute Knowledge," reason's knowledge of its own requirements, and some satisfaction that these requirements are not merely subjective and so positive, what we happen to require of any coherent experience, but that they are absolute, that "what is, is rational." On such a view, Hegel could accomplish such goals if he could show that the true "subject" of self-determination was a Divine or infinitely self-determining Absolute Subject (= "Absolute Spirit"), progressively becoming more self-conscious and so more adequately self-determining in time, all in a way somehow connected with the development of human cultural and political history; and if, metaphysically, Hegel could show that a kind of romantic monism was true, that all there was, "really" was such an infinitely self-determining Spirit, and so that dualisms like those between mind and body, subject and object, finite and infinite, or contingent and necessary, and so forth, would finally have been understood as "overcome" somehow in this Absolute Spirit's knowledge of itself.

It is of course very unlikely that any of this stands much of a chance of being true, or even that it could be made much more intelligible. Viewing such a position as the outcome of a consistent radicalization of Kant's modernism might then be viewed as a kind of *reductio ad absurdum* of the whole idealist enterprise, and might prompt a search for where we could have gone so wrong. It certainly suggests that there is little of Hegel's basic position that could play an important role in any contemporary discussion of modernity, or nihilism, or postmodernity problems.

By while the scholarly issues involved are endlessly complicated, it is possible here to note a different reading of Hegel's position, one more consistent with the Kantian line we have been developing and ultimately much more fruitful in thinking about Hegel's version of the modernity problem. I have attempted an extensive defense of this reading elsewhere, but for our purposes in this context, consider the issue this way.[26]

As we have seen, while Kant may have claimed that reason "frames for itself with perfect spontaneity an order of its own according to ideas," in Kant's actual theory, the spontaneity in question is far less than "perfect." The understanding's spontaneity is constrained by the forms of human intuition, reason's spontaneity by a pre-existing, internal architectonic, and so on. Hegel's project, by contrast, or his "experiment," insists on a rejection of all such qualifications, and the attempt at a complete avoidance of any reliance on the "positive." It radicalizes, that is, critical philosophy's attempt at reason's reliance on itself alone in accounting for experience or evaluating action, but it attempts to do so without any certifying appeal to intuitions, facts of reason, or logical forms, and by avoiding or denying any assumption that such self-determination should be understood as "imposing" itself on a foreign manifold or object. While in Hegel's system there are still distinctions between such things as "the given" and "what we do with it," such distinctions themselves are shown to emerge within an extended historical process of rational self-examination. There is, in other words, only "what we have come to regard" as given, or as under-determined by the given. Whatever comes to count as a constraint or limit on thought's self-determination is itself viewed as a kind of product or result, at a higher or more comprehensive level, of thought's self-determination, and, in Hegel's most difficult claim, that self-determination is viewed as always already "in relation to" or determining, objects. And it is this radically extended critical (and not metaphysical or theological project) that is involved in such extreme Hegelian claims as, "This pure being-on-our-own belongs to free thought, to it in its free sailing out on its own, where there is nothing under it or above it, and where we stand in solitude with ourselves alone."[27]

Clearly this project does involve a kind of expansion of the Kantian idea of a transcendental subject, Kant's formal way of considering "what any subject" must think in representing an object. Kant had paved the way for this issue by showing how little of the structure of experience or the performance of an action, could be said to be determined by the immediate or given, and had tried to account for the "subject's contribution" in this "transcendental-logical" way. On Hegel's account, there is no such thing as "any such subject." Hegel proposes to think of human subjectivity collectively and historically, such that individual philosophers at some point in time necessarily take up and continue a legacy of reflection, failure and re-formulation already inherent in the terms of the problems they take up, and the options taken to be open to them. And, while not denying that there are lots of things about the world we come to know empirically, at the appropriate or "Notional" level, Hegel thinks he can both show a completely autonomous self-determination, and undermine a scepticism about the objectivity of such results. As we shall see in more detail below, such a "collective, historical subject" is viewed as completely self-forming in time, and so is supposed to do justice to, at some trans-individual level, the critical demand for spontaneous self-determination. Of course, such a notion also introduces a number of problems, such as how such a continuous collectivity in human history, or a logic, a rationality, of self-transformation, is to be defended, but these problem, however finally intractable, do not involve any dubious metaphysical commitments and can clearly be said to be extensions of Kant's critical project.

Thus Hegel's essential answer to the question of why we have come to think about things as we have, to categorize our experience and evaluate our activity in ways so fundamental that they cannot be said to be due to experience itself, but must be already presupposed in experience and action, is that we have come to think some way or other because of prior attempts at such categorization and difficulties encountered in such attemtps. The question of the justification of what he come to count as an authoritative explanation of events or evaluation of actions is thus radically historicized, made to depend on some prior authoritative procedure or set of practices, and, or so Hegel thinks he can show, the internal breakdown or collapse of such a "shape of Spirit," and its determinate resolution by a new set of criteria. This is something Hegel had promised early in his career, in the *Difference* essay (1801) when he had claimed to be able to show that the being of the "intellectual" and "real" world, "its being as a product" had to be "comprehended as a producing."[28]

Moreover, there is much more at stake for Hegel than the issue of how to understand account-giving or justification in philosophy. This is so because Hegel understands all the basic institutions of a historical society as sustained by a kind of ongoing, implicit consensus, a collectively shared view of criteria for evaluation, the good life, the highest things, etc. Such implicity held views are taken to be authoritative because of some complex shared understanding of their worth and of the ground or legitimacy for ascribing such worth to them. Hegel believes he can describe a general "process," a development, in a community's emerging self-consciousness about such criteria that can account for the periodic breakdown of such consensus and the emergence of a new self-understanding. In a word, Hegel is an idealist; he believes that communities are the way they are basically because of how they understand themselves and what they value, and these criteria and values are the way they are because of the determinate insufficiencies of prior attempts at self-understanding and self-legitimation.

Thus, in Hegel's account of why we have come to regard some set of rules or a practice as now authoritative or then as discredited, his system has a place in it both for the "logical" insufficiencies of the "forms of thought" deeply presupposed in such activities, and the social or "existential" manifestations of such insufficiencies in concrete historical life. The latter appears most prominently in the great work of his youth, the *Phenomenology of Spirit*; and the former concerns seemed more of interest to the mature Hegel, of the *Science of Logic* and, especially, the *Encyclopedia of the Philosophical Sciences*. And, periodically, he was fond of insisting that both kinds of stories were essential to his project, prompting a major industry in Hegel scholarship, the "what is the *Phenomenology's* relation to the rest of the system?" problem.

But the general point about a collective, progressive, historical self-determination is all we need here. Earlier we noted that when Kant's own critical theory was accused of a kind of positivism or dogmatism, a reliance on undischarged assumptions, it looked as though any sort of answer that could be given to the kind of question Fichte was asking would inevitably be subject to the same counter, that we had painted ourselves into a corner, an inevitable reliance on a dogmatic appeal. Hegel's attempt to see every principle or axiom or methodology or intuition or *telos* as historically provisional, itself a product of some collective self-determination, was, in the interpretation I am sketching, an attempt to meet this difficulty, and so to make this process of "thought's self-determination" itself "infinite," in Hegel's language, or "all there is" to justifying and evaluating. On this account, the question of what comes to count as, in general, an authoritative explanation of objects and events, the decisive classificatory procedure, or evaluative criterion, can never itself be resolved by appeal to an ultimate explanatory principle, or general regulative ideal, or basic argument strategy. There are, finally, no rules to tell us which rules we ought to follow in regulating our discursive practices, no intuitions certifying the axioms out of which such rules should be constructed, and no transcendental argument for the necessary conditions of any experience. What we always require is a narrative account of why we have come to regard some set of rules or a practice as authoritative. In Hegel's "phenomenological" version, such an account must always appeal to a pre-discursive context or historical experience (sometimes simply called "life") as the origin of such authoritative procedures and rules (even while Hegel also maintains that such a context or experience is itself the "product" of a kind of prior reflective principles, now become implicit, taken for granted, in everyday social life). Our account of our basic sense-making practices is thus tied to an account of the *aporiai* "experienced in the life of Spirit," and so such a justification is everywhere, to use the famous word, "dialectical," and not "logical." Moreover, Hegel tries to argue that this self-determination should be conceived in a radically "holistic" way, not as a kind of intellectual self-examination guiding practical affairs. In his ambitious project, a political crisis or economic revolution are just as much matters of "Spirit's" self-interrogation and self-determination as a great conceptual shift in philosophy. Both are manifestations of Spirit's coming to self-consciousness and neither is reducible to, or explicable without, the other.

All of this of course immediately raises new suspicions: whether there really is such a self-determining, internally self-correcting, process or not; whether this Hegelian totality, Spirit, so coherently self-determining in its political, aesthetic, religious and philosophic manifestations, can be defended.[29] Before we raise such problems, however, we should also stress that Hegel does not want merely to appeal in a general and vague way to such a dialectical origin. He does think he can account for the emergence of such *aporiai*, and show how a fuller or more reflective position would resolve them and so come to exercise a certain social authority. Thus, for a variety of reasons, he would insist on a far stronger version of "dialectic" than that recently defended by Richard Rorty. Rorty is in favor of some version of Hegelian "dialectic," but only when understood as "the attempt to play off vocabularies against one another, rather than merely to infer propositions from one another," or as a "partial substitution of redescription for inference." He considers this practice just a "literary skill" rather than an "argumentation procedure."[30] However, event though Rorty indicates, in his criticism of Habermas, that we still require some sort of "replacement" for religious and philosophic accounts of a ground for modern institutions, and that a "historical narrative"[31] will provide such a replacement account, he also undermines the possibility of any genuine narrative by insisting throughout on a kind of radical contingency in conceptual and social change. That Europe simply "lost the habit of using certain words and gradually acquired the habit of using others"[32] or that the use of a new language "with luck ... will also strike the next generation as inevitable,"[33] makes it very hard to see how such a narrative could be a narrative (rather than a list of social events) and how it could function in the way Rorty suggests. From Hegel's point of view, the appeal to chance or luck or contingency is simply another species of dogmatism, an appeal to "the positive" or "what simply happens," as if such an appeal were possible.[34]

And we should also pause to note the general relevance of Hegel's approach for the larger modernity issues we have been raising. It should be obvious by now that Hegel's position, or what little of it we have discussed, does not fit easily into the categories already developed. In the first place, it is clear enough that Hegel is a committed proponent of the modern revolution. He is dead serious when, in this *Lectures*, he tells us that with Descartes, "we are at home, and like the mariner after a long voyage in a tempestuous sea, we may now hail the sight of land."[35] The "land" we have sighted is a full or complete self-consciousness and so the achievement of "absolute freedom," the modern principle. But Hegel affirms such a principle in a way unique among his modern colleagues. Hegel regards the emerging reliance by Western civilization on the authority of reason, and the emerging understanding of reason as a fully critical self-determination (as absolute freedom) to be deeply continuous with the pre-modern tradition. Modernity itself is then not a "revolution," or autochthonous or self-grounding; it is the whole of human history that must be seen as "absolutely" self-supporting or self-grounding, and modernity is just the beginning of the final realization of this self-consciousness itself, as well as a realization of a *telos* already implicit at the origin of the Western experience. (In fact, as we shall see in more detail in a moment, in Hegel's account of what he calls "negativity," the dissatisfactions responsible for historical change, they stem from an original failure of self-consciousness, an original inability to understand the self-determined character of human history and its institutions and so an inability to account reflectively for those institutions or to defend them from sceptical attack.)

Or modernity's self-understanding (the absolute rejection of dogmatism) can be given a historical justification, all as long as Hegel can also justify history itself as "the whole," as the totality of human

experience, "outside" of which there is only "positivity," or uncritical
metaphysics, scientism, religious and traditional mystification, etc.[36]
(Again, the latter claim means most directly: no reliance in a philosophical account on any principle or faculty or axiom or procedure,
without a "phenomenology" of why we have come to regard such
a procedure as indispensable, and a "logical" reconstruction of the
categorial commitments of such an enterprise.)[37]

What could it possibly mean, though, to conceive of such an
extreme, post-Fichtean expression of self-determination as somehow
the "realization" (*Verwirklichung*) of as well as the overcoming and
completion of any pre-modern ideal? This question again raises the
chief issue – why we should believe in Hegelian teleology, and for
many commentators, the most useful focus for raising that question
has been Hegel's attempt to reconcile various consequences of the
modern notion of autonomy (consequences he appears to accept)
with various pre-modern notions of community, or an organic view of
the human place within the whole. This is itself a book-length topic,
but we can make use of the issue briefly at least to sketch the chief
problem now beginning to emerge.

On the one hand, in his practical philosophy, Hegel clearly accepts
a modern, essentially Kantian criterion for evaluating the worth of
actions. To act freely is to act rightly, and to act rightly is to act in a
way consistent with the will of all, or to act universally, and to act in
some sense with this intention as a reason. But, in an argument
indebted to his general idealist position, he does not believe that we
can formulate the content of such a universal law except by reference
to the history of ethical institutions, the history of what we have come
to regard as counting as universal, as what all others would or could
accept as a maxim.[38] Just as when we attempt to "judge objectively"
or "determine the truth," we inherit an extensive set of rule-
governed, historically concrete practices, so when we attempt to "act
rightly," and attempt to determine our action spontaneously, we
must see ourselves as situated in a complex collective and historical
setting,[39] a dependence on setting very much like that implicitly
asserted by the narrative form of the modern novel. (Indeed one of
the oddest things about Hegel's *Phenomenology* is that it much more
resembles a novel in its account of social and ethical institutions than
a philosophical treatise.)[40]

Thus it could be said that, in a way much like the classical ideal of
freedom as "realization within the whole," Hegel too tries to show
how the attempt at self-determination requires (at least at some,
often very implicit, level) an understanding of oneself as occupying a
"place" within a larger whole, except in his view that the whole is

not nature or the cosmos, but the history of a collectively self-determining subject. More concretely, it means that Hegel thinks he can show that one never "determines oneself" simply as a "person" or agent, but always as a member of an historical ethical institution, as a family member, or participant in civil society, or citizen, and that it is only in terms of such concrete institutions that one can formulate some substantive universal end, something concretely relevant to all other such agents.

And here again we are pushed back to the issue of whether we should regard any such modern institutions as more than wholly contingent, as really the products of some historical, even "rational, self-transforming, self-correcting "process." This is obviously the most implausible aspect of Hegel's claim, and generates a number of questions that we should at least survey.

First, we might ask, why wouldn't it be more plausible to think of the origin of our most important, seemingly indispensable classificatory and evaluative categories in a more straightforward way. Let us admit that some empirical or purely rational justification of some schema is impossible. Why then not move to an non-cognitive, or explantory rather than justificatory approach, as if such conceptual schemes are themselves products of some non-conceptual ground. That is, why shouldn't the rise and spread of Christianity have much more to do with the economic conditions of the Roman empire than with the internal deficiencies of the Greek view of subjectivity and the Roman notion of the person? Why isn't the modern version of the nation state better regarded as the seizure of power by the property-owning classes than the "actualization" of the modern notion of right? And so forth.

Quite consistently, if still problematically, Hegel would clearly claim that all such appeals to causal origins or functional correlations, or to unconscious motives, etc., are themselves claims of a certain sort, embedded in complex, historically specific theoretical projects, projects that require their own account or phenomenology, if they are to be legitimated. We would first have to understand why we have come to find it plausible to look for this or that category as *explicans* before we could set off in search of "the answer." Or, from Hegel's point of view, there is no "outside" or extra-conceptual *explicans*. There is only what we have come to regard as an indispensable *explicans*, and the narrative we need to give concerns that "coming to regard."

This sort of response, however, could simply provoke a more radical rejoinder. Let us assume that Hegel has successfully linked the question of the rational justifiability of various cognitive and evaluative principles with something like their historical sufficiency, with an account of how such principles emerged as resolutions of an experienced and "logical" crisis in a community's self-understanding. Let us also assume that in making his case for this progressive view of conceptual change Hegel is not, as it is put in the Hegel literature, "presupposing the Absolute," or justifying this claim for progression by an appeal to some theory which just presupposes that basic conceptual change is to be understood as a process of some monistic subject's self-enlightenment. Given the above rejoinder to more sociological or empirical accounts of conceptual change, and, now, a denial of any metaphysical foundation for a faith in teleological progression, why should we believe that there should be any overall progression, or even that we could account for such conceptual change at all? Perhaps such changes are in a general sense "historically motivated," are "responses" to historical *aporiai*, but maybe any determinate "resolution" is just one of many others that could have emerged then, and these basic shifts are just fundamentally contingent, and so *alogos*, not subsumable under any single narrative.

We have already seen something of the spirit of Hegel's response to such suspicions in the discussion of Rorty above. In the first place, he would be quite critical of any account which implied that communities could suddenly, in some radically contingent way, "change the subject," could simply invent a new agenda or basic self-description. Communities ("Spirit") don't just have or adopt such agendas; the authority of basic principles and criteria are linked to shared assumptions about the justifiability of such norms, and we could not arrive at any account of the determinacy of a new agenda without some accompanying account of what went wrong in such a consensus and why that going wrong would lead to this resolution. In Hegel's view, resigning oneself to a description of such "changing agendas" would be like trying to do science by simply recording *seriatim* all one's observations.

So much for what we cannot rest content with. In Hegel's view, what sort of narrative is possible?

4 Hegelian Teleology

Hegel's claim that human history is dialectically and progressively self-transforming is much more controversial and (apart from the

obvious case of Marx) much less influential than his general "histor-
icization" of Kant's transcendental enterprise. Indeed, a very great
deal of the thought of later European philosophers, starting roughly
with Schelling's Berlin lectures, could be categorized by understanding their differing sorts of opposition to Hegel's account of the progressive logic of conceptual change and his case for the significance
of that conceptual change in social, religious, political and aesthetic
practices.

Consider the issue this way: Let us assume that early modern
philosophers understood modern liberation and a quest for independence as freedom from religious and traditional authority and a new,
hard-headed allegiance to "nature" as an ultimate standard, whether
understood empirically or rationally, that Kant effectively criticized
such appeals to nature and re-interpreted true Enlightenment as the
human subject's knowledge of its own self-legislating activity, and
that Hegel showed that the form of such contributions by the subject
could not be determined by a transcendental analysis, but required
some sort of a continuous historical narrative. Then, much post-
Hegelian European thought could be understood as an attempt to
come to terms with an acceptance of this entire idealistic progression,
coupled with a vigorous denial of any possible continuity in this
Hegelian narrative, and so a new appreciation of the role of utter
contingency in the formation of what we come to regard as an
authoritative practice or criterion. If history turns out to be as
purposeless as nature (the "slaughterbench" Hegel himself described), unavailable as some whole within which to orient and assess
collective and individual possibilities, then the agenda facing Kierkegaard, Schopenhauer, Nietzsche, and Heidegger appears on the
horizon.[41]

It will not be possible here to deal in any responsible way with the
nature and adequacy of either Hegel's general case for historical
teleology, or the application of that theory in his complex assessment
and partial defense of such modern institutions as the bourgeois
family, civil society, the modern nation state, idealist philosophy,
Protestant Christianity, romantic art, etc. But we have seen enough
of his position at least to suggest that we should beware of falling into
superficial characterizations, and that his insistence on an idealist,
internally rational view of historical change might prove very difficult
to reject, even if it all leaves us with a variety of *aporiai* that invite the
"determinate negations" of Nietzsche and Heidegger.

For example, as I have presented his position, there simply is no
Hegelian guarantee or deduced necessity that human history is

<u>progressive</u>. In the first place, Hegel is interested only in a relatively small range of historical phenomena, and within that range, his interest is smaller still. He is perfectly willing to admit that vast areas of human experience are unconnected and have no rational relation to the past. What is at stake is only *Wirklichkeit*, actuality, or the basic structure of reality and the supreme criteria of evaluation, not mere existence, or the mere happenings of human events. Roughly, Hegel's idealist account of such actuality ties the issue of "what there fundamentally is" or what is fundamentally right or good, to our non-derived criteria or categories and he is chiefly interested in the development of these categories. It is by no means an easy task to extract from Hegel a clear definition of what is everywhere the central focus of this historical reconstruction, what he calls *der Begriff*, or the "Notion," but it is clear that such a reconstruction is the heart of his analysis, and everything else of interest he has to say is made to depend on it. As we have seen, this means that Hegel's chief interest lies in those conditions which could be said to make possible the identification of a determinate object of experience or a discrimination in individual cases of the right, and ultimately the good. Hegel too accepts the now widespread post-Kantian anti-empiricism: the "world as such" does not come to us pre-categorized; at a sufficient level of generality, it should be conceded that it can be cut up and evaluated in all sorts of different ways, and so the relevant question is to account for what we end up collectively sanctioning as the decisive kinds of "cuts," the Notions ("cause," "substance," "essence," "appearance," "law," "individual," "science/non-science," etc.).

Yet, as I have portrayed the Hegelian experiment, no such account could itself be said to find some sort of ultimate source for such categorization, whether in the forces of production, our hard-writing, or our best collective interests. Any such account would merely reflect the current authoritative criteria of contemporary sense-making institutions. Hegel's account of wisdom or absolute knowledge has (on this reading) noting to do with providing some final account for such a question, along the lines suggested by the above alternatives. Rather, such a full or complete self-consciousness would only involve a defense of the claim that the formation process of such Notions is as Hegel says it is, everywhere a historical product, assessible only in terms of its potential, determinate superiority to past standards, and concretely available options. There would be, then, no *telos* to such a process in any standard sense, only some sort of realization of the "ultimacy" (in Hegel's language the "absolute" status) of such historical "excitation" itself. And finally, Hegel thinks he can show that, given the conditions for the very possibility of self-directed or distinctly human doings and conceivings, the historical process responsible for the determinate principles governing such activities must be understood "rationally," that the process would not be intelligible, and so neither would the activities, unless the "movement" of such a process were narrated by reliance on the idea of concrete, determinate, progressive negations. (Said most globally, even if paradoxically, on Hegel's reading the sort of "reconciliation" promised ideally by modernity is neither something that can be simply achieved, once and for all, nor something that can be abandoned, or forgotten. Both alternatives would require a kind of regression into a new form of "positivity.")[42]

This is part of what Hegel means when he makes the sweeping and otherwise unintelligible claim, at the conclusion of his *Science of Logic*, that

> The identity of the Idea with itself is one with the process; the thought which liberates actuality from the illusory show of purposeless mutability and transfigures it into the Idea must not represent this truth of actuality as a dead repose ... by virtue of the freedom which the Notion attains in the Idea, the Idea possesses within itself also the most stubborn opposition; its repose consists in the security and certainty with which it eternally creates and eternally overcomes that opposition, in it meeting with itself.[43]

Thus, there is both a stronger and weaker version of teleology that might follow from this claim. The weaker version just amounts to a kind of "historically situated" version of rationality, or account-giving; sense-making in general. On such a theory, the question of the justifiability or legitimacy of some dominant practice or method could only be answered in terms of, let us say, its historical sufficiency, by means of our ability to understand the determinate emergence of such a "paradigm," and its resolution of earlier difficulties. (All of which also assumes that we have also "correctly" identified the nature and significance of such earlier difficulties, a thorny problem on its own.) And Hegel's own version of such a "legitimation strategy" will only be as good as the details of his case in individual instances, and its ability to withstand objections and counter-proposals from competitors. It may end up that no good account can be given of the concrete or sufficient, historical rationality of contemporary "ethical institutions" like the family, bureaucracies, geo-politics, mass culture, academic philosophy, etc., but (a) such an attempt can at least be placed back on the agenda without fear of committing oneself to a jejune, optimistic progressivism and (b) any denial that this is the way to go about an assessment of our "life-world" will have to deal with charges about the positivism and critical *naïveté* of a more heremeneutical or historicist approach, or the ideological and insufficiently reflective character of a more critical or traditionally rational approach.[44]

Of course, even at this level of modesty a number of problems are both obvious and ominous, problems that make the post-Hegelian reaction we shall soon discuss and understandable. This sort of reading of Hegel as a kind of radical, post-Kantian modernist, in effect shifts the real burden of his argument away from a "meta-physical" core, from which so much is supposed to be "deduced," to a more programmatic and methodological center, the strength of which is a function of its superiority to other approaches and its ability to "deliver the goods." And Hegel's great success in the former (or so I have argued elsewhere) does not insure any success in the latter. It may be that a detailed Hegelian reconstruction of contemporary life will simply fail to find any convincing "traces of reason" to use Bubner's[45] phrase. Or, Hegel may have suggested the only possible legitimation of modernity, even if that possibility cannot be realized. There are certainly undeniable problems in his own speculations about the resources or "traces" within his own society. Some historical intimation of this looming failure would be inspira-tion enough for, say, Nietzsche, simply to abandon the prospect as a dead-end, as we shall see.

Beyond this more modest approach, however, Hegel himself clearly thought he could also defend a more ambitious theory, and the problems he creates for himself when he suggests such ambitions are well known. As we briefly noted earlier, he thought he had a very general explanation for the emergence and bread-down or internal collapse of various Notional candidates in the past. That account appealed to incomplete or insufficient self-consciousness; that, some-how, not realizing the self-constituted nature of such Notions made a full assertion and defense of such criteria impossible, requiring, in some determinate way or another, a "more" self-conscious position, and so that therefore, the "realization" of a number of the themes of post-Kantian critical idealism was "implicit" in the original Greek attempts at philosophy, and that difficulties with such "ultimate" philosophical notions, construed as these sorts of difficulties, were "responsible" for a variety of other crises and *aporiai* in the social and religious life of Western communities.

In my view it is very unlikely that Hegel can account for as much as he would like by an appeal to this emerging idealist self-consciousness. But the details of that problem need not concern us now. What I have been trying to suggest is that Hegel's position (at least the weaker version described above) represents a certain sort of appropriate terminus in philosophy, once the problem of a genuinely modern revolution, a new insistence on an "independent" self-determination, is raised. I have spent so much time with the details of his way of framing the problem because, as I hope now to show, many of the issues raised by his radicalization of Kant's rejection of dogmatism will re-emerge, in significant and pointed ways, in two modernity theorists who insist that Hegel and the whole idealistic, the whole modern enterprise, is, respectively, dogmatic, still motivated more by a kind of atavistic faith than anything else (Nietzsche's view), or that Hegel, and the idealists, and even Nietzsche himself, are all prime examples of a great self-delusion endemic to the whole post-Platonic enterprise, an apotheosis of philosophical subjectivism and the forgetting of being.

4

"Nihilism stands at the Door": Nietzsche

1 Nietzsche's Complaint

The modern experience could be said to raise several problems, or to create a wide variety of reactions and deep dissatisfactions. Some of these are distinctly social, and have largely to do with the emergence of new class relations, and the growth in power and influence of the property-owning and professional classes. For many thinkers, this phenomenon raised disturbing questions about various entitlement issues and about the modern organization of work and distribution of wealth and opportunity. Some problems have to do with the nature of modern culture, especially with the emergence in the late nineteenth century of what would later become the contemporary "consumer society," and with the effects of such a mass society on taste, moral sensibility, on what had been both high and folk culture, and on aesthetic experience in general. Many other problems have to do with more philosophical worries, concerns about the consequences of the Enlightenment attack on religion, or on classical, teleological models of explanation, or about the possibility of a genuinely secular foundation for moral and political life, or about the nature of the modern "individual," so celebrated as the great result of modern liberation.

Since (for the thinkers I am dealing with) these more philosophical concerns are often presupposed in the social and cultural and aesthetic dimensions, and especially since the very perception of a problem or dissatisfaction with some aspect of modernization often relies on some such philosophical assumption, I have concentrated above on an attempt to provide some comprehensive view of such issues. This has led us to a concern with the multifaceted issue of autonomy, the modern attempt at critical, social, political and aesthetic "self-rule."

Nietzsche, I want now to claim, represents a third, alternative approach to the "discontinuity" and "continuity" views we have so far discussed.

Nietzsche's views on modernity can be initially summarized in three claims. First, there is, for him, no radical, modern origination. Nietzsche is a thoroughgoing continuity theorist. (Descartes, for Nietzsche, with all his grandiose pretensions about a modern founding, "was superficial.") Secondly, however, this is so not because of any development, or progression, and certainly not because modernity represents any final success or culmination of what had been, in some implicit way, premodern ends. Neither, despite occasional appearances, does Nietzsche argue as a "perennialist," as if, because of some unchanging human situation, origination is simply impossible.

In the account we shall examine below, Nietzsche places a great deal of emphasis on two influences, or "institutions" in his narrative of the Western experience, institutions he calls "Platonism" and "Christianity" (which he also calls "Platonism for the people"). According to Nietzsche, all the major institutions of modernity – modern science, with its reliance on causal, deterministic explanation, liberal-democratic politics, romanticism, humanism, "free thinking," socialism – should be interpreted as essentially Christian, or as expressing the kind of psychological and moral interests promoted by Christianity. (As we shall see, these include such things as asceticism, self-denial, *ressentiment*, weakness, a slave mentality. At the most basic level of Nietzsche's analysis, all such phenomena should themselves be interpreted as consequences and implications of the most basic "drive" prominent in Western institutions, what Nietzsche calls the "will to truth."[1])

Of the many things Nietzsche wants to address by insisting on such a continuity claim, one, especially in this context, is central and highly controversial: the claim that, ironically, all forms of the much ballyhooed modern claims for "independence" actually represent a deep fear of genuine independence, and a disguised or self-deceived form of dependence, even a "slavish" form. Being genuinely "free," or in his language truly "active," and "self-affirming," has nothing to do with realizing one's nature within the whole, with any reliance on a "certain" methodology, or a complete, critical, self-consciousness, whether historical or transcendental, or with the rational will, or with merely an unconstrained successful satisfaction of one's interests. In his account of the emergence of a nihilism crisis, all such versions of the realization of freedom have very specific, self-deceived, and ultimately self-undermining origins. (So "Christianity," while an immensely powerful and attractive form of asceticism, is, especially now, avoidable, not in some sense historically "fated," given any attempt at self-determination, as it roughly is in Hegel's account.)

As the very terms of such a summary indicate, however, this often bitterly critical attack on the pretensions of Enlightenment modernity still contains a somewhat experimental and original attempt to insist even more decisively on some kind of self-determination, "truly" becoming "who you are," on an "Overman," or on a "self-overcoming," a modernist duality clearly present already in much we have seen before, in Rousseau's invention of the problem of culture, in Kant's "critique," in Baudelaire's ambiguities, and in Hegel's "dialectic." Sometimes Nietzsche even seems quite comfortable invoking Kantian language, identifying his opponents as "dogmatists," and, for all his contempt for the "great Chinese of Königsberg",[2] attempting in effect to "trump" or "out-criticize" the post-Kantian attempts to trump Kant, accusing all philosophic attempts to justify or legitimate modernity of such "dogmatism," and contrasting such an approach with his own more radically self-conscious "perspectivism."[3] This strain leads Nietzsche to propose what could be called the "German" version of autonomy – a complete and so self-determining, even hyperbolic, self-consciousness – even as he confusingly seems to reject any traditional version of such a goal, and promotes instead what seems a new sort of "immediacy," even a "kind of second innocence." (For many recent commentators, all of this has come to mean that Nietzsche's version of the attempt at autonomy entails an "artist's metaphysics," an invocation of the post-Kantian fascination with the "autonomy of the aesthetic" and a grand extension of the scope of the aesthetic-as-creative, as if everything were a matter of *l'art pour l'art*. To live is to "be an artist," and to be an artist is to be essentially self-creative. I shall try to show that this is an incomplete interpretation of what Nietzsche was after.)

To return, though, to his modernity interpretation: Even if all of these extraordinary critical, deflationary claims could be established, it would still not follow that there was any problem with the modern project, or that we should be at all bothered by its unique extension of "Platonic/Christian" ideals, even if we might have to give up any premodern/modern contrast. But Nietzsche also claims, in his third and in many ways most difficult major thesis, that there is something historically distinctive about modernity, particularly as it manifests itself in the late nineteenth century. His claim is that we live in an age in which there are numerous "signs" revealing (to those with eyes to see) that this entire post-Platonic project has begun to collapse under the weight of the dilemmas and *aporiai* it created for itself, to terminate in an anomic, directionless "herd society," and most fundamentally in an experience of worthlessness and enervation Nietzsche calls "nihilism" or "the radical repudiation of value, meaning, and desirability."[4] His own more precise definition of this "failure of desire" states simply that the arrival of nihilism means that "the highest values" (those Platonic-Christian values distinctive of the Western tradition) "have devalued themselves."[5] In a claim that will require considerable explanation, Nietzsche asserts that it was the historical experience that resulted from attempting to pursue such highest ideals that itself produced a "dawning" realization that the ideals were worthless; that where once there had been value, there is now the *nihil*, nothing, that we live in the age of the "death of God," the death indeed of all the moral and philosophical gods, the age of the "last men," the "twilight of the idols." It is clear that Nietzsche regards this historical or social event as itself decisive philosophically: what has been undermined is the very "possibility of value," as value has always been understood, and so we must now seek a complete "transvaluation of values," a way of thinking "beyond good and evil."

So in *The Twilight of the Idols*, for example, "the modern" is defined as a "self-contradiction," although Nietzsche gives this dialectical notion a unique spin by calling it a "physiological self-contradiction"[6] (a qualification we shall return to). Or modernity has in some sense, ended, terminated in some sort of double bind or nihilism in which subjects must still evaluate, will and act, but in which they have rendered themselves incapable of such affirmation, so dubious about the possibility of any ideal or end implied by affirmation that they have become enervated, sick, "modern scep-tics."

All of which seems to have made Nietzsche central in everything "European" and raised the stakes considerably in any Nietzsche interpretation. (At stake is often a position on the meaning or very possibility of "modernity," or "reason.") Commentators who would disagree about most everything else often agree about at least the centrality of Nietzsche's diagnoses. For Habermas, Nietzsche re-presents "the entry into post-modernity": he "renounces a renewed revision of the concept of reason and bids farewell to the dialectic of enlightenment."[7] By this Habermas means that Nietzsche broke with Hegel and the other early modernity critics who saw clearly many of the intellectual insufficiencies of modernity's self-understanding, and many of the disastrous effects of social and economic modernization, but who did not want to throw the baby out with the bath-water, who wanted their recognition of these very problems to form the basis of a "dialectical" reformulation of the modern project. Nietzsche, according to Habermas, was the first who claimed that you had to throw out the "baby" too, especially the hopes for a socially and politically integrating, reconciling appeal to reason in public life and private morality.[8] (We have already seen enough to be suspicious of such popular characterizations, since Nietzsche is trying to hold the Enlightenment to its own standards, to show its own "self-contradiction," and such doubts about the autonomy and integrative function of reason itself are as old as Rousseau's complex speculations about its contingent, or "non-natural" origins.)

Some commentators, like Charles Taylor, simply characterize all influential contemporary European philosophy as "neo-Nietzschean,"[9] and Stanley Rosen does not hesitate to claim that "Friederich Nietzsche is today the most influential philosopher in the Western, non-Marxist world."[10] Even those not much interested in the postmodernity issue point to Nietzsche's role in raising powerful, necessary questions about modernity's self-understanding. Leo Strauss has claimed that it was Nietzsche "who ushered in the second crisis of modernity – the crisis of our times,"[11] and Alasdair MacIntyre that Nietzsche "is *the* moral philosopher of the present age."[12]

For many, many others who have written about Nietzsche, from the summary just given, it would be fair enough simply to add his name to the long list of European intellectuals who identify a kind of cultural crisis as the heart of the modernity problem: that egalitarianism, the intrusion of market considerations into every aspect of life, the effects of a mass, eventually media-dominated society, or the narcissism and impatience created by modern institutions, each or all signalled some vast decline in the moral sensibilities or taste essential for a vital, or noble civilization. From literary modernists to critical theorists to conservative Platonists, Nietzsche's power stems largely from his undeniable rhetorical skill in articulating this great distaste with modern banality, vulgarity, and kitsch.

Yet, to return to the approach I shall pursue in assessing the three components identified above, Nietzsche's own view of the "revolution" now needed seems, somewhat traditionally, to have a very great deal to do with how we come to understand Plato, Socrates, the Christian tradition, Kantian moralism, etc., that, as he put it in *Beyond Good and Evil*, the "greatest events" of an age are its "greatest thoughts."[13] This is the "idealist" and incontrovertibly philosophic element in Nietzsche which continues to make him attractive to those interested in maintaining that there is something of great political and cultural importance in, say, the critical or deconstructive analysis of literature or of all "texts," the kind of thing that could lead de Man to write that "I have always maintained that one could approach the problems of ideology and by extension the problems of politics only on the basis of critical-linguistic analysis,"[14] or could lead J. Hillis Miller even farther, to say that "I would even dare to promise that the millennium would come if all men and women became good readers in de Man's sense."[15]

I propose to examine Nietzsche's account of modernity's nihilism crisis in the following way. First we need more detail on just what Nietzsche thinks has gone wrong, not just with modernity, but with a whole tradition so influenced by Greek thought and Christianity. This will involve a brief summary of his account of how the highest values have "devalued" themselves, or why modernity should be understood as a "physiological self-contradiction."

Since Nietzsche is not interested merely in listing symptoms, we shall then need some account of his "diagnosis" of the modern illness, his "genealogy," explaining why we have produced the age of the "last men," without desire, or a goal. This will involve some of the most complicated and disputed elements of Nietzsche's case, since he seems to have a number of different sorts of answers to this question. Many are strictly historical; that is, they involve some sort of historical narrative, a story about what happened when we tried to regulate our conduct by allegiance to certain moral values ("good" versus "evil"), and how we came to experience the *aporiai* or even self-contradictions involved in such an attempt.

However, as we shall see, Nietzsche is not just interested in a historical genealogy, a way of showing how such ideals actually arose as a response to a specific social situation, and how difficult it came to be for us to accept this realization about their local and contingent origin. If this were the case, there might be no general philosophical significance to these results. We might be a bit surprised to realize how much the appeal of early Christianity could be plausibly traced to rather ignoble motives of resentment and fear, but we need not be convinced that all this has anything to do with the contemporary institution, or with the instrinsic worthiness of the ideals of universal brotherhood and equality. (The same would be the case with any realization about the all-too-human interests of scientists and philosophers.) Nietzsche realizes that he needs some way to disabuse us of any notion of intrinsic worthiness ("the good in itself"), and some way of preventing any marginalization of his historical genealogy.

This will turn out to be complicated, but we can introduce the issues by noting that in his account of the significance of such appeals to origins, Nietzsche often appeals to what we would call hermeneutical considerations. He says frequently that he is interested in such things as "the meaning" of "the ascetic ideal" or in showing that "the Christian interpretation" and its "meaning" are "counterfeit."[16] And when he wants to marshal evidence to support his views about social phenomena and religions, he appeals often to etymologies ("good," "bad," "evil," "guilt"), to texts, and to the work of artists, poets, and musicians. And so this whole approach, at least initially, seems to presuppose that some model of interpretation is the only one capable of revealing such a meaning. When we ask ourselves questions like: what were Christians actually doing in promoting the practices of self-denial, what were they after, or what was the point of Socrates's promotion of dialectic, definition and logos, we are asking not for any fact of the matter but for some compelling and persuasive re-description, some reading, as if we were to ask why Emma Bovary was so dissatisfied in marriage or about the meaning of Charlus's psychological and social disintegration. (And, just as in the latter question, we are not concerned simply with a psychological individual, or in Nietzsche's case a historical event, but with general questions of significance, history, what has become possible for us, and we have no method or formal approach that will resolve disputes about these issues. The issues are such that there can be no such thing as the resolution of disputes, and Nietzsche is one of the first to think about that fact in ways that avoid jejune relativism, or a too easily achieved, cynical nihilism.)

Thus, however much we are driven to try to extract one from his texts, this whole approach seems driven by no general theory of interpretation, or no decisive claim that there could only have been such specific and contingent origins, and that the meaning of such ideals is exhausted by placing it within some interconnected, unified narrative. Nietzsche readily admits that all interpretation, including his own, is a "subduing," a "becoming master,"[17] that "wisdom" he is interested in is "mocking," "violent," and "always loves only a warrior,"[18] so that his own view is simply a competitor in some eristic discourse, subduing and becoming master by a kind of poetic force, rather than an appeal to truth. The idea seems to be not that Nietzsche has claimed to identify "the essential meaning" of a phenomenon, but has succeeded in some other, essentially rhetorical sense of showing why "it ought to be read as having such a meaning." The key issue will be what this might mean.

For now, we need only note that Nietzsche does seem to have some sort of account of the "possibility" of a phenomenon being meaningful, or value being a value, or a claim to truth counting as an authoritative claim to truth, and that this possibility rests on the omnipresence of interpretation, of a self-construal undetermined by the facts or nature, both for the original participants and the Nietzschean hermeneuticist. And that all of this is presupposed in his influential indictment of modern culture.

Sometimes, as in the first essay of *Beyond Good and Evil*, he seems to baptize such a position as if it were indeed a straightforward, easily accessible philosophical theory; it is a "perspectivism," a radical, quasi-metaphysical claim that asserts, in effect, "to be is to be interpreted." At other points, in the notes, he even seems to have something approaching a kind of reductionist or naturalistic account, one that claims that all our sense-making or evaluative activities represent or are expressions of "the will to power," as if the latter were a "drive" that counted, again, as an account of the "possibility" of intelligibility and value.

Finally, Nietzsche draws a number of conclusions from his diagnosis, and even proposes a "grand politics" for the future, consistent with his case against modernity. This aspect has proven the most unsettling with many otherwise sympathetic readers, since this is where appeals to an *Uebermensch* or in some translations "Superman," occur, and where Nietzsche discusses such things as eugenics, how women really ought to be treated, praises cruelty, scorns democracy and, it appears, unleashes his "blond beast." Yet, in a way more friendly to recent postmodernist and literary approaches, Nietzsche also insists on the omnipresence of irony in his work, rejects all the political movements, including anti-Semitism, often associated with him, and seems more interested in playing the provocateur, or simply in playing. All of which will finally raise the question: what in Nietzsche would it mean not to be "modern"?

2 Modernity as "Twilight" Zone

Nietzsche's central claim about the historical situation of modernity is that "nihilism stands at the door."[19] As we have seen, this is supposed to mean that contemporary European culture has begun to lose faith in its sustaining "values," its sense of purpose and so its self-confidence. "The aim is lacking; "why?" finds no answer."[20]

Typical of his sweeping claims about this state of affairs is the following:

> What has happened, at bottom? The feeling of valuelessness was reached with the realization that the overall character of existence may not be interpreted by means of the concept of "aim," the concept of "unity," or the concept of "truth." Existence has no goal or end; any comprehensive unity in the plurality of events is lacking: the character of existence is not true, is *false*. One simply lacks any reason for convincing oneself that there is a *true* world.[21]

But while it is clear enough from these and many similar indictments, that Nietzsche himself has become convinced of such claims, it is not initially clear why Nietzsche feels entitled to claim that this feeling of valuelessness simply "was reached" as some sort of historical event, or that in general "one simply lacks" reasons that would convince one of a "true world."

Sometimes, although rarely, Nietzsche does try to point to actual historical "symptoms" of such "feelings." In one of his notes, he lists some "chief symptoms" of the cultural "pessimism" he interprets as a prelude to full-blown nihilism. These include,

> the *dîners chez* Magny; Russian pessimism (Tolstoy, Dostoyevsky); aesthetic pessimism, *l'art pour l'art*, "description" (romantic and anti-romantic pessimism); epistemological pessimism (Schopenhauer, phenomenalism); anarchistic pessimism; the "religion of pity," Buddhistic premovement; cultural pessimism (exoticism, cosmopolitanism); moralistic pessimism; I myself.[22]

For the most part, however, Nietzsche does not rely on any direct or obvious manifestations of "social distress" or "physiological degeneration" as evidence of any nihilism crisis, and he admits freely, that, on the contrary, "Ours is the most decent and compassionate age."[23] And even though Nietzsche turned out to be a very good prophet, and this "feeling of valuelessness," particularly after the First World War, would indeed become very widespread, most of his own writing about the present age does not rely heavily on identifying such symptoms as the above, or on any prophetic promises.

Nietzsche, that is, is well aware that among almost all of his contemporaries there is very little sense of any great moral crisis, or even any disaffection with modern ideals. The bourgeois, modern civilization he describes in *Thus Spoke Zarathustra* as the "city of the many colored cow" is as stolidly contented as that bovine characterization implies. When, in the prologue to that work, Zarathustra first enters this town, he proclaims the possibility of a new kind of human being, the "Overman," and so a new way of thinking about how we come by our highest ideals and how we affirm and sustain them. By contrast, he encourages his audience to have "great contempt" for their present "happiness," that it is in fact "poverty and filth and wretched contentment."[24] Zarathustra, speaking in an elliptical, parabolic language, characterizes his historical age as the advent of the age of the "last men," the "most contemptible" type. These men "no longer shoot the arrow of . . . longing beyond man," and so the "time is coming when man will no longer give birth to a star,"[25] when "humanity" will have no "goal," and so humanity itself "will still be lacking."[26]

All of this is jeered at and ridiculed by Zarathustra's audience. They have experienced no crisis, are quite satisfied with their goals, treat Zarathustra as a clown and madman, jokingly plead to be turned into these "last men" and they "jubilated" and "clucked with their tongues."[27] The question this obviously raises is how Nietzsche wants us to understand this "crisis" and "failure" that is somehow experienced as contentment and the achievement of "freedom."

In this work, though, there are only a few details available to suggest Nietzsche's answer. For one thing, such "last men," when they announce that they have "invented happiness," "blink," suggesting a kind of rote, or dulled, unthinking recitation of their virtues. They do not understand the terms used by Zarathustra and ask directly about the language with which he upbraids them. "What is love? What is creation? What is longing? What is a star?" they ask, and again, this last man "blinks."[28] Such a reaction implies a kind of stupefied bewilderment at Zarathustra's exhortations, a reaction that indicates they do not any longer understand how much they have given up in order to be contented. Such a last man "is no longer able to despise himself"[29] and so can only "blink" in wonder at Zarathustra's perorations. The community Zarathustra describes has "settled" for what in other contexts would be described as the paradigmatic bourgeois virtues – peace, security, and the rational, efficient, satisfaction of one's (rather narrowly defined) "interests" – and has "forgotten" that this is a way of life chosen among many other possibilities, and whose conformist, timid spirit represents great losses as well as some gains.

And their blinking reaction to Zarathustra's prophetic pose also prefigures another of Nietzsche's favorite images of modern existence: they begin to drift off into a kind of permanent, peaceful, untroubled, "sleep."[30] In this sense, then, their contentment not only does not count against Nietzsche's claims about the absence of any value or ideal; the terms of their contentment, their lazy, thoughtless, "low" self-satisfaction, or conflict. They do not define or "overcome" themselves, and so are content with whatever satisfactions they can achieve collectively with as little pain or struggle as possible.

It is of course more than a little controversial to interpret modern liberal culture this way, to suggest that a commitment to pluralism or respect for each person's choices and their possible happiness reflects not a new, genuinely modern goal, but a kind of nihilism, or an absence of any goal worth "discipline" and sacrifice. To those who would point to, say, the French Revolution as evidence of the risk and sacrifice undertaken in the name of modern freedom, Nietzsche appears to respond a bit like Flaubert – that these revolutionaries were self-deceived, this was yet another "slave" revolt the true meaning of which is much more visible in Homais, or in the vapidity of the Second Empire in general rather than, say, in Napoleon.

Many of these issues will return later. For now we need only note that Nietzsche wants quite deliberately to claim that one of the chief characteristics of the nihilism crisis is that very few people experience the modern situation as any sort of crisis, that the last men have not only given up any attempt to pursue a goal, to create and affirm in any way that counts as genuine affirmation, but they have settled so comfortably into their contented lives that they no longer even realize what they have done, or what else might be possible. One Nietzsche's understanding of being human (which we shall look at more closely later) they thus barely count as human, or self-defining creatures, and may be the "last" men, the prelude to a race more like sheep than men. So in a section of the *Twilight of the Idols* called "Criticism of Modernity," he claims that, "The entire West has lost those instincts out of which institutions grow: perhaps nothing goes so much against the grain of the 'modern spirit' as this. One lives for today, one lives very fast – one lives very irresponsibly: it is precisely this which one calls 'freedom'"[31] Or we interpret "the loss of instincts out which our institutions grow," as our institutions, proclaiming our collective uncertainty about any end worth a sustained effort as the "achievement" of pluralism, tolerance, freedom. This means, Nietzsche had claimed in *The Gay Science*, that "All of us are no longer material for a society; this is the truth for which the time has come."[32]

Thus Nietzsche's claims go considerably beyond those of other nineteenth-century philosophers also concerned about the effects of a mass, commerce-dominated society on public taste, values, and ideals. He shares some of, say, Mill's concerns, and would also prefer to be a "Socrates unsatisfied, than a pig satisfied," but his criticism is not so much concerned with the difference between true or higher and false or lower pleasures. Pleasure and happiness are of no interest to him, since what counts as pleasant is a result of what one esteems. And so "esteeming" or "valuing" and its proper conditions are his focus. On Nietzsche's reading, the question most at issue in modernity concerns the fate of modern ideals and their weakening hold on us. These values include liberty, equality, moral duty, selflessness, rational consensus, toleration, and so forth, together with what Nietzsche claims is a parallel opposition to any "order of rank," egoism, tragedy, or nobility. He wants to show first how deeply we have misunderstood our own ideals or any possible ideal and so that "the time has come when we have to pay for having been Christians for two thousand years."[33] It is as a consequence of this two millennia long self-deception that the "modern" may be "defined as physiological self-contradiction."[34] Our most immediate, powerful and deepest sense of things, our "instincts" or moral sensibilities, have been trained in a certain way, trained to esteem or value in only one, divinely sanctioned, or objectively grounded way. And there are signs everywhere that we have lost confidence in that way, and can see no other, can see only "nothing." These signs include actual expressions of scepticism and pessimism, and the hypocrisy and vulgarity of institutions that still proclaim an allegiance to Christian or modern, "progressive" ideas.

Parenthetically, we should also note that Nietzsche's general characterization of the modern moral problem tends to highlight such things as liberal-progressivism, romanticism, Christian humanism, socialism, and egalitarianism as prototypical of modernity, and often ignores strains in modernity that share few assumptions with such camps (e.g., Machiavelli, Hobbes, Spinoza).[35] His view seems to be that such a sweeping characterization is defensible since all the qualifications and distinctions we might make are irrelevant. Any other "strain" in modernity we might identify still relies on a view of its own authority that requires a dogmatic and self-deceived "will to truth," and the whole "moral" apparatus that comes with what he considers such a moral ideal.

The basis for this view will emerge in the next section. For the moment, we can add a final, very frequent Nietzschean characterization of modernity. If the fundamental problem is modern "morality," then *"Morality in Europe today is herd animal morality."*[36] For the most part, especially in *The Genealogy of Morals*, he explains this notion by contrast with an aristocratic, or "master" society.[37] Since modern, Christian, democratic man has become so unsure of his various "idols" (e.g., natural right, the state, humanity, science, reason), or unwilling to deal with what is emerging as the disintegration of the justification traditionally provided for such idols, he has taken refuge in another form of security, a "last" form of justification. What he now affirms are the kinds of ideals that the maximum number of people could affirm without conflict, for they are the safest bet for a people which views itself as essentially a "herd," concerned above all that no one be elevated above them. Nietzsche implies that in the anxiety created by doubts about divine authority, and in the chaos created by so many irreconcilable attempts at a secular basis of moral order, we have, in a kind of panic, taken refuge in each other, in safety, or the lowest common denominator. We have degenerated into creatures who can will to do only what all others are willing to do, and this primarily out of fear and a timid hesitation about the consequences of any full realization of the contingency and plurality of human ends.

So, what is celebrated in modernity as an adherence to reason – the claim for example that no action of mine or social policy can count as justified unless it can be shown to be universally justifiable, that all those affected by it would or actually do accept the act or policy – is not for Nietzsche some sort of unavoidable imperative in human life. His concern with such an ideal goes well beyond those who worry about how to specify "what others would will," or how to include any historical detail in that counter-factual speculation. He interprets the entire ideal as merely a contingent way of life, arising at a certain point in history in reaction to the failure of traditional or religious ways of life, and as essentially motivated by fear of and resentment at, the strong, or independent creators of value.[38] In his narrative this interest in universalizability, or reason, however spelled out, should be understood as a search for some sort of reassuring protection against what is emerging in modernity as nihilism crisis, a collapse of faith in any "external" or divine or objective good. Moreover, this sort of reliance on reason, or insistence on the universality of one's principles, (a) is to be understood as simply an extension of the Christian demand for equality, itself a "reaction" by "slavish" and "weak" communities to the threats perceived to exist in the strong or masters, and (b) requires, when pursued, such narrow and ultimately empty values as to result in a self-denying, repressive conformism, again providing social harmony at the price of stultification, anomie, and tedium.

Nietzsche even goes so far as to suggest that the ever growing authority of natural science or the naturalistic world view should be understood as part of this frightened, conformist reaction, that the appeal of a view of the world in which we are all subject to the same natural laws, where there is "everywhere quality before the law" is "a fine instance of ulterior motivation, in which the plebeian anta-gonism to everything privileged and autocratic as well as a second and more refined atheism are disguised once more."[39]

Clearly, if we are to accept Nietzsche's view of what "now stands at the door," we are going to need a more extensive discussion of the terms within which he poses this modern nihilism crisis. Why should we believe that the modern promotion of rational debate, a universal method for investigating nature, equality of rights, or moral univer-salism all somehow essentially "express" a Christian, reactive fear of strength, difference, or the "chaos" we would have to confront with-out such artificial impositions of order? Why, said another way, shouldn't we understand Nietzsche's fulminations against modernity as "premodern" rather than in any sophisticated sense, "post-modern," or, like the views of Burke, or Carlyle, or Arnold, or even Tolstoy, a mere nostalgia (fueled by bitterness and a grandiose sense of self-importance) for the era of privilege and clerical authority, and the oppression and self-serving doctrines of nobility that go with it?

3 Origins and Perspectives

Nietzsche's call for a complete self-consciousness about "origins," his sensitivity to the thin line in modernity between a rational social integration of individuals and a "herd" or conformist society, and his search for a "noble," genuine form of independence, a "pathos of distance," an "active nihilism" that would finally realize the modern, secular goal of autonomy, all make his concerns central to the issues we have developed thus far. But Nietzsche has his own controversial reading of what makes prior attempts at such autonomy failures and why they have resulted in a widespread nihilism crisis. And Nietz-sche has several different ways of persuading us that his reading of the modern scene is the correct one. Taken together, they clearly separate him from the level of discussion common in reactionary critics and in the legion of socially conservative literary modernists, the likes of Eliot, Joyce, or Pound. His answers will raise their own problems, but they suggest an ambitious hermeneutical strategy well aware of many other things that have to be addressed if the interpretation produced by that strategy is to be defended.

Nietzsche proposes a sweeping historical "genealogy" of the origins of the tottering moral distinctions he claims are at the center of the Western and especially modern experience. In general, his account has two main components. His central question, "under what conditions did man devise the value judgments good and evil"[40] is, he claims, best answered by a story of historical "degeneration," the reaction of a large, but weak and powerless social group (the "slavish"), eager to rewrite the terms of moral discourse in a way more favorable to their position and prospects. Originally a different distinction and agenda (that between "noble" and "base") had dominated public life, literature, and religion, and this "slave revolution" story constitutes the best historical account of the new agenda. As we have noted, Nietzsche also believes, as a separate element in his account, that this whole project was doomed from the start, that, in order to succeed, it needed to tell a very different story than the true one about its origin and status, a story, he claims, that eventually could not withstand the imperatives of truthfulness and self-consciousness promoted by that very point of view.[41]

But Nietzsche's position is not exhausted by this historical genealogy, and it is his account of the significance of that genealogy that raises the stakes considerably in his account. For Nietzsche is not only interested in showing that such a moral ideal would have been attractive to people in such a powerless situation, and that they would have found it difficult to admit that so much of their attraction to such an ideal was based on resentment, fear, envy, and even self-hatred. He also frequently writes as if believes that such moral ideals must always reflect the contingent perspectives of those who adopt them, that no universal perspective is possible, and that a general account can be given of the nature of all such perspectives: they are expressions of "the will to power." An allegiance to a measure or criterion in evaluation is not just sometimes, or incidentally, motivated by a broadly self-promoting and contingent point of view.[42] Identifying such a perspective and its relation to the advancement of power identifies "the meaning" of the moral ideal and its very possibility. Or, answering that first question ("under what conditions did man devise these value judgments good and evil?") also answers the second of the two questions *On the Genealogy of Morals* asks: "and what value do they themselves possess?"

This latter dimension in Nietzsche's diagnosis will return us directly to many of the large themes already introduced in previous chapters. For, as suggested earlier, Nietzsche's whole project involves both a deep suspicion of the optimism and self-understanding of modernity, as well as an attempt to radicalize, complete, and thereby overcome the limitations of such a project. The modern "faith" in rationality, or its secular "ascetic spirit," is supposedly shown to be merely a contingent strategy in a long struggle for power between the weak and resentful, and the strong and self-assertive. It is rendered a mere "event," to use Foucault's word, and cannot be said to represent the universal interests of mankind, the necessary conditions of any affirmation or esteeming. Modernity thus has naively misunderstood itself, and Nietzsche, as he conceives himself, thus can be said to represent, somewhat ironically, a more enlightened, fully self-conscious position.

But this of course must mean that the Nietzschean terms of "enlightenment," or the realization of this messy interplay of the psychology and sociology of power in intellectual and moral institutions, do not themselves in any straightforward way recreate the Kantian enlightenment ideal of full, or critical self-consciousness. There are obviously connections with the spirit of that enterprise in Nietzsche, but for him Kantian and Hegelian criticism (not to mention "the English psychologists," or modern sceptics, or Darwinians, or others who share some of his genealogical spirit) presuppose "values" whose origin remains for them unquestioned. They too are dogmatic and promote a kind of impossible transcendence, naively presuming that they can secure universally and necessarily the values they promote. (Or, again, such modern philosophers formulate the issue of philosophic or moral or critical autonomy in a Christian way, recreating by various strategies the Christian notion of a separable soul, still under the sway of the assumption that independence requires a denial of the body, contingency, a mastery over the unthought and unseen. And this is the assumption Nietzsche means to undermine.)

This means first of all that Nietzsche must somehow defend his reading of modern institutions, his claim that they culminate in a realization of the wholly unsecured nature of all evaluation, the impossibility and destructive consequences of any attempt at a "self-reassurance." And he must do so without reliance on the "perspectives" and "values" he has exposed or undermined. And this will all again, we shall see, recreate in Nietzsche (to some extent directly and intentionally, in other respects, indirectly and with consequences he wants to avoid) the interplay between a typically modern demand for radical critical autonomy – no reliance on any foundation or origin or value without showing how and why we have taken it to be a foundation or origin – and the limitations encountered in such an attempt at a full self-creation, the interplay between what Hegel would call the "infinite power of the negative" and finitude.

It is in the third essay in *On the Genealogy of Morals*, "What is the Meaning of Ascetic Ideals," that the two strains in Nietzsche's account noted above come together and begin to raise many of the issues just noted. In the first essay, Nietzsche had defended his interpretation of the origin of the moral ideals of selflessness, duty, and a "pitying" concern with others, or with universality, typical of the Western moral tradition, and had, by his rhetoric, lauded the "pathos of distance" accepted by the "noble, powerful, high-stationed and high-minded," his seizure "of the right to create values and to coin names for values"[43] with no concern for others. In the second essay, he tries to show the vast metaphysical and moral-psychological system that had to be created to justify the moral point of view favorable to the slave, the notion of a separate, immaterial soul (untouchable by the master's power), individual "responsibility," conscience, etc.

In the third essay, his account is deeper and somewhat less strictly historical. He notes that the general form of the moral ideal he is interested in can be said to be an "ascetic ideal," or a vast regimen of "life-denying," repressive, even self-mortifying practices. We have produced, he claims (when viewed from a high enough altitude), in our philosophers, intellectuals, religious leaders, even artists (at least artists like Wagner) a type, "the ascetic priest" who "juxtaposes life" with "a quite different mode of existence which it opposes and excludes"; life itself is viewed as a mere "bridge" to a "higher" or more "spiritualized" form of existence. We can reach this higher life only if we "turn against" and "deny" life, "the whole sphere of becoming and transitoriness."[44]

Such a generalized view of our moral situation is now not treated only as a historical reaction to the rule of the stronger. First, as we might expect, no practice can be successful if wholly reactive, defined, or trapped by the terms of its opponent. The Socratic-Christian point of view also involved a bold, even powerful "active" stance, a determined and successful seizure of power from the "nobility" and an enforcement of strong "discipline." Nietzsche now points out that the particular form taken by the slave revolt was motivated by its own very large concerns with existence itself, indeed chiefly by a fear of the transitoriness and pointlessness of existence. We created ourselves as a "life-inimical species ... in the interest of life itself that such a self-contradictory type does not die out."[45] (The "active" and "reactive" are necessarily intertwined, and cannot be formulated as if in strict opposition.) This great illusion of a "true world," whether of a Platonic or modern mathematical character, and the spiritual sacrifices necessary to achieve it, "made life possible," allowed us to exert power over life, to redeem it, justify living to ourselves, and so avoid the great *horror vacui*, the fear that suffering and pain really are without significance or purpose.

In *Thus Spoke Zarathustra*, his account is painted in even broader strokes, as Zarathustra claims that all prior Western moral ideals are based on a "revenge" against time, an inability to accept the transitory and purposeless nature of existence,[46] and that now, "For *that man may be delivered from revenge*, that is for me the bridge to the highest hope, and a rainbow after long storms."[47]

What is especially significant in such claims about the origin and meaning of the ascetic ideal is that Nietzsche associates the pursuit of the ideal, and his account of its false pretensions, disastrous consequences, and immanent historical collapse, even with those modern intellectuals who "certainly believe they are as completely liberated from the ascetic ideal as possible," those "pale atheists, anti-Christians, nihilists; these skeptics, ephetics, hectics of the spirit."[48] These modern sceptics and nihilists (unlike, presumably, Nietzsche himself) still "embody" the ascetic ideal, indeed, they are "its most spiritualized product, its most advanced front-line troops and scouts," all because "they still have faith in truth."[49] And this of course raises immediately all the questions suggested above about the status of Nietzsche's own diagnosis and remedy of the "modern sickness," a diagnosis that somehow can accept its own partiality and perspectival character. Nietzsche here prefers to leave all the questions raised by this claim unanswered in this book. He ends his discussion simply by asking,

> what meaning would our whole being possess if it were not this, that in us the will to truth becomes conscious of itself as a *problem*? As the will to truth gains self-consciousness – there can be no doubt about it – morality will gradually *perish* now: this is the great spectacle in a

'truth' is exclusive, hence denying

hundred acts reserved for the next two centuries in Europe – the most terrible, most questionable, and perhaps also the most hopeful of spectacles.[50]

If, then, "the entry into postmodernity" as Nietzsche see it, will most fundamentally involve some sort of new self-consciousness about the problematic status of the will to truth, what will all that involve? What is involved in this rendering problematic, and what will follow from it?

Nietzsche of course does not offer us a "critique of pure truth," but in some books, such as *Beyond Good and Evil*, he does offer formulaic and much quoted summary statements of his position on the problematic status of the will to truth, that "It is perhaps dawning on five or six minds that physics, too, is only an interpretation and exegesis of the world (to suit us, if I may say so) and *not* a world-explanation,"[51] and "There are no moral phenomena at all, but only a moral interpretation of phenomena."[52] In a section of his *Nachlass* organized under the title "Will to Power as Knowledge," there are similar Kantian-like or idealist claims: "facts is precisely what there is not, only interpretations. We cannot establish any fact 'in itself'"[53] and "Logic is the attempt to comprehend the actual world by means of a scheme of being posited by ourselves; more correctly, to make it formulatabe and calculable for us."[54]

All such claims stake out what we would today recognize as a general anti-realist position, a relativization of claims to truth to general "criteria" of truth, accompanied in Nietzsche by claims that there can be a plurality of such criteria, and that an assessment of such criteria cannot depend on any notion of correspondence or greater or less approximation of the real. This is not then a metaphysically idealist position (the existence of objects is not said to depend on our thinking or interpreting), nor a Kantian position. We are not "cut off" from and made ignorant of things in themselves by our perspectives. The idea of such a world in itself is alternately treated as "nonsense," or itself a "fiction," a perspective designed to "suit" certain purposes.

So, from the point of view of the old "dogmatic" perspective, what Nietzsche is claiming is that "untruth" is a "condition of life," that the unavailability of the dogmatic notion of truth in itself, or the absence of such a ground, is precisely what makes a coherent or intelligible life possible, what requires created perspectives.

But what kind of non-dogmatic "authority" can all of this claim? None of this means that Nietzsche is a kind of tolerant pluralist about the issue of the perspectival nature of intelligibility. It is not enough to think of Nietzsche as simply "experimenting" with theories concerned with the possibility of intelligibility, or with possible interpretations themselves, since Nietzsche not only clearly holds that his general claims about perspectivism cannot be denied without *naïveté*, without in effect being "uncritical," positivist, but he goes on to "rank" various perspectives, to indict the dominant Western, modern perspective (itself a denial of perspective, or will to truth) and to elevate a new noble point of view. It is not enough to note that he presents all of these in a defeasible, non-dogmatic way. What one wants to know is how and why he affirms what he affirms. It is clear enough that this affirmation is not based an any appeal to the truth of Nietzsche's views, but it is also clear that he is not merely proposing a possible view or a possible model for life, as if in a kind of passionless game, or as if he thinks that "looking at things this way" will be pragmatically useful.[55] The central interesting fact is that he is addressing us, that he is attempting to create (at least among the right, "higher types") a social consensus about how we might view what has happened to us and what we should do about it, and that some part of his success depends on the proper reception of that appeal. So we have pursued the question of the authority of Nietzsche's interpretation of modernity ot the question: What counts as such a reception?

And again this returns us to a kind of dilemma in the reflections on modernity we have been pursuing. The story we have been telling is of an attempt at radical self-sufficiency, an attempt to kick away one's ground or support, what one has been merely handed by tradition or authority, or self-evident reason, or intuition, and to re-establish such a foundation or ground in some wholly self-made, or at least self-determined way. Occasionally, in the story Nietzsche and Hegel (and lately Girard) tell, this enterprise has led us to each other for some sort of support, suspended above the void, all resulting either in a disastrous and unsatisfying conformism, or in a new theory of social and historical rationality, depending on one's point of view. We might now ask, does Nietzsche's participation in this project succeed in finally kicking away the last prop, the attempt to see ourselves in any sense as we "truly are," or the "faith" in the "will to truth" and so realize the modern "dream" of complete self-sufficiency (however now re-formulated non-ascetically); as if we can finally escape self-deception or dogmatism?

No discussion of this problem can avoid the fact that the language Nietzsche often uses suggests he has a rather conventional answer to this question, one founded on a kind of armchair science about nature and human nature. In a famous passage from *Beyond Good and Evil*, he writes,

> Suppose, finally, that we succeeded in explaining our entire instinctive life as the development and ramification of *one* basic form of the will – namely as the will to power, as *my* proposition has it ... then one would gained the right to determine *all* efficient force univocally as – *will to power*. The world viewed from inside, the world defined and determined according to its "intelligible character" – it would be will to power and nothing else.[56]

It is noteworthy that there are ironic qualifications, as it were, "scrawled" all over this passage. The whole passage is a mere "supposition"; Nietzsche emphasizes that this view is his view, not "the" view; the idea of a "univocal" perspective had just been undermined throughout the first part of the book; the idea that the world has an inside, or even an "intelligible character" are both very frequent objects of Nietzschean sarcasm.

However, many readers of Nietzsche have been more impressed by much less qualified formulations culled from his unpublished notes (collected together as the "book," *The Will to Power*). There he writes such things as, "The criterion of truth resides in the enhancement of the feeling of power."[57] And there are several other passages from the 1880s notes that suggest that "everything is will to power" is to be taken as an explanation for things being as they are, as if human beings, plants, asteroids, sets, and spaghetti, are, by "maintaining themselves," by virtue of some omnipresent drive, not merely for self-preservation, but for a kind of supremacy, by "opposing" and negating others.

It is of course extremely unlikely that Nietzsche has anything like a biological or naturalistic theory in mind by these remarks. The notes themselves continue a sustained critique of the possibility of any metaphysical or scientific identification of the basic "forces" in the universe, as well as of any possible use of the notions of "cause," or "explanation," or "law" that might be involved in any such appeal to a universal "drive" for power. Rather, again, even in the notes, Nietzsche most often associates the will to power with interpretation itself, suggesting again that all intelligible categorization and evaluation is a function of values or ends pursued in ways that cannot be secured or grounded through the use of any procedure or by appeal to any fact of the matter.[58] Or the basic cuts and divisions and moral discriminations in our experience are as they are because we have made them; we have not made them in any sense because they are found to be as they are. And Nietzsche's frequent way of making this point is to say such things as "The will to power interprets ... it defines limits, determines degrees, variations of power ... In fact interpretation is itself a means of becoming master of something"[59] and in a passage that will be one of the most important for Heidegger, "To impose upon becoming the character of being – that is the supreme will to power."[60]

Life then is will to power because life is or everywhere requires a kind of "unsecured" interpretation, one without the possiblity of a methodologically or practically "re-assured" consolation. True "modern" independence will somehow involve a refusal of such consolation, a refusal motivated by a realization of the contingent and self-destructive, now failed agenda originally driving the great modern experience of self-conscious doubt. It is in this sense that a hyperbolic self-consciousness wil undermine the enervation produced by modern self-consciousness itself and so make possible a self-overcoming and genuinely "joyous" legislation.[61] The authority of the guiding principles (or values) of various interpretive strategies are now understood to stem only from the authority bestowed on them, or on the authority that can be bestowed in some historical situation or other. We cannot even say (at least with any illumination) that these interpretations arise "as an attempt to gain power over existence and others," since what counts as power is also up for grabs ("everything is will to power") as in the conflict between Christian asceticism and the aristocratic legislation of values.[62] This is all something we try to avoid or deceive ourselves about, but "now" the time of reckoning for such deception is at hand; the contingent nature of such perspectives is more and more impossible to avoid, and we shall be called on the adopt and pursue our goals, to produce our art, to marry and educate and deal with fellow citizens, all in the light of this realization. What will that mean?

4 The "Pathos of Distance"

We have already seen enough to know that it cannot mean that Nietzsche's position should be viewed exclusively as that of an aesthete or litterateur. I mean the kind of position persuasively attributed to Nietzsche by Nehamas's recent book and long influential for many who see Nietzsche as an apotheosis of aesthetic modernism. Much of Nehamas's interpretation is motivated by a realization of how many insoluble self-referential paradoxes are created by traditional metaphysical, biological, naturalistic, even, in general, "philosophical" readings of Nietzsche. To avoid these, the various questions we have raised should, we are told, be answered more in the language of "literature" rather than philosophy. Nietzsche "wants to be believed, but not unconditionally"; he wants to avoid "sef-deception" about the "conditions under which views are accepted as true," to announce everywhere and openly that his views are "only his," and to persuade, in some sense of that term, by making "his presence as an author literally unforgettable,"[63] by fashioning a compelling "literary character" out of himself, out of someone "whose views are exclusively philosophical."[64]

To get to the heart of the matter raised by such considerations, we must pass over a number of very important features of Nehamas's account, particularly his treatment of Nietzsche's views of the Will to Power, Eternal Return, his attack on traditional views of the unity of the subject, and his rejection of all absolutist, universalist moral codes. What is important to us is Nietzsche's general views of narrative, which clearly play so large a role in his diagnosis of the ills of modernity, and the question of a literary model for such a narrative.[65] Nehamas argues that at the center of Nietzsche's project is an individual act of self-creation, that by viewing life itself as literature or interpretation, Nietzsche is called on to fashion himself into a literary character whose views on his own and his tradition's past will end up cohering as a compelling, inter-related "model self." The paradigm for what Nietzsche is doing is "the perfect narrative, or perfect story. In such a story no detail is inconsequent, nothing out of place, capricious, haphazard, or accidental."[66] The material of Western history is, literally, senseless unless narrated in some sort of coherent whole, or made into a kind of novel, a whole somehow relevant to the character "Nietzsche," who happens to view his own fate as essentially tied to the fate of such a tradition. This literary conception of a "controlled and coherent whole"[67] serves as a standard for evaluating the success of such a narrative, although there is no claim that only one, or even one sort, could possibly satisfy such a criterion.

Nietzsche says so many things about an "artist metaphysics" and an "aesthetic justification of existence" that such a characterization of Nietzschean "life" as "literature" is undeniably important. But the interpretation also raises several problems, problems, I think, Nietzsche was himself well aware of, and which render the aesthetic reading not so much incorrect as incomplete. As we shall see, Nietzsche's sense of the contemporary historical significance of art or "the poetic" in the long "quarrel between philosophy and poetry" itself relies on more than can be contained within the category of the "literary" or aesthetic. This is especially true if we do not consider Nietzsche as simply a self-created author (already a category too close to Flaubert's famous aesthetic asceticism), but understand him within the oscillating celebration and defamation of modernity so characteristic of European thought after Rousseau. If we do, we encounter an issue we have encountered before: whether everything of significance in human life can be viewed as "inside," or the product of, an autonomous self-legislation, here, "an interpretation."[68] It is one thing to look to aesthetic criteria and the honesty with which they are applied, when evaluating a character or practice, and it is another to have decided that such criteria are of paramount or even exclusive importance in all evaluation. Creation would then threaten to become meaningless, or one would have no means with which to discuss and comprehend the significance of interpretive activity in general. Any such sense of its significance – any appeal to the historical context which requires such a point of view, or of the utter failure of non-perspectival projects, or of the "conditions" under which truth claims can and cannot be accepted – would all be, not comments on, but moments of, a Nietzschean "poem," and so could not count as a comment on the significance or meaning of literary creation itself.

Before exploring such an issue further, we should also note that, in fairness to Nietzsche, such issues must be stated carefully, lest the question simply be begged. Nietzsche, after all, is one of the first thinkers in the modern tradition to have fundamentally challenged the very possibility of "transcendental" or formal-logical or "critical" or "purely" aesthetic, or, roughly, autonomous points of view in philosophy or thought, any viewpoint from which the essentially Christian hope for autonomy, whether conceived philosophically, morally, or poetically, could be realized. (The "artists," too, after all are "valets of some morality, philosophy or religion, ... all-too-pliable courtiers of their own followers and patrons, ... cunning flatterers of ancient of newly arrived powers".)[69] For him, all such positions simply represent timid attempts to re-conceive a Christian dualism, a safe, pure haven for thought, and so to promote a kind of ascetic "denial of life." But, as the aesthetic reading, and the evidence for it, makes quite clear, none of this represents a reversion to a precritical dogmatism, or a positivistic naturalism or materialism.[70] There can be no purely self-defining self-creation without an acco- modation with an essentially Christian view of aesthetic autonomy, and yet there is no appeal to any "ground" or anything "outside" the artifices of human making without a regression to dogmatism. In Nietzsche's work, this led inevitably both to a claim for the essential contingency of our central perspectives, or sense-making practices, and an extremely elusive attempt to characterize and affirm that contingency, to render it intelligible, without reliance on a theory that would deny that (and our own) very contingency, that would see it as the inevitable outcome of perennial psychological or social "forces." In this respect, Nietzsche's central problem is indeed the problem of a great deal of twentieth-century European thought, a problem for which the very notion of a "resolution" seems not only impossible but inappropriate. That central *aporia*, already visible in Rousseau's ambiguity about culture and nature, freedom and happi- ness, in the Kantian antinomy, in the difficulties created for Hegel by "nature" and a "philosophy of nature," is still fully manifest in what Blanchot has called Nietzsche's double refusal: his "refusal of im- mediacy," and his "refusal of mediation."[71] And if this turns out to be the terminus of Nietzsche's position, it will be fair enough to conclude that he has not "broken free" of modernity but only inten- sified its *aporia*.

Nietzsche himself may have occasionally dealt with the tensions created by this problem through promoting what he called "a kind of second innocence," and championed an "active forgetting," his way of attacking all the reflective ideals of the tradition. But it is hard to see how innocence (like Paradise) once lost, is ever regained. (One always remenbers that one is trying to forget.)[72] This is especially true once one has once doubted that one can count oneself as a genuine origin of interpretation, or wonders whether the terms of the narration and the values promoted in a certain kind of narration themselves come from "outside" the interpretive activity, whether as the unconscious, social forces, the Logic of the Concept or whatever.

To return to the central issue in Nietzsche's own account, for all the inevitable questions it raises, it is still the case that for him a reliance on an interpretive activity akin to novel- or poem-making is clearly provoked, or called for, by what is claimed to be the failure of sense-making practices that deny or suppress this interpretive element.[73] And this sense of historical significance carries an enor- mous amount of weight in Nietzsche's account, a weight so heavy as to invoke all sorts of powerful, even apocalyptic images.

Nietzsche himself is quite clear that the "modern pessimism" he sees as a prelude to the "active nihilism," or "aesthetic justification" he celebrates, is itself but "an expression of the uselessness of the modern world – not of the world of existence.[74] This means for him that, as a condition of the significance of his own "active nihilism," we need to understand that the modern world has, or "should be interpreted as having," an "ambiguous character," that "the very same symptoms could point to decline and to strength." Nihilism could be a "sign of a crucial and most essential growth, of the transition to new conditions of existence," or "genuine nihilism."[75] If this apocalyptic sense of the modern "twilight" is to make sense then Nietzsche cannot be merely offering us "his own" narrative, for his own purposes, but must be trying to account for and motivate the origins of such self-consciously contingent approach to moral character and the future.

None of which means that he can do this, consistent with the restrictions he has imposed on himself, that he can appeal to factors "outside" his own literary constructions from "within" them. Given the terms within which Kant originally defined many of these issues, that is a problem becoming ever more acute in those who, like Nietzsche, are dissatisfied with modernity, realize they cannot go "back" or "away" but wish to remain modern, and instead "to rise," presumably, beyond its too limited self-understanding.[76] We shall see in the next chapter how Heidegger argues that almost all the major presuppositions in Nietzsche's emphasis on *poesis* (or "subjectivity"), even if, for Heidegger, an "ontological" category, capable of bearing the weight of the "significance" questions raised above better than a wholly aesthetic reading, remain completely "unthought" in Nietzsche.

But we need here to note that this general problem cannot be avoided or resolved by the litterateur approach, even as we should admit that this whole issue does not simply represent a deficiency or failing in "Nietzsche's theory." When viewed with a wide enough lens, the problem of Nietzschean self-understanding is, I am trying to suggest, *the* problem of modernity's self-understanding, particularly when Hegel's promissory notes are regarded as unredeemed, or unredeemable.

Viewed within such a lens, Nietzsche's view creates the following dilemma. The outcome of modernity's rigorous self-criticism is this: all human sense-making practices are perspectival. To appropriate, deal with, communicate about, the world, we require a "net" of concepts and evaluative criteria whose structure cannot be fixed by any appeal to the "world (or the good) in itself" (including any "world" of purposes, ends, or basic desires); such a world in itself is "chaos." And such perspectives are wholly conventional. It is not only true that there is no realist or intuitional or methodological way to secure or anchor such a structure; there are and can be no "good reasons" at all for them (whether transcendental or historical). Such an appeal would only reflect other conventions.

However, as Nietzsche notes in a famous passage in *The Twilight of the Idols*, when we abolish the "true" world, we also abolish any so-called "apparent" world. "Acts" of interpretation, if considered in themselves, are but moments in a "chaotic flux" and so can themselves have a significance only if one is created for them. But there is then no compelling reason, however understood, to create such a significance, or at least no ground more compelling than withdrawing to "passive" or despairing nihilism. As we have seen, without an appeal to something like "the historical occasion" of such a celebration of interpretive activity or creation, Nietzsche's recommendations for the future turn out to be, and only to be, "personal confessions," not diagnoses, revelations, prophecies, unmaskings (which he clearly takes them to be).[77] But, for a variety of reasons, such a reliance on our collective history and cultural inheritance (if it to avoid the passivity of historical relativism, which Nietzsche abhors) would also seem to push Nietzsche in a "Hegelian" direction, one he already rejects.

There are certainly indications in Nietzsche (and indirectly in Nehamas's interpretation) that the problem is recognized, and that Nietzsche means to push his account in a direction that will take account of them. That is, there are indications that the "post-Hegelian" dilemma keeps re-appearing, the tension between the modern commitment to autonomy as a kind of spontaneity and full self-determination, and the need for a "reconciliation," created by that very commitment, most concretely a form of reconciliation with others, a form of substantive social unity that does not appeal to premodern *teloi*, and is consistent with that commitment to autonomy. As we shall see, it keeps reappearing because no form of modern self-consciousness can be said to conclude or resolve "the fate of modernity" or the "possibility of valuing," or, really, to resolve, decisively, anything, if the problem of dogmatism has been correctly posed. In Nietzsche this will mean that some form of "reassurance" necessarily re-emerges with the problem of reconciliation, and can only be avoided by a kind of Fichtean insistence on absolute self-determination already undermined or exposed by Nietzschean genealogy.

Nehamas himself notes that one may always wonder whether what one thinks of as a "unified" literary creation really is, that there is a "distinction between the fact and the feeling of unity."[78] (Nehamas concentrates on doubts about unity, but one could also contrast the fact and feeling of creative power itself. One may understand oneself to be "creating" and may simply be "reflecting" a variety of inherited social prejudices. Or one might question the difference between feeling the significance of creative activity, and reassuring oneself about that "fact.") And he admits that such a doubt would send one "outside" one's own self-understanding.

> Nietzsche, of course, constantly emphasizes the importance of evaluating oneself only by one's own standards. Nevertheless, especially since he does not believe that we have any special access to knowledge of ourselves, such questions are finally decided from the outside. This outside, which includes looking at one's own past, may consist of a very select public, of an audience that perhaps does not yet exist.[79]

This sort of consideration suggests that Nietzsche must not only appeal to factors "outside" interpretation, to history, in order resolve doubts about the significance and possibility of interpretation, he must appeal to another sort of "outside," or an audience, others, in order to resolve doubts about the power, cogency and unity of individual interpretations. Perhaps Nietzsche embodies the fate of the modernist dynamic this way: there is no ground or external basis for the self-reassurance of modernity, in whatever manifestation. We should be content instead with aesthetic projects, images, metaphors, sketches of future lives, creative narrations of the past, compelling and competing accounts of what "noble" lives might be possible now. These creative projections take hold with others, within a certain audience, if they do, and establish the agenda for the postmodern age, only by chance; if the rhetoric and imagery of such projects manage to create an audience receptive to them, a "collective identity," strong enough to risk and sacrifice, then and only then can one be, in a fragile, tenuous way, "reassured" about one's own identity, sense of worth, creative hopes. There might be all sorts of problems, discussed above, with how we could be said to have come to "understand" that this is the "fate of modernity (or even to have understood that there are only interpretations of the "fate of modernity") but perhaps the only sort of re-assurance possible about those doubts too is aesthetic and ultimately, in this attentuated, minimal sense, "social."

But this admission raises all sorts of interesting questions. Recall first how much of Nietzsche's diagnosis of modern nihilism depends on a claim that we have become a herd society, full of slavish pity and so abject dependence on each other. We have "lost" ourselves in an ever more absorbing, routinizing mass society. In the broadest strokes, the question of what it would mean to "no longer be modern" comes down to what it would mean to give up such dependence, and to achieve independence. A radical or complete assertion of independence, though, raises the problem noted above, the danger of celebrating a mere "feeling" of independence, of self-delusion. As we have seen, for Nietzsche, at least in books like *On the Genealogy of Morals*, the clearest examples of such self-creation can be found, not only in literary creators, but also in premodern, especially Greek, forms of "noble" independence. Since such examples immediately and more clearly raise a variety of social issues, perhaps they will help with this problem.[80]

In *Beyond Good and Evil*, and in many other places, Nietzsche regularly emphasizes his standard view, that it is only a "slavish" or weak type who cares at all about the "opinions of others." He stresses the "characteristic right of masters to create values" and claims that it is only the "ordinary man" who "always waits for an opinion about himself and then instinctively submits to that."[81] In *On the Genealogy of Morals*, the "noble" or "high-minded" are said to have "felt and established themselves and their actions as good." He goes on to say that "it was *out of* this pathos of distance [from the "low-minded" or "plebeian"] that they first *seized the right* to create values and to coin names for values."[82] While it is a mark of *ressentiment* to attempt to establish or justify such posited values, or even to "persuade themselves, *deceive* themselves that they were happy",[83] nevertheless Nietzsche still invokes the language of a "seizure of right," "justified" by this great "distance" between types.

This all gives us a clearer and somewhat harsher picture of what interpretive self-creation (here the "positing of values") actually involves, since it focuses attention on the conflict engendered by such activity. In *Beyond Good and Evil*, Nietzsche is very clear that this original "pathos of distance" also requires a "keeping down and keeping at a distance,"[84] that the right to create and realize such values is partly a matter of the successful exercise of power (even if nowadays a literary or rhetorical power). In a way, one's status as a

Master-Creator is indeed confirmed from "outside," by one's success in avoiding absorption in the concerns of the many, or dependence on the views of others, and by one's success in preventing the many from interfering with one's pursuit of one's ideals.

There are already historical problems in Nietzsche's use of this "active/reactive" schema to interpret antiquity. There just are no characters in Greek literature or history who are accurately captured by it. While it is true that Achilles or Odysseus or Antigone or characters in Thucydides are unconcerned with whether the values they pursue have any universal status or hold for all rational agents (they always clearly hold only for Greeks of a certain class), this does not entail that they are asserting individual "rights to create values." There is no active self-legislation by any such character; their sense of such values comes from (is "dependent" on) some larger sense of place within some whole. They are always quite sensitive to the justification of their values and do not simply "feel themselves" to be happy. Their privilege "flows" from some sense of the function of a chieftain in the army, or some general view of human nature, blood, tradition, the ancestors, the gods, etc. And the same is obviously true of the Scandanavians, Romans, barbarians, and others used by Nietzsche to make his point.

All of which ought to make us immediately suspicious about the very notion of a "pathos of distance" as well as the notion of a supremely self-sufficient affirmation, unaffected by doubts (doubts, say, about whether one is "truly happy") engendered by even a minimal self-consciousness. In the first place, a sense of one's nobility established or confirmed by such a pathos is still a form of "dependence," a certification of one's "characteristic right to create values" by a successful opposition or negation of others. Nietzsche clearly wants to deny that the fact of mastery itself in some philosophical sense "entitles" the "winners" to rule. Their victory simply means that they do rule, and determine their values for themselves, and any other value, such as a demand for justified entitlement, is a reaction to this victory, a contingent strategy of opposition. But all of this requires that there be others of such a type and that they cooperate in, especially, not interfering with the realization of the master's values, something presumably insured by force or the exercise of power. In Nietzsche's great, original drama then, while the Master does not care whether the Slaves actually do recognize his right to Mastery and so is not dependent on their opinions (or the universal validity of the values he posits), his own certainty about his "right" and status is nonetheless mediated by others.

And, as Hegel long ago pointed out, such a pathos of distance is a profoundly unstable notion. In his language, one "recognizes" oneself as superior and entitled to value-creation by contrast with those *whom one does not recognize*. The pathos of distance "out of which" one seizes the right to create values is, strictly speaking, meaningless to the Master; he confirms himself by a contrast with those who refuse to play his game, and so his actual success in "keeping" the slavish "at a distance, is a worthless or at best marginal achievement. It doesn't certify or confirm or establish any "right" to create values; strictly speaking, one is merely brushing aside impediments to the realization of one's values, the right to which one must already have established or somehow assured oneself about.[85]

And as Hegel also pointed out, this should shift our attention to the conflict among those who continue to insist on their independence, to the unavoidable struggle between Masters. Here Nietzsche has a great deal to say, but it is still profoundly ambiguous. In *On the Genealogy of Morals*, in a passage concerned with such issues, he stresses again his characteristic description of the Master Creator as wholly spontaneous, active, and independent. This means that among such "strong, full natures in whom there is an excess of the power to form," one would be "incapable of taking one's enemies, one's accidents, even one's misdeeds, seriously for very long."[86] One acts in supreme indifference to others (even in indifference to oneself and one's past), even others who oppose one's pursuits.[87] However, this emphasis is almost immediately countered by a different direction taken in the same paragraph. "How much reverence has a noble man for his enemies! – and such reverence is a bridge to love. – For he desires his enemy for himself, as his mark of distinction; he can endure no other enemy than one in whom there is nothing to despise and *very much* to honor."[88]

This passage greatly qualifies Nietzsche's more official claims for an aesthetic version of the modern dream of autochthony or self-creation. Here, it is implied, the values one creates in one's narration of oneself can only have some sort of "distinction" if they are somehow "reflected" in the opposition of a worthy enemy, an opposition that must also reflect some shared view of what is worth fighting about, even, Nietzsche goes so far as to hint, a shared "love" of values and so each other. Without this shared view and noble, agonistic sense of creation, the passage implies, there is no way for an individual to experience the worth or seriousness of his values, what or how much is at stake for him in pursuit of them.[89] There is only the "feeling" of assertion or power, and a great potential gap between that feeling and the "fact."[90]

But one can only push Nietzsche so far in this "Hegelian" direction, a direction in which the "road to the self leads through the other." As we have so frequently seen, he also constantly stresses the spontaneity of the noble type, his, in some sense, unselfconscious affirmative stance. We have already seen enough in Kant and Hegel especially, to doubt the possibility of such a second innocence, or new form of joyous immediacy.[91] That side of Nietzsche, as some passages in his own work indicate, seem a dead end, a slide into "positivity" and the pre-critical. And Nietzsche's own distaste with social or inter-subjective versions of justification of the rational or good, is so intense, that the hints of a reliance on sociality in passages like the one above, cannot go very far for Nietzsche to remain "Nietzsche."

Moreover, it is also unclear just how much would be gained by attention to a small elite of mutually recognizing masters. Collective self-affirmation is no less subject to the danger of self-deceit than individual self-affirmation. And the dynamics of such mutual recognition are difficult to understand from a Nietzschean perspective. One either succeeds in having one's own views recognized by others, in which case, they become dependent and so unworthy opponents; or one comes to relect in one's own valuations some commonly held value, in which case one becomes dependent oneself, ceases to "become who one is" and "becomes who they are." Or, one engages in a ceaseless struggle, and we are back to the problem of there being nothing "outside" one's self-certainty.

Both Hegel and Nietzsche, in other words, represent a rejection of the transcendental, critical, or formal conception of philosophical autonomy, but both still somehow want to affirm the modern imperative: become [honestly, freely] who you are. One last way of contrasting their options could be put more directly this way. Tracy Strong has argued[92] that the difference between Nietzschean and "Hegelian/ liberal" politics, defined as a politics of "selves meeting each other and seeking forms of mutual acknowledgment," is that "For Nietzsche, the problem lies deeper: it is the having of selves at all that is first in question."[93] This is probably how Nietzsche would put the point, but it is important to note that such a Nietzschean point constitutes Hegel's famous criticism of the liberal/contractarian tradition, his attack on the very possibility of atomistic agents negotiating the political order, and the whole point of Hegel's famous argument in the *Phenomenology of Spirit* is to show that "being an individual self" necessarily requires a "struggle for recognition" with others.[94] The dispute with Nietzsche turns rather on this issue: whether this profound implication of one's identity with others, with the contingent, quite specific community one simply inherits, and the eventual mutuality it seems to demand (the achievement of some fully "collective identity," to use Strong's phrase) ultimately involves a kind of weakening, homogenization, or flattening of any "vital" self (Nietzsche's view), or whether it finally ennobles, enriches, even "realizes" the self, and so makes possible being any sort of "self." Looked at this way, it is more often Nietzsche who is close to liberal sentiments (or suspicions about sociality), not Hegel.[95]

Finally, many of these problems are reflected quite directly, as, I think, *aporiai*, in Nietzsche's hermetic work, *Thus Spoke Zarathustra*. For one thing, the difficult problem of "reconciliation" is a major theme of the narrative itself, manifest first as comedy, in Zarathustra's relations with the townspeople, and then as tragedy, in his relations with his disciples; as is the tension in Nietzsche between his perspectivism and his revolutionary rhetoric.

The four parts of the book divide, as I have argued elsewhere[96] by reference to Zarathustra's reaction to one "great event," the Soothsayer's suggestion of the Eternal Return of the Same. In the first two parts of the book, Zarathustra has identified himself as a revolutionary prophet, a harsh critic of what modernity had beocme, and as one of the few who sees what is truly possible now. He has understood history itself, has correctly understood the significance of the "last men" of bourgeois society, and so knows the reactions to that fate now possible. The possibility that "everything recurs eternally," entertaining the image of a vast, senseless, non-progressive cycle, the realization that his own "Overman" represents no decisive revolutionary moment, but a contingent moment in such a senseless cycle, itself of no intrinsic or historical significance, all literally makes him sick. He ceases referring to any Overman, and no longer, in the second two parts, seeks disciples. His own (perhaps Nietzsche's own) revolutionary spirit is revealed as another attempt at "revenge" against time, as would be all attempts to secure a so-called modern age (or postmodern future, for that matter). Zarathustra's "love of man," his eagerness, like the original ascetic priests, to find a way in which man could continue to affirm, long for "the stars," etc., has led him perilously close to an ascetic version of the will to power, and of his own autonomy, and to deceptively "decisive" historical ruptures. He wants to redeem man, and so had affirmed a Christian view of history, as if a new Incarnation is possible, after which all will be different. Instead, all recurs eternally, he now understands, and the entire language of a nihilistic moment which we might overcome or resolve properly is undermined.

None of which means that Zarathustra loses hope for man or returns permanently to the the life of an isolated, wholly self-defining hermit. (The book had begun with an implicit rejection of that stance and a return to man, something many commentators do not take seriously enough.) Zarathustra does leave the city and return home to a cave, but dissatisfied and eager for signs of his "children," signs that will make another return possible (which seems to occur as the book ends). As he presents the issue, Nietzsche, oddly, much like Hegel, cannot be satisfied with the modern myth of autocthony and autonomy, nor with the conformist or nationalist or romantic or "socialist" subjection to the herd, or the "new idol, the state." In a perfect statement of the duality we have been tracing, he explains his necessarily "double will."

> This, this is *my* precipice and my danger, that my glance plunges into the height, and that my hand would grasp and hold on to the depth. My will clings to man; with fetters I bind myself to man because I am swept up toward the overman; for that way my other will wants to go. And therefore I live blind among men as if I did not know them, that my hand might not lose its faith in what is firm.[97]

Zarathustra's movements "up" and "down" are central to the narrative, and are here affirmed as equally dangeorus and inevitable, "up" or back to the cave on the mountain and the false security of a literal independence, and "down" inevitably back to some human reconciliation, one necessary for Zarathustra to be and overcome himself.

This all merely introduces an issue tht would require a detailed reading of *Thus Spoke Zarathustra* to explore. Here we can only note that the outcome of Nietzsche's own deflationary genealogy of Zarathustra's (and his own?) hopes, effected by the "eternal return" image, is ambiguous. The narrative details themselves are not very reassuring about the social and political prospects opened up by this realization. It is striking that Zarathustra rejects a life of loneliness, will not stay in his cave with his animals. His contempt for the *hoi polloi* does not extend as far as Plato's, for whom escape from the cave is escape from humankind, up and away from the earth, towards the sun. Zarathustra is contemptuous of the sun ("what would you be had you not those for whom you shine") and is a "lover of earth," even a "lover of man." But, to make a long story very short, he fails, at least in this text, to find or create any "re-assuring" community among the citizens or with his disciples. His last remarks, as an old man, that his "children are near," that he will or might find such a community strike me at least, given what we have seen throughout the book, as ironic, perhaps even pathetic.

Yet, just as any passage in Nietzsche celebrating an artist legislator or self-creation can be balanced by one pointing to the "unthought" in every thought or the self-deceit involved in art or self-legislation, passages full of so much contempt for the modern herd animal, or the last men, can be balanced by Zarathustra's enduring "love of man," and his continuing commitment to the project of a grand politics. This at least suggests something again similar to some of the conclusions drawn from the earlier discussion of Hegel.

One could consider the situation this way. Traditionally, Aristotle's twin definitions of the human animal are understood as linked; it is because we are the "animal having reason" that we are "the political animal." Political life is made possible by a common faculty, imprecise, but reliable enough to identify the objective ends of collective life, ends all could be persuaded (or educated) to pursue. Even with the demise of such a substantive notion of reason, that faculty still functioned as the supreme social mediator, fundamentally making possible a cooperative life. The possibility of a formal or procedural standard for resolving disputes made possible a modern, secular notion of justice, as did appeals to an efficient, reliable "system" for the satisfaction of individual interests. If we regard such criteria as having no internal authority, as the products of various, original historical conditions, now much altered (or as "fragments" of an old and now irrelevant moral language), the Nietzschean question about politics emerges: how is political life even possible? And besides the scepticism about that possibility already noted, Nietzsche's continuing interest in some form of a new social reconciliation (Zarathustra's search for an audience), implies, at the very least, some new possibility.

It is as if he sometimes hopes that the exposure of the fragility and contingency of these "mediating" principles will also make clear the timidity and fear in which they were conceived, the ascetic assumption that such sociality would only be possible by a repressive narrowing of human possiblity, a self-discipline born out of a great contempt for the human animal, and a belief that only some sort of absolutely authoritative, "objective" and universal principle would allow us to deal with each other. By contrast, he sometimes intimates, "now," a much more direct and unmediated sociality is possible, a sort of "we're all we've got" realization will dawn and a "race" of proud, independent, but not falsely autonomous or fearfully subservient beings can emerge. Whether that is so, though, and in what sense in might be so, would, I can only suggest here, strain beyond possibility the boundaries of the kind of discourse Nietzsche has created for himself.

That discourse itself is also best understood by linking it with Zarathustra's "abysmal thought," since it introduces us to the omnipresence of irony in Nietzsche's thought. Irony emerges as a way of saying without saying, of experimenting with possibilities that cannot be fully affirmed. Irony is a style that avoids what we have identified as the great enemy of self-conscious modernism – dogmatism – just by being a kind of style, by not being a substantive teaching, and only "a way" of approaching the paradoxes and self-referential dilemmas of any "modernist" affirmation. Nietzsche's love of masks, his creation of so many "Nietzsches" as authors of so many books, and so, in standard terms, his inconsistency, obscurity, and unsystematic playfulness, all make him one of the most interesting and representative modernist authors to read.

But it does not make him satisfying. One cannot even take much comfort in being dissatisfied, in being told that the experience of reading such an ironic author, one who never fully identifies with any of the positions he tries out , simply embodies the dissatisfying (and exhilarating) experience of the uncertain, always changing modern age itself. If one could be somehow assured that this was the significance of one's dissatisfaction, then one would be reassured, even satisfied. But there is no possible ironic defense of such irony. And if this question of a "defense" itself seems to beg the question, to presuppose the integrity of such self-doubt and the authority of reason-giving and justifying that Nietzsche is attacking, what one wants to know is how one can "forget" to ask it.

As we have been tracing it, the philosophic idea of liberation and the achievement of autonomy began with and was largely defined by, an attack on scholasticism, religious authority, and fedual power in the name of method, sceptical inquiry and universal, disinterested reason. It progressed to a deeper, critical investigation of the "possibility" of such reason itself, a kind of question that broadened into a social inquiry and so a critique of social self-consciousness or eventually of ideology (an account of the "possibility" of modern social institutions which claimed rationality). Reading Nietzsche as suggested here would place him within and at the end of such a sequence. If that very self-consciousness begins to undermine rather than realize all modern notions of autonomous reflection, then Nietzsche's position is one of the few conclusions one could draw. Nietzschean irony promises such a hyper-self-conscious sophistication as to move beyond any reflective or "well grounded" self-reassurance to a new immediacy, an undermining of the self-conscious doubts which themselves originally destroyed or infected the experience of immediacy. This is supposed to lead to an affirmation of immediacy as perspective, plurality, difference, the "unthought" and so forth, but one in which affirmation itself is now understood in a new way, nondogmatically, not as the result of an "inference." Modernist irony in this sense is not enervating but the final liberation, the realization of autonomy.

There is a great deal more to be said about the resources within Nietzsche for making this approach more intelligible and more plausible. But it is time to consider whether this whole idea of a modern revolution, whether as an Enlightenment promotion of rationality and freedom, or as modernist dissatisfaction and hopes for a radically novel, aesthetic redemption, or as some sort of new, ironic affirmation, is misconceived from the start, whether all the strategies of self-critique, historical self-consciousness, genealogy, irony, or reconciliation, share a disastrous common orientation, that "The essence of modernity is fulfilled [in Nietzsche] in the age of consummate meaninglessness."[98]

5

"The Age of Consummate Meaninglessness": Heidegger

1 Failed Autonomy

Since Heidegger's reflections on the fate of modernity are the most neologistic and difficult to discuss economically of any we have considered (even when measured by the Teutonic standards of Kant and Hegel), it might be a good idea to begin here by summarizing the context so far developed, the problematic within which I would like to situate the following account of Heidegger's Nietzsche lectures and articles.

As we have seen, there are all sorts of ways in which one might raise the "problem of modernity." One might even raise it by attacking the very idea of a problem, arguing instead that too many diverse phenomena are being unfairly lumped together, that while it might be possible to speak of genuinely modern institutions in one context (say, natural science, or liberal democratic institutions), there is no reason to expect that vast areas of "post-Enlightenment" social existence, or literature, or religion, or human passions in general, should reflect any similar evidence of modernization, or, even if they do, should be uniform or similar enough to warrant inclusion in any one topic.

In other words, as we first saw in discussing the origin of the idea of a modern epoch (and the discontinuity and secularization issues that surround that topic), the historical category itself raises philosophical problems. These especially concern the relation between human self-understanding and history (particularly the idea of "historical autonomy" suggested by the very idea of modernity), and the relative scope and weight one ought to give such self-understanding in accounting for diverse kinds of historical change. As we have seen,

much of the modern tradition understood itself as essentially a philosophical revolution, and understood the social and economic and
political dynamic of modernity as a whole to depend for its authority
and self-sustaining confidence on the success of this philosophical inauguration. As we have also already seen, even in non-philosophic
contexts like literature and art, the emergence of a variety of doubts
about the initial promises of the modern enterprise can only be fully
understood by linking such experiments and formal innovations to
the underlying philosophical claims and counter-claims at stake.
One ignores such large issues only at the expense of ignoring the
significance of such innovations and dissatisfactions, of myopically
treating the emergence of the modernist sensibility as a fad or a
movement, or as driven by aesthetic issues alone.

    Put more concretely, the historical category raises as a problem
what Blumenberg called the "self-assertion" of the modern epoch.
The question raised thereby is whether a genuine origination in
Western civilization occurred in roughly the sixteenth and seventeenth century (or whether it could have occurred, or what origination might mean), whether our epoch, however continuous in other
ways, is, or is potentially, independent of classical and religious
assumptions, or whether it still depends on mythic, religious, or
perennial human expectations and hopes.

    This is also the form of the most persistent kind of question
continually asked within modernity; whether a specific form of collective or individual independence, true self-determination, is possible;
and if not, how to understand and state the nature of our "dependence" on tradition, nature, biology, history, in general how to understand our finitude.

    In a brief look at the social dynamic portrayed in the modern
novel, we could see the emergence of a pervasive scepticism and
irony about political and social forms of such independence, everywhere pursued or simply assumed by modern men and women, but
nowhere truly realized. In contrast, these modernist suspicions about
social and intellectual pretensions to autonomy (or bourgeois optimism in general) helped generate at the same time (and somewhat
paradoxically) the hope that art itself (for its own sake, as non-
representational, *sui generis*, self-defining) would both be, and in
dress, taste, personal style, be a model for, a renewed modern view of
self-definition. We also briefly considered the limitations of such
modernist hopes, that its (ultimate if not initial) refusal to "depend"
on any conventional, moral or philosophical frame of reference would
eventually mean an insistence on art as either a purely formal game,

self-enclosed, reductionist, sterile, (or would conclude in a self-destructive attack on the category of art itself as dogmatic) or as an eventually exhausted, co-opted, everywhere displayed and commercialized "culture of rupture."

All of which helped set the stage for a consideration of Kant's inauguration of a philosophical modernism, the attempt to determine, without appeal to foundations or origins or intuitions, the conditions for the very possibility of knowledge and self-determining agency. The modern question of independence became itself a philosophic issue in Kant, the reflective attempt by reason to determine the rules of its own activity, to set for itself its ends, to determine its own limits.

It was this critical project that, in its denial of the possibility of any epistemic role for immediacy, givenness, simple "presence" in experience, elevated the role of a self-determining subject in experience and action in ways that soon exceeded the limits or transcendental conditions Kant tried to place on them, and created the most influential and comprehensive issues of modernist philosophy. The focus in German Idealism shifted immediately to the complex nature of such self-determination, and its own origins in a process or "living nature" inaccessible to transcendental analysis (Schelling), or in some new form of immediacy or intuition, as in Fichte's account of the self's immediate presence to itself, the "I's positing of itself". In this tradition, it was Hegel who most tried to resist what he saw as these reversions to a new dogmatism (the "dogmatism of thinking" rather than "being"), and to formulate some view of the internal logic and phenomenology of an "eternally" self-determining, collective subjectivity, of Spirit.

Historically at least, Hegel's inability to persuade his successors that such a historical process of self-negation and self-determination was in any sense of the word, "logical", progressive, or rational, inaugurated the "left-right" Hegel wars familiar to so much later European thought. Hegel's project fell apart into camps which shared assumptions about the failure of traditional hopes for the autonomy of philosophy, or even critical reflection, but who rejected Hegel's attempt to redefine human autonomy as a historical project of collective self-consciousness. Autonomy was instead an issue of "praxis," an achievement of "real" historical actors engaged in a struggle for social power, or it was understood as a matter of self-definition inaccessible to reflective justification, whether couched in theoretical or practical terms, as in Kierkegaard's famous anti-dialectical essays in *Either/Or*.

Looking at the context this way defines the issues Nietzsche eagerly embraced. The unavailability of any traditional appeal to nature as a ground or source of value or of any self-determination, coupled with what Nietzsche regarded as the equally impossible dogmatic attempt to appeal to any transcendental subject (or "necessary conditions") or to the self-transformations of the historical process, all meant the historical, internal collapse of the most distinctive Western hope, the "will to truth." Self-determination or Nietzschean "affirmation" could now no longer be linked in any way to the cosmos, one's true self, real happiness, complete, rational autonomy, or one's realization within the historical community. What the idea of a modern epoch had sown and what Kant had cultivated, Nietzsche would now reap.

The lack of a "link" between self-determination and such origins opened the door to a very complex and problematic kind of self-assertion, or affirmation in Nietzsche. On the one hand, on Nietzsche's terms, an individual could not simple "value" himself (or his *ex nihilo* decision itself) as the "source" of meaning and value, as in Sartre's existentialism, since the language of any ultimate "source" and "origin" is denied in Nietzsche's radical hermeneutics. One's view of oneself as the "free" center of an "absurd universe" is as much the product of interpretation as Platonism, and cannot be authorized by any claims about "the" universe or by any ponderous ontology of "being and nothingness." But, on the other hand, as we saw, the act of interpreting cannot, within Nietzsche's account, possess any significance without some sort of prior, independent evaluation of history or even of the "possibility" of sense-making in general, which all conditions or motivates the role of interpretation in the "age of nihilism," even if that evaluation is a matter of some contingent social consensus, or reconstituted politics. And such requirements proved difficult or impossible for Nietzsche to fulfill, at least not without reverting to what he would regard as dogmatism or a social consensus he would regard as a "herd mentality."[1]

Said summarily, what all this means is that the modern sense of its own novelty and historical superiority can be said to have helped generate in philosophy the search for some way of demonstrating the autonomy, the self-grounding authority of modern thought and therewith modern culture. Kant's enterprise is the heart of such an attempt, but historically, the "all-destroyer" was more successful in attacking the possibility of traditional and early modern formulations of such claims for self-grounding than he was in defending the idea of a "spontaneous," self-legislating Reason. The link between spontaneity and law was too fragile to preserve, and, in effect, spontaneity "won out."[2] Hegel managed to add to the problem by introducing the issue of the historical dependence of any putatively self-determining thought, but, for most of his successors, did not succeed in re-establishing some collective, dialectical sense of self-ruled, universally achieved, or collective independence. And clearly, with Nietzsche and with many modernist claims for the authority of the aesthetic, with the eruption of suspicions everywhere about the contingent, local, or irrational nature of all self-understanding, all such attempts to establish, or legitimate, or defend the modern hope for a collective or rationally formulated version of independence were over. Autonomy required not philosophy, but now and henceforth, bravery; integrity, in some strange way the one enduring value throughout these transformations, would now and henceforth be as much a matter of refusal and denial as of affirmation.

It is possible to conclude from all this that such a narrative of modernity – as the story of "failed autonomy" – might have a great deal to do with the way in which such a *desideratum* was formulated in the first place, that there is something flawed, exaggerated, perhaps deeply hubristic in the traditional sense, in the spirit of all modern attempts at self-assertion. And that suspicion brings us, finally, to Heidegger.

This is so because it is Heidegger who has formulated the most profound, disturbing and influential criticism of such a modern spirit, most of it focused on modern philosophers, especially Descartes, Kant, Hegel, and Husserl. This criticism culminates in his Nietzsche interpretation, his claim that even Nietzsche, for all of his insight into the "nihilistic" fate of Western philosophy, has not escaped the nihilism of modernity, that he is the last and in some ways most typical "metaphysician of the West." With Heidegger, many of the issues we have discussed before as "dissatisfactions" in later modern European high culture, such things as distaste with bourgeois smugness and doubt about modern optimism, prudence, and progressivism, worries about the effects of mass culture and consumer societies, suspicions about the historically and socially contingent nature of basic criteria for justification and evaluation, all take on a new and vast importance. The fundamental philosophical issue at stake now is not historical discontinuity, or autonomy, or self-consciousness, or the will to truth; it is the meaning of Being in modernity.

2 Modernity as a "Metaphysical" Problem

Heidegger has always had a great many things to say about modernity, and especially about the connection he sees between the modern experience and "technology," the transformation of nature into mere "material" for use by self-defining human agents. In one of his essays he lists some of the "essential" aspects that, for him, define such a modern experience. These are said to include the institution of science, "machine technology," art's "moving into the purview of aesthetics," or its becoming the object of a merely "subjective" experience, the emergence of the notion of "culture" in understanding human activity, and what Heidegger calls the "loss of the gods."[3] Although he comments in other places on most of these characteristics, in this essay, in discussing modern science, he quickly and typically comes to focus on an issue that dominates most of his important discussions. He insists that in the modern emphasis on method, on the security of a repeatable means of achieving reliable results, there is, surprisingly, a great "metaphysical" (and not epistemological or historical or pragmatic) issue at stake. Within modernity (especially but not exclusively) "knowing" is construed as essentially a "representing," and therefore "being" as a kind of result of such attempts to represent and secure one's representing. We understand ourselves as "picturing" the world, and the world as whatever can be successfully pictured by us. And so the "fundamental event of the modern age is the conquest of the world as picture";[4] we live in the "age of the world picture." Or, as he put it in the Nietzsche lectures, "At the inception of the modern age the beingness of beings changed. The essence of that historical incepton consists in this very change. The subjectivity of the *subiectum* (substantiality) is now defined as self-representing representation."[5]

This event, "the uprising of man into subjectivity," an event that "transforms that which is into object"[6] is not only said to be the chief metaphysical characteristic of modernity, it is also a characteristic Heidegger makes use of in accounting for what he, with Nietzsche, describes as the utter nihilism of modernity. With the "age of subjectness ... driving towards its consummation," it is clear to Heidegger that "The essence of modernity is fulfilled in the age of consummate meaninglessness,"[7] an event, we shall see, that Heidegger interprets somewhat differently than Nietzsche. This means that many of the themes which have made Heidegger important to some contemporary academic philosophers – his critique of post-Cartesian theories of representation, his emphasis on the role of unthematic, practical engagement as essential, even prior, in any relation to and within the world, his influence in transforming much of the enterprise of philosophy itself into "hermeneutics," and his insistence on the limitations of standard, discursive language in accounting for the most fundamental of issues – are all themes that are also of central importance in a dimension of Heidegger's work until very recently less well received in the academy: his sweeping account of "the history of Being" and its "consummation" in nihilism in modernity.

So the issues we have been concerned with should, according to Heidegger, be re-thought, framed in a deeper, more comprehensive way, as "metaphysical" issues, and doing so will allow us to see how and why such an age of consummate meaninglessness has been reached. Moreover, a crucial aspect of Heidegger's discussion of such an issue involves the interpretation of Nietzsche that he developed in a series of lectures in the nineteen-thirties and forties, and in a few related articles. This is so because, first, Nietzsche himself correctly "interprets the course of Western history metaphysically, and indeed as the rise and development of nihilism,"[8] but more importantly because Nietzsche's attempt to "overturn" metaphysics "remains only a self-deluded entanglement" in such an enterprise, and so Nietzsche's "own experience of nihilism" is "itself a nihilistic one."[9] Nietzsche therefore fully embodies "modern metaphysics," which "as the metaphysics of subjectness, thinks the Being of that which is in the sense of will,"[10] and so he is the "last metaphysician of the West."[11] Nietzsche is right about the exhaustion and completion of modern metaphysics, but the "break" required with such a tradition will have to be far more radical yet than anything Nietzsche imagined. Nietzsche, indeed, is still a "Cartesian," and only Heidegger represents a "new path."[12] Thus, virtually all of what Heidegger wants to say about modernity is on view in these Nietzsche lectures, and especially, how he means to justify his apocalyptic claims about the failure of Western "reason," the most "stiff necked adversary of thought."[13]

This is not to say that the Nietzsche lectures are easily accessible or do not raise many problems of their own. There are lots of controversies surrounding such things as (a) Heidegger's concentration, almost exclusively, on Nietzsche's unpublished notes, rather than his written works (as if what is "unthought" in Nietzsche will appear in what is unpublished); (b) the way in which Heidegger construes the history of philosophy, not as a continuous conversation between individual philosophers, challenging and correcting each other, but as the history of Being itself, of Being's destiny or fate, as if each thinker is "called on" to "think his thoughts" by Being, construed, as itself a "happening" or "e-vent";[14] (c) the way Heidegger casually admits that he is not much concerned with "what has been taken from Nietzsche's words and what has been added to them,"[15] that he is interested in a genuine "confrontation" (*Auseinandersetzung*) with Nietzsche rather than an interpretation, all in preparation for the "supreme exertion of thinking";[16] and (d) the extremely unusual sense in which Heidegger claims to be able to "turn" or "twist" away from, the metaphysical tradition, to have achieved in his "destruction" or "deconstruction" (*Abbau*) of the metaphysical tradition, not a new beginning, a *Überwindung*, itself a "metaphysical" notion, but a *Verwindung*, a much trickier and elusive notion, as we shall see.[17]

But the complexities of Heidegger scholarship need not detain us here.[18] What is of interest is whether Heidegger succeeds in reinterpreting the problem of modernity as a "metaphysical" issue that reaches a kind of crisis in Nietzsche, one from which Nietzsche cannot disentangle himself. Looking ahead, we can anticipate that if he does, then a great deal of the "postmodernist" or even "postphilosophical" spirit of the last twenty years ought to be taken serious account of. For what Heidegger would have shown is that the most comprehensive and fundamental assumptions of the whole negative and dissatisfied modernist sensibility we have been examining must still obscure and evade precisely what most needs clarification and confronting; that in Nietzsche, the most powerful and sustaining assumptions of all Western thought are "gathered and completed in a decisive respect,"[19] preparing the way for the possibility of a whole new orientation and sensibility, the enterprise Heidegger sometimes simply calls *Denken*, thinking.

Let us begin with the claim that Nietzsche's work and Nietzsche's own narrative of the Western tradition ought to be read "metaphysically." In his first lectures on Nietzsche in 1936, Heidegger insists that Nietzsche will not be approached as a vague "poet philosopher,"[20] but that his "thinking proceeds within the vast orbit of the ancient guiding question of philosophy, "What is it to be an entity? (*Was ist das Seinde?*)"[21] Nietzsche's central thought, "the will to power," is said to be an "answer to the question,"what is it to be an entity?"" and so to be a "metaphysical" doctrine, a "name for the basic character (*Grundcharakter*) of any entity (*Seinde*)."[22]

Such an interpretation of Nietzsche is, Heidegger clearly realizes, doubly complicated. In the first place, it seems quite foreign to the spirit and unsystematic nature of Nietzsche's work, even to the "context-less" fragments collected as *The Will to Power*.[23] Heidegger must be invoking an unusual and relatively non-standard under- standing of "metaphysics." Secondly, even while Heidegger appeals to the notion of metaphysics to affirm the importance and even "rigor" of Nietzsche's thought, the characterization is additionally complex since that same description is meant to imply the nihilistic consequences of Nietzsche's enterprise, his "completion" of the whole metaphysical tradition in "meaninglessness." It is hard enough to think of Nietzsche as a metaphysician; it is harder still to think that he is somehow paradigmatically representative of a continuous way of thinking stretching from Plato, through Descartes and Hegel, and culminating in "machine technology," the tradition that is said to be "murderous in a most extreme sense, because it absolutely does not let Being take its rise, i.e., come into the vitality of its essence."[24]

"Metaphysics" is thus being used first to illuminate a dimension in Nietzsche's thought ignored in traditional attention to his culture criticism, attacks on traditional morality and religion, and indict- ments of mass, democratic cultures (issues which Heidegger virtually ignores in eleven hundred pages of lectures). Although in Nietzsche's published works, claims about "the will to power" are noticeably rare and not made much of, Heidegger proposes to focus most of his attention on that topic (and its relation to four other "fundamental thoughts in Nietzsche"), and to interpret it as Nietzsche's answer to the traditional questions, "What is there?" or "what are the beings?" And he also wants to show that Nietzsche's way of asking and answering this question has a very great deal to do with how philo- sophy has always asked and answered such questions, a way which continually obscures a deeper and more fundamental question, al- ways assumed in, but forever foreclosed by, "metaphysical thinking": the question of Being (*Sein*) itself.

Towards the close of his 1937 lectures (focused mostly on Nietz- sche's account of the "eternal recurrence of the same"), Heidegger devotes two lectures to an exposition of this notion of metaphysics and its place in Heidegger's Nietzsche analysis. In "The Essence of a Metaphysical Position," Heidegger makes a great deal of the fact that the central question of metaphysics, alternately expressed as "what is being, insofar as it is viewed as being? *Ti to on hei on? Quid est ens qua ens?*,"[25] should be considered the "guiding question" (*Leitfrage*) of Western metaphysics. In posing such a question, we want to know not what makes a number a number, or a value a value, or a species a species, but what it is to be at all, what "everything that is," every entity, is, or is "fundamentally." These are the kinds of questions answered by Plato's Ideas, Aristotle's forms, the Christian notion of being as "being created," Descartes's two substances, Leibniz's monads, Wittgenstein's facts, materialism's "whatever current physics says," and so forth.

Almost everything of importance in Heidegger's work depends on understanding the next point he makes about this enterprise. He wants to claim that there is something common to all such attempts at asking about nature or the world, common to philosophy, scientific research, theology, moral thinking, almost all instances of aesthetic and technical activity; an orientation towards the world that is fundamentally limited in some way, that forecloses an even deeper and more important question from being asked. Most of what he wants to say about this issue is summarized in one dense, elliptical passage in this lecture: "Inasmuch as beings (*Seinde*) are put in question with a view to the *arche*, beings themselves are *already determined*. If we ask whence and in what way being (*Seinde*) rises and, as rising, comes to presence, being itself is already defined as the upsurging and as what holds sway and presences in such upsurgence."[26]

In keeping with his frequent characterization of the original Western orientation with respect to the question of being as a "decision,"[27] Heidegger emphasizes the contingency and distinctness of this emphasis on "presence," or on the mode of being of enduring entities in Western metaphysics, especially prominent in the original Greek notion of "nature" or *physis*.[28] Something fundamental has been prejudged by this "guiding question," something only very rarely "developed" by fundamental thinkers, the very different "ground question" (*Grundfrage*) already presupposed but rarely in view. This deeper question is said to concern the "beingness of beings" (*Seindheit des Seins*), or what the Greeks called *ousia*, and what Heidegger explicitly formulates as the Being of beings, *das Sein des Seinden*.

This claim for an "ontological difference" between an unthought, concealed question of Being (*Sein*), and a traditional "metaphysical" attention to the nature of entities (*Seinde*), turns on, first, Heidegger's claims that traditional metaphysics "already determines" the question of Being by unwittingly assuming a notion of presence, or "standing presence" (*beständige Anwesenheit*) as definitive in its interrogation of beings (that to be is to endure through time, to "arise" and persist as "entity," or later "object"), and, secondly, his claim that this predominance itself reflects a kind of subjectivism or humanism in Western thinking, a desire to "measure" being by reference to the demands and needs of human *logos* and human self-satisfaction (that such a view would only have come to dominate within some self-understanding as "subject," a representer or account-giver).

The first issue is best understood by contrast with a "fore-having" or unthematic "sense" of Being Heidegger tried to find a proper formulation for since *Being and Time*. Such a sense or meaning is not something that could be understood as the content of a proposition, or a belief a subject could have, but is embodied in existence, is itself a mode of existing, a way of being. In his famous analysis there of our "concernful" dealings with objects and others in the world, Heidegger tried to show the misleading and superficial implications of treating as primary any understanding of being taken to be the result of our encounters with entities simply "there," present before us, objects which we represent to ourselves as having these or those characteristics, or which we regard as mere material, to be assigned values or uses according to subjective intentions. Such a view of objects lying around before us, independent, real, persistent through time, and of ourselves as independent, judging, acting, self-determining subjects, is, Heidegger tries to show, itself already a highly abstract and historically motivated interpretation, one geared, he thinks he can demonstrate, to the subject's attempt to manipulate and gain "dominion" over entities, and one that is hardly original, fundamental or immediate. While we thus tend to think of truth as a matter of successful assertion or well-founded claims about being, for Heidegger, truth is a matter of the pre-predicative in experience, what originally "lights up entities" in this or that way, to be then apprehended and manipulated by us. Truth is an original "unconcealment," (as in Plato's image, the "light" itself and not the entities illuminated by the light), and so not the achievement of an assertion. And the way in which Being is originally "cleared" or "lighted" (Being as "presencing" (*Anwesen*) rather than "standing presence," (*Anwesenheit*), as he sometimes puts it), pre-judging so there may be entities to be judged, is the "fundamental ontological" issue for Heidegger.

In that 1927 work, this issue was pursued by reference to a human agent's (*Dasein's*) "care," the nexus of practical concerns within which (and, adding a complex transcendental dimension to the work) only within which, the world could be originally encountered as a piece of "equipment" or, subsequently, abstractly thematized as a "standing object," "present at hand." On this view, there is no Cartesian, spectating mind "viewing" either its own ideas or the substance of the world; neither is there a transcendental subject legislating to nature, outside of history, its own desires or language. All such views count as founded interpretations in Heidegger, ways in which we have come to regard ourselves for various purposes,[29] and so both count as derivative, founded (in ways often explicitly denied) on a more immediate, "lived" experience, one Heidegger originally tried to approach through a radically revised version of Husserlian phenomenology.

As noted, Heidegger is also interested in why the idea of independent, enduring (present), especially eternally enduring, objects should have come to exercise such a hold over Western thought, should have defined in effect, the enterprise of metaphysics, and subsidiary disciplines like science. As we shall see in the next section, he answers that question by pointing to the importance throughout Western thought of understanding human being as a subject, an underlying agency, responsible for ordering, assessing, evaluating its "ideas" or notions, and directing its actions. The notion that the world is just "there" to be apprehended or acted upon, in other words, requiring a "subject" who can represent it accurately and manipulate it successfully, is all a historically contingent perspective and Heidegger frequently gestures in the direction of some fateful human self-assertion (some willful insistence on human autonomy, in the terms used here) as an "explanation" of Western metaphysics. (And thereby already revealing the crucial importance of modernity in affirming this intention, and of Nietzsche in insisting on it most directly.)

Later in his career, Heidegger shifted his interest somewhat, away from a phenomenology of an individual *Dasein*'s always already prior concernful involvement "in" a world, to the thrownness of any "people" (*Volk*) or community in history itself, the history of Being, all as a way of making similar points about the founded and secondary nature of representing, picturing, object-talk, etc. His attempt to show what is fundamentally unthought (and indeed unthinkable) in such guiding questions led him to broaden his frame of reference considerably, and so to connect themes like our "forgetting" of the Being question not just with themes so prominent in his early (and distorted) appropriation by "existentialists", such as "inauthenticity," "falling," and "the They," but with the "destiny" of thought and mankind, "technological existence" and its inherent nihilism.

This, then, is the metaphysical enterprise with which Nietzsche is linked, and the nihilistic fate in which Nietzsche is supposed to share. What is especially useful about this approach is that, if successful, it will help a great deal with a number of problems raised in the previous discussion of Nietzsche. The idea, say, that the struggle for power between masters and slaves, and the subsequent resentment of the losing slaves, should all somehow "count" as "the meaning" of Christianity and Christian institutions, or that an anxious "revenge" against the transient, impermanent nature of existence, should count as the central or essential meaning of the ascetic spirit, and should so "be" what post-Platonic philosophy and modern science "are," led us back to a very unstable and unsatisfying account of perspectival interpretation, and Nietzsche's own will, rhetorical power, irony, etc., none of which addressed the issues raised adequately. Heidegger is suggesting that Nietzsche's interpretations are convincing because he is identifying some sort of fundamental orientation in such institutions, their reliance on a notion of Being tied essentially to an affirmation of human subjectivity and power. Since, Heidegger maintains in his own voice, all intelligibility or "meaning" derives from such fundamental ontological orientations, Nietzsche's success in unveiling the deeper metaphysical issues at stake in Western notions of reason, or equality or justice, his showing that they all are tied to "the supreme will to power," "to impose upon becoming the character of being,"[30] means that he has established the fundamental "level" of interpretation required for him to make the sweeping claims about the significance of his results.[31]

Before examining how all that is supposed to work, and before thereby returning to our concerns with the modernity issue, we should note more emphatically the unusual nature of this characterization of metaphysics.

As should be obvious by now, Heidegger's discussion of metaphysics detaches the issue from its traditional close links with epistemology. Metaphysics is often treated as itself a special domain of knowledge, characterized by such features as apriority, necessity, and eternality, or as requiring intellectual intuition, *noesis*, or some other special sort of justification. Heidegger is not much interested in such issues, and links metaphysics instead to a kind of "unconcealing" or interpretation of being that cannot be "regulated" by methodologies or argument strategies. (The attempt to do so has been what has defined the problems of, especially, modern metaphysics.) This means that in some sense poets and painters, as well as unclassifiable writers like Nietzsche, can be said to "have a metaphysical teaching," to have illuminated some aspect of our understanding of the beings for the most part covered up or passed over. (In Heidegger's language, borrowed, as Schürmann shows, from Kant, metaphysics is not a matter of "knowing" but "thinking.")[32]

Heidegger very well realizes that for a modern reader, this makes for a great deal of insecurity, even anxiety. We usually want there to be some sort of possible "contest" among such various views, governed by fair, clearly defined rules, so that only the "winner" deserves our attention. Without such rules, as Kant long ago worried, we suspect that we are dealing with the various "dreams" of various "spirit seers." As we have been seeing, Heidegger thinks this whole intuition comes from an ungrounded, discredited agenda, and, anyway, prejudices the issues in a particular "anthropological" way from the start.

Moreover, by focusing on the will to power as a metaphysical doctrine, Heidegger can appear to give the impression that he interprets Nietzsche as proposing a straightforward, quasi-naturalistic theory about all the beings, about the "nature" of every single thing that is. There are certainly passages in Nietzsche that read this way,[33] and Heidegger is not always careful about his own formulations, but the balance of the lectures suggest otherwise, or suggest that Heidegger does not think that Nietzsche means us to believe that everything, from numbers to rocks to dogs, "is" by constantly striving to enhance its power, even at the risk of its own preservation. As we saw in the last chapter, Nietzsche's appeal to the will to power is meant precisely to suggest the absence of any "truth" about the nature of everything, or to suggest the all-determining role of interpretation in the identification of "what anything is."[34]

Heidegger, particularly in the early lectures, stresses just this aspect of Nietzsche's thought, and thereby links Nietzsche and his whole modernist project with the Idealist tradition, citing Nietzsche's own citations from "the best and greatest tradition of German philosophy, ... Leibniz, Kant, Hegel and Schopenhauer"[35] (all quite appropriately, from the point of view developed in this book). Although Heidegger is eager to avoid implications of "subjectivism" or even traditional idealism, he himself also often emphasizes that Being is only accessible within the horizon" of man's concernful dealings, within the "presencing" made possible by man's "openness" to Being.[36] In the early lectures, Heidegger had invoked his own key notion of "resoluteness" (*Entschlossenheit*) to gloss Nietzschean will to power, suggesting both a willing and a "resolute openness to oneself."[37] It is by means of such resolute openness that we are said "to find ourselves particularly attuned [*gestimmt*, another key term from *Being and Time*] to beings which we are not and to the being which we are."[38] It is in this sense that the will to power functions not as "the willing of any particular entity," but involves "the Being and essence of beings; it is this itself."[39]

And this co-dependence between human (historical, embodied) existence as a kind of horizon for any understanding of Being, and the historical "presencing" or illuminating of Being as a horizon for *Dasein*'s self-understanding and dealings with the world, when transferred to the interpretation of Nietzsche[40] is especially stressed when Heidegger wants to claim that Nietzsche has misinterpreted this co-dependence, and is guilty of a one-sided elevation of human subjectivity – just like the Idealist tradition before him. He has interpreted human existence as "will to power" and so sees metaphysics as "imposing upon becoming the character of being." We need now to see what that means.[41]

3 The "Vollendung" of Metaphysics

In a 1940 lecture series ("Nietzsche's Metaphysics"), Heidegger lists the five fundamental expressions of Nietzsche's metaphysics: "'will to power,' 'nihilism,' 'the eternal return of the same,' 'the overman,' and 'justice.'"[42] Since, for reasons we shall not trace here, Heidegger interprets the eternal return doctrine as essentially linked to the claims of will to power (it is the "way" in which Nietzsche means to affirm the totality of will to power, "how" he means to render of vast, indeed "eternal" metaphysical significance the role of a groundless, self-defining subjectivity),[43] the overman as the teacher of the eternal return and therewith the will to power,[44] and "justice" as a kind of "homoiosis"[45] or accordance with the wholly temporal realm of becoming (and so again as expressing the totality of will to power), we shall be able to concentrate here, as Heidegger does, on the relation between the will to power doctrine, the Western tradition, and nihilism.

The extravagant claim that Nietzsche, the great demystifier of metaphysics, should be understood as "the thinker of the consummation of metaphysics,"[46] is clearly meant provocatively by Heidegger, as a way of pointing to something neglected both in Nietzsche and in the metaphysical tradition, something that becomes harder to deny, or is more on the surface, in modernity. The metaphysical tradition, understood as "affirming the predominance of beings over against Being, without knowing what is involved in such an affirmation,"[47] can be accounted for, or, in some sense, this predominance can be explained, by understanding how much of Nietzsche's destructive account is correct, that such an orientation should be understood as kind of human self-assertion, a relegation of Being to human will. This in turn will enable us to understand Nietzsche properly, that Nietzsche is "the transition from the preparatory phase of the modern age – historically the time between 1600 and 1900 – to the beginning of its consummation."[48]

We have seen enough, I hope, in this and in the last chapter, to understand what Heidegger means to affirm in accepting so much of Nietzsche's reading of Western philosophy. For Nietzsche, what was important to see was the central role of "value" and the act of valuing, in the metaphysical positions that have predominated in the West. Nietzsche was right, according to Heidegger, to see that all prior claims for metaphysical truth are no more than "estimations of value," and were undertaken for the "preservation and enhancement" of "life."[49] The Western fascination with a supersensible-sensible contrast, with mathematics, monotheism, Christian asceticism, with law, universality and equality, can all be accounted for by Nietzsche's inclusive appeal in *Thus Spoke Zarathustra* to a "revenge against time," a resentment against chance, contingency, against the brute particularity of existence. Metaphysics especially is a strategy of human self-empowerment, a way of rendering the whole manageable by human agents, comprehensible and so less fearful, as well as technically manipulable.

Nietzsche is thus right that Platonic *eidos* and his own notion of *Werte*, value, belong together, and right too in seeing the rest of the Western tradition as dominated by this attempt at self-empowering and a securing of the beings through value. According to Heidegger as well, "the begining of metaphysics in Plato's thinking is at the same time the beginning of 'humanism'."[50] Plato, Kant, "and the whole conception of the essence of absolute reason in the metaphysics of German Idealism (in Fichte, Schelling, and Hegel)" [are] to be accounted for by reference to the "poetic essence of reason,"[51] or what Nietzsche called the will to power.

Heidegger of course wants to deepen this claim by articulating the special terms within which the most fundamental issues in metaphysics should be understood. What Nietzsche is really talking about, according to Heidegger, is the domination in our thought of the idea of presence, the role of entity-talk and entity-thought in our ontology, and so the avoidance of any serious interrogation of the (one might even say) "formal"[52] process by which entities come to dominate our thought, the presencing or historical clearing that, Heidegger tries in so many elusive ways to claim, is the "happening" of Being, of what

comes, contingently, from "nowhere," to count for us as "real."[53]
There is a particularly direct passage in the 1939 lecture series that
summarizes this claim well.

> This [Nietzsche's] ruthless and extreme anthropomorphizing [*Vermens-chlichung*] of the world tears away the last illusions of the modern
> fundamental metaphysical positions; it takes the positing of man as
> *subiectum* seriously ... Nietzsche would claim with equal right to have
> brought a metaphysically necessary subjectivism to completion ...
> In Nietzsche's thought-path to the will to power, not only modern
> metaphysics, but *Western* metaphysics as whole is accomplished [com-
> pleted, *sich vollendet*].[54]

Although such claims are controversial enough, what is important
for our purposes is how this whole appropriation of Nietzsche functions in Heidegger's account of modernity. This is an especially tricky
issue since that problem is inextricably intertwined with Heidegger's
presentation of Nietzsche's (and so modernity's) failure to escape the
nihilism of the Western tradition. (And, to note an even more complex point one final time: this is all made trickier still by Heidegger's
protestations that he is not attacking or criticizing Niezsche or modernity or metaphysics, that the priority of the beings over Being itself
represents "a peculiar dominance of Being 'over' beings as a whole
[in the veiled form of Being's abandonment of beings]."[55]
Much of this strategy of double association, of Nietzsche with the
essence of modernity, and modern metaphysics with the nihilistic
essence of the Western tradition, comes to a head in several lectures
on Descartes in the 1940 lectures on "European Nihilism." There
modernity, in a relatively straightforward sense, is understood as the
"emphatic positing of the subject," so that the "guiding question"
ceases to be "What is it to be a being?" but a question of "method,
about the path along which the absolutely certain and secure is
sought by man himself for man himself."[56] In his most sweeping
claim about the moden epoch, one which raises virtually all the
questions we shall ask in the next section, Heidegger asserts,

> The securing of supreme and absolute self-development of all the
> capacities of mankind for absolute dominion over the entire earth is
> the secret goad [*geheime Stachel*] that prods modern man again and
> again to new resurgences, a goad that forces him into commitments
> that secure for him the surety of his actions and the certainty of his
> aims.[57]

This project is clearly in Descartes, according to Heidegger, whose insistence on the priority of the problem of "representing" the world reflects an attempt by human being to "decide in advance and everywhere on his own what can and should be accepted as well placed and permanent."[58] And this is all "the first resolute step through which modern machine technology and along with it the modern world and modern mankind, become metaphysically possible for the first time."[59]

As Heidegger had argued in *Being and Time*, this emphasis on representation and epistemological security makes it impossible for Descartes, or the legions influenced by him, to raise the "ground question," the question of the Being of the subject doing the representing and calculating, to ask what has made possible or "cleared," "lighted," the subject as a quest for radical certainty. The *"sum"* in Descartes's famous *"Sum res cogitans"* remains unexplored, treated, if at all, in a question-begging way, only according to the requirements of a representing subject, as a kind of object, standing over against the representer himself, a "substance" with essential and accidental properties.[60]

While Heidegger realizes that there is little in Nietzsche that resonates with any interest in substance metaphysics or "the new way of ideas" in general, (Nietzsche's teaching is not "the same," *das Gleiche*, as Descartes's) he does try to show that Nietzsche and Descartes are "thinking the self-same (*das Selbe*) in the historical fulfillment of its essence."[61] This self-same has again to do with the metaphysics of subjectivity, that, even though Nietzsche rejects Descartes's faith in the transparency of consciousness to itself and the role of conscious thought in general (all in favor of the "unthought," drives, the "living body", etc.), even though he does not share Descartes's faith in mathematics as securing the subject's domination of beings (insistent instead on the "poetic essence of reason"), nevertheless Nietzsche maintains an "even more rigorous commitment to the subjectivity posited by Descartes," than Descartes himself, and so, "For Nietzsche, not only is what is represented as such a product of man, but every shaping and minting [*Prägung*] of any kind is the product and property of man as absolute [*unbedingt*] lord over every sort of perspective in which the world is fashioned and empowered as absolute [*unbedingt*] will to power."[62]

Simply put then, Nietzsche's ruthless honesty in exposing what metaphysics has always been, what it more clearly came to understand about itself in Descartes, and then progressively in Kant, Fichte, Schelling, and Hegel, has now made it impossible to continue to affirm metaphysics. The "essential possibilities of metaphysics are exhausted,"[63] and "European nihilism" has begun to "unfold in the history of Being."[64]

Nietzsche clearly believes that this honesty alone makes possible a culmination and overcoming of metaphysics, but, Heidegger claims in many different ways, Nietzsche's own emphasis on a "trans-valuation of values," his celebration of the will to power, creation, affirmation, and so a kind of divinized humanism, betray the persistence of metaphysical assumptions, a "murderous" refusal to "let Being be" and so a lingering nihilism in his own position.

Now, by nihilism Heidegger means something of his own; he means obviously that the question on which all other questions depend, What is Being?, can no longer be asked, and so "here the age of consummate meaninglessness begins."[65] In this age (the "essence of modernity") Being is understood through mere "machination" (*Machenschaft*), wherein Being is taken to be infinitely malleable, subject completely to human will. This attitude "prevents any kind of grounding of the projections that are under its power and yet are themselves nonetheless powerful."[66] We live in an age in which "world views are invented and promulgated with a view to their power,"[67] (and an age of "ungrounded truth")[68] and this absence of "ground" is what Heidegger means to point to by this reference to nihilism and meaninglessness. He tries everywhere to make clear that he is not encouraging a return to traditional notions of "meaning" or purpose. Those too are human projections, expressions of a quest for self-satisfaction and security we are well rid of. Instead Heidegger tries to refashion the issue in his difficult, neologistic language. In his own terms, 'When Being lacks the clearing, beings as a whole lack meaning," [*Das Lichtungs-lose des Seins ist die Sinnlosigkeit des Seienden im Ganzen*] a fate which means that modern man's projections must emerge as "essentially violent,"[69] successful only by establishing their "rule" through power alone.

Nietzsche was thus correct to pronounce that "God is dead," and correct in understanding that this exhaustion had to do with much more than the Christian religion, that the fate of all metaphysical thinking was involved. But he could not free himself from the "value thinking of metaphysics," and insisted, in a kind of final, apocalyptic way, that modern humanity "will itself as the executor of the unconditional will to power,"[70] perpetuating and even radicalizing modern "thoughtlessness," its inability to ask itself the one question that most needs asking. This thoughtlessness is as apparent in the mindless subjugation of the earth to technology, the point or significance of which no one knows how to raise, as it is in Nietzsche's own celebration of the will to power, the content of which is equally (and equally dangerously) "open," ungrounded.

Said in Heidegger's own vocabulary, Nietzsche was right that where metaphysics had tried to determine an *arche*, or principle, there is nothing, "no being." But, "What if in truth the nothing were indeed not a being but also were not simply null?"[71] In that case, Heidegger remarks elliptically, "Nihilism would then be the essential nonthinking of the essence of the nothing."[72] By contrast, presumably, a genuine turn from the nihilism of metaphysics would consist in actually "thinking" of the essence of the nothing.

Said more prosaically, the absence of a metaphysical, unifying, principle in late modernity, the unavailability of any appeal to nature, or reason, or the transcendental subject, or history, is not to be understood as mere absence, an unavailability required by the final triumph of modern subjectivism or the culmination of the disintegration of critical idealism in Nietzschean perspectivism. That would render the human subject the "last" metaphysical *arche*, constrained by "nothing" in its quest for autonomy, and most visible in the way modern life is "enframed" in the *Gestell*[73] of a limitless technology. Just this position insures modern "thoughtlessness," fundamentally unaware of the conditions or possibility of its ascendancy, profoundly forgetful and "closed."

Heidegger struggled during his whole career to find some way of articulating this experience of the "originary" as absence, or nonbeing, but "not as null," and throughout his career, it remained what made his language and style so difficult, even forbidding.[74] In our context, his claim is that the collapse or end of the metaphysical project of modernity should not be understood as it is in positivism or atheism, as the certification that some claims "thought to be true" are now "known to be false." Rather it means (or could mean, Heidegger hopes) the possibility of an experience of genuine "presencing," of some sort of recognition of the way in which our discourse, action and thought comes to be oriented, has a certain "directionality," that simply happens, of an "origin," in some infinitely complicated sense, that is a "non-origin."[75]

In *Being and Time*, Heidegger made use of a radically revised phenomenology to focus attention on the way in which the "meaning" of human being came to light in "being-towards-death," in some authentic anticipation of one's not-being. The famous account there of an "anxious" realization that the "ground" of one's own being was a "nullity" was immediately misinterpreted in "existentialist" terms (the "meaninglessness" or "absurdity" of existence, the heroic nature of human freedom, etc.) but even in this text, Heidegger is clearly interested in this experience as "preparatory" for a fuller understanding of the meaning of Being in general as presencing, (a no-thing that is not null), a "framing" of existence always prior to language, method, moral judgment, but "not," as an event, itself subject to a *logos*. In this "fundamental ontological" context, however, the modern Cartesian or technological comportment toward the world is characterized in language that, despite demurrals, suggests some sort of resistance, some opposition between "authentic" and "inauthentic" existence. Around the mid-thirties, Heidegger's language began to shift, this language dropped out and the much discussed Heideggerean "turn" to the en-framing of an epoch, and the language of passivity, mittence, shepherds, and so forth, began.[76]

With respect to the Nietzsche interpretation, the question being raised is, for all the extremity and unfairness of Heidegger's "interpretation," a profound one, especially as it concerns the fate of modernity. As it has been presented here, Nietzsche's own understanding is, however unique, recognizably modernist: he means to offer a critique, a genealogy or unmasking of all possible appeals to origins. He means to end metaphysics and all dogmatism. According to Heidegger, because of what is "unthought" in Nietzsche, the way he goes about this insures the re-emergence of some appeal to the (typically modern) subject as metaphysical origin, a "grounding" in "the will to power." One can finally see in Nietzsche that modernity's rejection of dogmatism is itself dogmatic ("unthinking"); so much so that modernity's self-confidence in the Age of Technology prevents more radically than ever before any "thinking" about the non-origin, or the radically contingent happening, the event or appropriation (*Ereignis*),[77] of all thought and action. The "oblivion" (*Vergessenheit*) of Being is great in any age, but "it reaches its greatest opacity in the technological age."[78] Modernity is not the realization of absolute freedom; it plunges us into absolute ignorance. Is this so?

4 The Turn, Turning Away, and Overturning

Basically I live an extremely dangerous life, for I belong to those machines which can explode.

F. Nietzsche Letter to Peter Gast, 14 August 1881

Heidegger's assessment of modernity does not of course end with the Nietzsche lectures or the later essays on Nietzsche. In fact, as we have briefly seen, his account becomes more extreme, less explicable in any traditional terms, and so considerably more difficult to understand. The language of the ontico-ontological difference, already elusive, is recast in terms of "world" and "thing," simple terms which have an extraordinarily concrete, special meaning in the later Heidegger; truth, unconcealment, *aletheia*, are recast as "event; "proximity" as "the four-fold"; the familiar *Dasein* as "mortal," and so on, all transforming a lexicon which still had many connections, through Dilthey and Husserl, to transcendental and critical concerns, into one, for want of a better word, "mythic."[79] However, while what we have seen so far only begins a much longer story, nothing in that story, I think, will undermine or avoid the criticisms I want now to suggest.[80]

Let us begin with the obvious responses to Heidegger's analysis of modernity. First, many commentators have remarked on the abstractness of the Heideggerean picture of the modern world, and especially of technology. The idea that the current, let us assume, predatory stance of modern man has less to do with the economic imperatives of market capitalism, the dynamics of the nation state and modern warfare, or even the darker, violent, and fearful side of human psychology, than with the metaphysical tradition stretching from Plato to Nietzsche, sounds to many so academic and implausible as to warrant a refusal to consider the matter any further.

However, while there are certainly many questions that need to be asked about the connection between the details of economic, technical, and scientific practice and Heidegger's elusive account of the fate of metaphysics, between concrete existence and some originary, direction-setting "presencing," we can at least avoid the confusion caused by thinking that Heidegger is trying to explain the empirical details of history by reference to the books philosophers wrote. In his account, philosophers, poets, and he often also says, political deeds, in some sense simply make manifest the way an age or "epoch" is "turning" or "closing," the event of presencing. He has no interest in "explaining" the origin of the technological "enframing." (And he also has no interest in any criticism of those who want to give such an account.) His interest is always focused on the issue of how some immensely fundamental "sense" of Being itself "happens" for an age (happens in a way that makes impossible that it ever happen *for* that age), and that interest avoids any concern with accounting for this or that moment. It remains on the "formal process," we might prosaically put it, focused only on the fact that there is always and only such a happening, a process that is one or unitary, he might put it, only by being multiple, everywhere different. His claim about the modern "age of the world picture" is that the currently dominant "sense" has made the most difficult yet even raising the very question of presencing, of Being; and that this event should be interpreted as continuous with the general way in which "metaphysical thinking" has always made very difficult the posing of this question of what is always prior to reason, or *logos*, or calculation. If Heidegger is right about the priority of this orientation, then his account is not "abstract" but "fundamental."

A better way to understand what Heidegger is interested in might open up by noting the objections raised by those more sympathetic to Nietzsche in this "confrontation." Many have argued that there are issues between them that are far more serious than whether Heidegger has interpreted the text rightly.

In the first place, there may be much less of a "confrontation" between them than Heidegger would like. Heidegger's attempt to interpret the Nietzschean account of "will to power" in terms so tied to traditional notions of modern subjectivity often creates a kind of straw man for him to attack. Accusing Nietzsche of attempting to establish man as an "absolute (*unbedingte*) lord," as if anything in Nietzsche could be "unconditioned" or absolute, and his association of Nietzsche with Descartes and the attempt by modern man to "decide in advance and everywhere on his own what can and should be accepted as well placed and permanent" should raise more that hermeneutical suspicions. Nietzsche frequently insists that he is attacking and thoroughly rejecting the modern notion of subjectivity as ground or unitary source; that the subject is a "plurality" of forces, and that "thoughts" come, "not when I will but when it wills."[81] There is much in Nietzsche, in other words, that suggests not so much the apotheosis of humanism as the beginning already of what we now call "anti-humanism," or at least a rejection of any notion of an individual or collective self-defining subjectivity, having its "source" in itself.[82] On this defensive reading of Nietzsche, the subject was "dispersed," its unity undermined and Western attempts to "measure" and calculate Being according to *logos* satirized and rejected – the true implications of the collapse of the modern project already detected – all long before Heidegger and his French epigones arrived on the scene.

These important qualifications and corrections of Heidegger, however justified, can, in this context, be put to one side. For such attempts to render Nietzsche as, if not even "more," Heideggerean than Heidegger himself,[83] cannot, I think, evade a basic issue. There is still something roughly accurate in Heidegger's association of Nietzsche with modern humanism, or with the modern project of achieving full autonomy, however much the "human" is "dismantled" and reconstructed, however much autonomy is reconceived as "self-overcoming" rather than self-realization. A deeper and more obvious confrontation between them can be discussed once we generally concede this point.

The important dispute between them (and between Heidegger and modernity) emerges when we note that Nietzsche would clearly suggest that Heidegger's famous "question" about Being itself still requires, cannot evade, a "human all too human" genealogy, that the emergence of the sensibility promoted by Heidegger – the dependence of any human self-assertion on "principles" that are themselves mere events or historical happenings – cannot itself be viewed "dogmatically," as a discovery, or truth or epoch-ending disclosure by Being. Heidegger's later philosophy, as well as the extraordinary popularity of "post" historical categories in contemporary discussions, depend essentially on the language of "closure," and completion, terms that return us, ironically, to the most paradigmatic forms of early modern, epochal self-consciousness, and that in Heidegger's hands immediately suggest a return to "dogmatism," at least in the form of some sort of appeal to historical positivity.[84] (I mean by this a return to a view that such an event should not be understood as a contemporary social achievement, the self-construal of a historical community, but as a "mittence," a gift "from" Being, or as a directly apprehensible event.)[85] Looked at from the point of view developed in chapters 3 and 4 above, however non-substantial, anti-metaphysical, and unprincipled the Heideggerean *Ereignis*, the enterprise of fundamental ontology/thinking/thanking, construed as a response to the *aporiai* of modernity, still betrays some hope for an intimation of ultimacy, for a "clearing," for what is "outside" of, and determines, human self-assertion, even as Heidegger affirms the "owning [*Eignen*] in which man and being are delivered over to each other".[86]

In other words, while Heidegger's position might not itself represent some hidden *metaphysical* agenda, a "dogmatic" notion of truth, a renewed appeal to origins, etc., "metaphysics" in this sense is not the real issue between Heidegger and Nietzsche, and therewith between Heidegger and modernism. Heidegger's appeals to the event of presencing might all be intricately formulated precisely to deny any new appeal to "origins" in any traditional sense, but the very claim for the impossibility of such origins, now finally, fully understood by Heidegger, and so the complete, thoroughgoing denial of the sufficiency of human self-reflection and autonomy, does appeal in some sense to an originary event as a limit (even if not a new "enframing"), and so establishes a fundamental closure, an end to the epochality ruled by principles of any sort.[87] And from the point of view we have developed, this does re-introduce the problem of positivity, whether metaphysically represented or not.[88] (Or, the post-philosophical starts to look like the pre-philosophical, raising problems we shall consider shortly.)

In this sense it is ironic that the one published text of Nietzsche's to which Heidegger does devote attention, *Thus Spoke Zarathustra*, itself suggests the complications of Heidegger's (and to some extent Nietzsche's own) attempt to "think historically." As we saw briefly in the last chapter, that book is structured around an episode at the end of the second part, Zarathustra's entertaining the idea of the eternal return of the same, which effectively ends Zarathustra's hopes for a decisive historical transformation. The doctrine of the Overman is dropped as Zarathustra realizes, in his illness and disgust, that the hope for such a redemption is itself a manifestation of a revenge against time, a transformation of the classical notions of transcendence and truth into the hope for a decisive historical reversal, for a revolutionary moment beyond which all would be different; in Heidegger's language that we would now, finally, start "thinking." Zarathustra (at least Zarathustra; the issue of "Nietzsche" himself being a much more complicated one) comes to reject the language of finality, closure, end, consummation, and it is a lesson Heidegger might have learned.

The more sophisticated commentators on Heidegger are, of course, intensely aware of this issue. In his recently translated series of essays (*The End of Modernity*), Gianni Vattimo stresses that Heidegger clearly wishes to avoid any "ultimate" and so paradox-producing claim about the "end" or consummation of metaphysics. The key issue in Vattimo's work is the historical event of the "weakening" of the hold that metaphysical assumptions have exercised over the Western tradition, an event that makes possible a kind of thinking that takes place in the light of this weakening, or a "weak thinking." This all turns out to have to do with a notion of postmodern or postmetaphysical "truth" in which the "experience of truth is an aesthetic and rhetorical experience,"[89] but his point of view suggests an interesting reading of the issue in Heidegger we are now pursuing.

For, Vattimo suggests, we ought to be particularly interested in those (relatively few)[90] passages where Heidegger stresses that his enterprise does not call for some epochal "overcoming" (*Überwindung*) of metaphysics, but instead for what is called a *Verwindung*, a word very difficult to translate. Heidegger himself told his French translators that it is not an "overcoming" but a "going beyond that is both an acceptance and a deepening."[91] Etymologically, the term suggests a convalescence from an illness, a twisting, or even distorting, as well as a resignation (one can be *verwunden* to a loss). It suggests both an acceptance of Western humanism, and a taking leave from it at the same time, much in the manner of the later Heidegger's remarks about the always intertwined nature of revealing and concealing truth. Metaphysics is not "responsible" for the obscuring of Being as presencing; Being always *must* be obscured as presencing.

And this all suggests that Heidegger's enterprise is not supposed to be revolutionary, a decisive origination that can make it seem as "metaphysical" as what it rejects, but a genuine *An-denken*, or re-collection of the metaphysical tradition; essentially a perpetual hermeneutics concerned with "where," in Heidegger's unusual sense, truth has happened by not happening.[92]

None of this, however, while it throws a moderating light on much of what Heidegger says (and often makes clearer the relation between Heidegger and Gadamer), resolves the central issue. It may be true that, "Both [Nietzsche and Heidegger] find themselves obliged, on the one hand, to take up a critical distance from Western thought insofar as it is foundational; on the other hand, however, they find themselves unable to criticize Western thought in the name of another, and truer, foundation."[93] But the important question does not concern their dissatisfactions with foundationalism, and their attempts to express these dissatisfactions without a new foundation. The question is whether both are appealing to a historical event in a way that treats it as some sort of directly accessible "event," and that thereby functions as a historical origin. In other words, even if the issue is a "weakening" or "convalescing," and not an overcoming, Heidegger and Vattimo elevate the significance of that event in a way that still suggests some decisive or revolutionary moment in history, all again as if that event simply "happens" to us, or is not itself the result of a complex, contingent, concretely motivated, collective self-interpretation. Thus Vattimo himself cannot resist the language of ultimacy and origin, and so still claims, after all this qualification about *Verwindung*, that nihilism "appears as the *one* possibility truly able to make possible all the other possibilities that constitute existence,"[94] and still talks about "the era of the "weakness" of Being,"[95] as if there simply "are" such things as "eras."

The same sort of problem emerges in Reiner Schürmann's apologia, which is much more explicit about the issue of "historicist" or "epochal positivism" in Heidegger.[96] He too claims that the historical "turning" promoted by Heidegger, "is the attempt at de-centering the network of phenomena by seeking its condition not in ultimate grounds, but in the simple event of coming to presence and its historical modalities."[97] But Schürmann denies that this reliance on the "event" of presencing, the "originary" throughout his book for all "thinking," is a "historicist or positivist concept."[98] This is so, he claims, because Heidegger still pursues a transcendental goal, "in that it seeks to reach in turn the conditions of these historical orders and breaks between them."[99] Heidegger, in other words, wants much more than a description of various epochs, or our own "post-metaphysical" epoch; he is quite aware that a wholly different issue is involved in the "transcendental" claim that Being occurs or happens only within such epochs, that such a historically contingent presencing is a "condition of the possibility" for any "unconcealing" or truth.[100]

However, from the, let us say, Hegelian point of view developed in chapter 3, it doesn't much matter whether the dogmatism or positivism in question is empiricist, historicist, epochal, or transcendental. The problem is still a regression to a kind of pre-critical point of view.[101] The language of transcendental conditions, however guardedly used by Schürmann and others, still carries with it the burden of a transcendental "deduction," a way of demonstrating some sort of "necessity" in what are claimed to be "conditions" for Heideggerean "truth," and I see little evidence that Heidegger wants to shoulder that burden. Not only would it seem to renew the whole subject-object and logocentric language Heidegger wishes to be free from, it would simply re-raise the classical post-Kantian problems of how human thought could be said to "discover" some extra-conceptual condition on which it "depended" (all as opposed to a way of thinking about ourselves that is only historically sufficient, a way in which we have come to regard ourselves).

There just does not seem to be any evidence that such an argument strategy plays much of a role in Heidegger's work.[102] And Schürmann himself appeals to a more recognizable Heideggerean diction, resonant indeed with a kind of "meta-historical" positivism, when, in responding to critics who are uncomfortable with Heidegger's "vengeful" attack on the tradition and his language of closure and completion, he says, "Many of these criticisms would collapse if their authors saw that what is at stake in the program of "deconstructing metaphysics" and the claim of an "end of philosophy" is an appreciation of the situation in which we find ourselves today, rather than a summary judgment of the past."[103]

Moreover, even if we focus our attention simply on the question of whether Heidegger has accounted for the "situation in which we find ourselves today," and especially on his account of modernity, there are questions enough to raise without introducing the "end of metaphysics" issues. Since, as we have seen in detail, the central philosophical dimension of modernity for Heidegger is "the uprising of man into subjectivity," we are owed some concrete account of what this "uprising," or "coming to be" means. Heidegger, that is, commits himself, especially in the Nietzsche lectures, to an answer to a question he poses for himself. "We are asking, How do we arrive at an emphatic positing of the 'subject'? *Whence* does that dominance of the subjective come that guides modern humanity and its understanding of the world?"[104]

Heidegger's remarkably brief answer to this question is one we have seen before; it involves a "secularized" salvation motive in modernity. "The essential Christian thought of the certitude of salvation is adopted, but such 'salvation' is not eternal, other-wordly bliss, and the way to it is not selflessness."[105] It now involves method, a "certitude by which man can by himself be sure of his own definition and task."[106]

We have already seen, in chapter 2, the limitations of such a secularization thesis, particularly one as crudely drawn as is Heidegger's. What it helps highlight here is the way in which Heidegger's account paints a historical picture that is colored by what appears to be a kind of "tragic" sensibility. Heidegger suggests here and throughout many of his comments on modernity that the central categories in understanding the modern experience are will and hubris, that with the decline of the Christian view of human power and security (the potential for eternal salvation), modernity emerged as essentially an act of human self-assertion, a reckless insistence on *human* power, dominion over the earth and self-sufficiency, all as a kind of "replacement" for Christian security.

This is all tempered and rendered more tragic by Heidegger's claim that this whole episode was not, as it were, "avoidable," that it itself is a "gift" of Being, an obscuring of presencing inherent in the event of presencing itself.[107] But that does not altogether temper the "how the mighty have fallen" tone in his comments on the rapacity, filth, and thoughtlessness of the modern world. And it also reveals that Heidegger is largely insensitive to the fact that the modern obsession with scepticism, method, certainty, the modern sense of a loss of trust in the lived, immediate world, are not all phenomena that simply result from some sudden radicalization of modern humanism.[108]

We have become so suspicious about the old, smug positivist myths about the ever progressive March of Science, rendering the need for religion and metaphysics ever more obsolete, that we tend now to forget that it is still in some sense true that the modern attention to epistemology and subjective certainty was not simply a continuation of Platonic metaphysics, nor a mere sudden "uprising" of willfulness, but was itself provoked by historical crises, inventions, growing paradoxes in the old paradigms, and the gradual "de-legitimation" of the vast network of premodern science. Nowhere does Heidegger seem sympathetic to the modern experience of an intense and well motivated disappointment with the premodern tradition, the experience of long-entrenched and spectacular error (the Copernican issue being only the most notorious example), or with the political consequences of "methodologically unsecured" belief (the wars of religion so intertwined with the seventeenth century, rationalist excitement about security and universality).[109]

In that historical context, viewed more sympathetically, from the "inside," the modern desire to bracket our natural, common-sense relation to the world, and then to re-establish a connection through some sort of methodologically defensible, or critically self-conscious criterion of knowledge, was, at the time, a perfectly legitimate, powerfully motivated, perhaps even unavoidable need. It marks not a radicalization of metaphysical self-assertion, a final forgetting of being, but a way of avoiding a disastrous, dogmatic, centuries-long self-forgetting. By contrast with this approach, Heidegger simply does not have a sufficient answer to his own question, "Whence does that dominance of the subjective come that guides modern humanity and its understanding of the world?"

As we have been detecting throughout, Heidegger sometimes seems to indicate that there cannot be anything we would usually recognize as an answer to this question, however he may have himself tried to provide one in the Nietzsche lectures. Heidegger is infamous for suggesting things like "In the most hidden ground of his essence, man truly is only when in his way he is like the rose – without why."[110] And "Why does it play, that great child of the world play seen by Heraclitus? It plays because it plays. The 'because' perishes in play. The play is without 'why'."[111]

Yet these and many other similar pronouncements are not meant to express a kind of scepticism or simple inability to answer a certain question about the origin of modernity. The articulate a Heideggerean view of an essential human dependence or finitude that dominates all his work. From *Being and Time* on, Heidegger's "corrections" of what he regards as the thoughtless, forgetful, hubristic, post-Cartesian spirit of modernity, read like what Hegel would call "indeterminate negations" or over-corrections and result, when thought through, in such curiously positivist appeals to the inexplicable play of "what happens." The famous notion of "Being-in-the-world," so useful and suggestive in Heidegger's early phenomenology, already betrays a notion of some kind of thorough practical "absorption" in the world, wherein entities, one's own activities and those of others, can be held before one, and called to account, or "represented" only "deficiently," by narrowing or forgetting this fundamental mode of being, or through its breakdown. Some richer dialectical notion of not simply being immersed in the world of concern, but also, in some sort of co-original way, always taking oneself to be immersed in a concrete way, self-consciously situating oneself, as well as merely "thrown," might have made possible a richer and less critically suspect account of existence. This in turn might have made possible a general view of human "transcendence," the ability to transcend or negate one's "thrown" situation, which is not tied so abstractly to the Heideggerean notion of "possibility," (resolute action or "hurling" oneself into the historical "abyss"), and so could have led to a richer and more concrete analysis of the origin and fate of modernity.

In particular, such a view, that one is never simply "absorbed" in a world, or a kind of "victim" of historical presencing, but absorbed in a particular way that depends on a certain self-construal, could have formed the basis of a view of modern technology more nuanced and less hegemonic than Heidegger's. That is, from the Hegelian point of view I am suggesting, it would never be possible to speak simply of "the" technological event or enframing. There could be no such thing as, simply, "technology," or *Machenschaft*, but only differing, historically situated, socially mediated experiences of human power and limitation, a "technology" appropriate to a certain social and economic order, experienced within a certain "ethical life," and differing from a technology expressing and functioning within a different historical community.[112]

Many of these issues, though, to be fair to Heidegger, would take us deeper into his project than this limited space allows. We have, though, seen enough to raise in a final, summary way the large, systematic issue towards which this discussion, as well as the discussion of Nietzsche and the idealist alternatives, have been pointing: the fate of the modern ideal of autonomy in the European tradition. My claim has been that Nietzsche and Heidegger fail to "break free" of, or go beyond or behind, modernity, that what they thought they had left behind simply re-emerges, and that this failure might give us ways to think about the great promissory note Hegel originally wrote on behalf of the modern enterprise. I want now to show, however briefly, that those who propose to go beyond or to deepen the thought of Nietzsche or Heidegger, also fail to break free of modernist imperatives, and to speculate in conclusion about that promissory note.

6

Unending Modernity

"Postmodernism is the Enlightenment gone mad."

S. Rosen
The Ancients and the Moderns

1 Modern Options

The original modern notion of Enlightenment was closely linked to a new view of nature, originally mechanistic, later more broadly materialist, and a tremendous confidence in a new, mathematically inspired method. For many philosophers, paradigmatically Hobbes, all this also meant a new view of human being as essentially a calculating, passion-satisfying engine, and so required a new theory of social life and political obligation. In the academic and intellectual life of much of Europe and to a much larger extent of Great Britain and the United States, these twin pillars of Enlightenment thought – the supreme intellectual authority of natural science (however, nowadays, historicized, shorn of foundationalist pretensions, itself "naturalized" or pragmatically interpreted), and the superiority of liberal-democratic institutions (however variously perceived by utilitarians, social democrats, Rawlseans, or libertarians) – have successfully and continuously supported and legitimated the major institutions of these societies.

In much of the European tradition, however, the situation has been different and in many ways immensely more complicated. The simplest, even a bit simplified, description of that difference concerns a much greater degree of dissatisfaction with various aspects of modernity and modernization, evident in much of the modern novel, poetry, and art, and in the closely connected philosophical agenda which has dominated much academic and non-traditional philosophy in Europe since Kant. I have suggested that the philosophical problem at stake in such dissatisfaction might best be examined as the problem of autonomy, or, more specifically, the nature of both the independence and the dependence or finitude of modern communities and individuals. This issue led us directly to Kant, who claimed, with great historical success, that the early founders of the Enlightenment project had not succeeded in achieving full "maturity" or self-direction, that they had not established an autonomously self-regulating reason. They, the rationalist and empiricist modernists, had appealed to methodological principles or psychological claims which could not themselves be justified, and were still guilty of a pre-critical dogmatism. Kant's dissatisfactions with the early modern project led him to a potentially explosive notion of a self-legislating and so purely spontaneous reflective reason, supreme in both theoretical and practical self-rule, a notion that became, in the story I have told, the focus for much of the debate about the philosophical possibility of modernity.

From what we have now seen, one can summarize that debate in a general way. Kant had argued for such an independent subjectivity, an understanding and reason underdetermined in all its claim-making activity by "the given," and unable to appeal to any "thing in itself," and an agent whose passions for actions became motives only if the agent freely determined them to be motives. And he had claimed that such a spontaneous, legislating subject realized itself as law. The understanding's spontaneity in judgment was constrained by rules for the very possibility of judgment, reason by ideas regulatively necessary for the organization of experience, and practical reason by a moral law binding on all reflective agents. Modern "critique" coincided then with rational self-rule, and so a universal, ordered life.

As we saw, Kant himself was accused of being insufficiently critical, of regressing to a dogmatism about just these twelve categories, or by appealing to carefully delineated human "faculties" and an inherent "architectonic" for human reason, or by assuming the universality and bindingness of a moral law; accused, that is, of not showing that such laws and rules could be said to be genuinely self-imposed. In the most sophisticated version of these criticisms, Hegel's, the modern ideal of autonomy was reinterpreted not as a transcendental requirement or condition for pure practical reason, but as some sort of historical achievement, all requiring a collective, developmental view of human subjectivity.

Much of the story told so far involves a denial of these attempts to realize the modern quest for independence in some form of self-imposed dependence, a dependence on rule or law in the case of

Kant, and, very roughly, on others (*Geist*) in Hegel. So the philosophical enterprise of modernity was supposed to have failed in an especially visible way in Kantian and Hegelian attempts at a radical, rational, or universally binding autonomy (independence as mutual dependence). It thereby eventually broke apart into Nietzsche's various "refusal," and his elusive, often problematic attempts at a wholly spontaneous affirmation, a new immediacy, and in a very untraditional, somewhat "mythic" invocation of human dependence and finitude in Heidegger.[1]

And in each case, the supposed failure of such a dialectic led the philosopher in question to a predictable set of tensions and *aporiai* on one side or the other of the issues. No "second innocence," it turned out, was possible for Nietzsche, no freedom from the quintessentially modern doubt about the possibility of one's affirmation of one's own freedom, creativity, self-overcoming, about the integrity, unity, or even beauty of one's creations, or about one's having actually achieved a "pathos of distance."[2] Nietzsche's celebration of a novel sort of independence, one more "modern" than the modern ideal (and so, supposedly, postmodern), one with no reliance on others, any essential or authentic or unified self, any view of the nature of things, or of the common human experience, terminated either in a wistful reverie of "active forgetting," the mere hope that one can forget or refuse to ask the kind of critical questions about one's dependence that mark the self-destructive modern spirit, or in some vague, poorly thought through and often contradicted accommodation to the claims of others, whether conceived through the image of an "overflowing" love of man ("no revenge!"), or by reference to noble enemies or worthy disciples.

Heidegger, gathering up both the pre-modern and modern tradition in the categories of "presence" and "subjectivity," sought to undermine the modern dream of self-sufficient subjectivity, and in many insightful and imaginative ways, pointed to the consequences of such hubris in the current fate of modern technological, "thoughtless" existence. But Heidegger's dissatisfaction with such pretensions was so intense that in his own position, with its notions of dependence, reception, passivity, thrownness, and ever-present obscuration and error, he lost hold of his own question about the "whence" of modernity. He implied instead an originary role for a kind of perennial human pride, and so lost touch with the concrete crises and paradoxes of early modernity. Secondly, speaking casually, he "overcorrected" the flaws he found in the modern tradition, and, in however unique and complex a way, returned us to the pre-modern, to a sense of religious finitude, and our own incapacities. This, though, would not only return us to an an-archic or unprincipled world of differences, plurality, and heteronomy celebrated in some postmodern thought, but also a world of conflict, war rather than play, and those who profess to "speak" for what cannot be "said" (a role as problematic as it is in those who speak for "what our community believes," "who we are," what "problems" we need to work on, as well as for spokesmen for the ontological happening.)[3]

We can begin now to summarize what all this might entail. To do so I want to try to bring the issues so far discussed to bear on some of the more influential contemporary accounts of the modernity problem, and to contrast this account with those. I especially want to consider very different, "critical" accounts of the inherent "dialectic of Enlightenment," and the now well-known attempts to "overcome" the modern and embrace the postmodern. These considerations will then provide an opportunity to consider some of the implications of the narrative presented here.

As always, I note again that treating so many complicated positions in a single chapter is already an admission that the treatment will not be adequate in any scholarly sense. I hope nothing said will be unfair or inaccurate, but in this context the important issue is the general contours of the contemporary understanding of the now long entrenched experience of a crisis in modern philosophical thought.

2 The Dialectic of Modernity

For the sake of argument, let us call the Hegelian or neo-Hegelian position on modernity roughly this: critical of the Enlightenment optimism about methodology and scientific rationality (*Verstand*) (whatever is thereby achieved leaves a good deal unthought or un-achieved, and unachievable by technical or methodological means), insistent on deeper or more fundamental self-consciousness by reason about itself, but, however sensitive to the profound failings or anti-nomies of modernity, equally opposed to an "abstract" negation of the modern project, arguing instead that the experience of the these sorts of limitations can lead to a reformulation and perhaps completion of such a project. Given the current international categorization of this dispute, such a position would necessarily invite comparisons with the various "negative" or more affirmatively "dialectical," "critical theory" attempts to defend similar positions.[4]

However, if the above account is correct, then we can first of all note that the original "dialectic" of enlightenment modernity should be understood in a very different way than that proposed in the famous, intensely critical account by Horkheimer and Adorno in *Dialectic of Enlightenment*. In a sweeping and unusually influential extension of Hegel's original worries about *Verstand*,[5] a critique of the "totalization" of "instrumental rationality" in the European Enlightenment and of the corresponding dominance of "identity thinking" (especially the "repression" and domination necessary to form the "unitary self" that could function as the subject of such "instrumental rationality"), Horkheimer and Adorno narrate a story which implies a kind of neurotic obsessiveness in modern subjectivity. Control, manipulation, exclusion of any deviance from the imperatives of systematic regulation of others and the environment, bureaucratic management, a subjugation of every issue to the demands of technical, efficient regulation, etc., were, for them, the marks of the modern view of self-empowerment. And in their interpretation of the unintended results of this movement, its "dialectic," they appeal to themes borrowed freely from Hegel, Marx, Nietzsche, and Heidegger and present their own version of what they regard as "the self-destruction of the Enlightenment."[6]

Their basic claim is that this insistence on the domination of nature requires a general view of reason and value that ultimately "de-legitimates" itself, renders unavailable any rational account of the purpose or significance of such control, and so ends up in a kind of cynical restitution of the mythic or irrational consciousness it was to replace. (Or the Enlightenment turns out to consist in the replacement of one sort of "mythic fear" by another; its dream of liberation leads a new form of enslavement.)[7] Practically what this means is that the anarchic impulses for happiness and pleasure repressed for the sake of domination and unity are quite unsuccessfully repressed and must re-emerge in ways naively unrecognized by official bourgeois optimism, secretly and in some more consistent cases (de Sade)[8] openly setting the agenda for technical activity.[9] So, "Ruthlessly, in spite of itself, the Enlightenment has extinguished any trace of its own self-consciousness,"[10] until "every specific theoretic view succumbs to the destructive criticism that it is only a belief – until the very notions of spirit, truth, even Enlightenment itself, have become animistic magic."[11]

While there are certainly elements of this narrative that ring true, from what we have seen it cannot claim to account for the dialectic of "the" Enlightenment.[12] In the post-Kantian tradition, that dialectic has involved, not a dialectic of domination and subsequent impotence, but instead a dialectic or mediation of spontaneity, an insistence on a radical self-determination by subjects of their own activity, and some reconciliation with onself and others. As we have seen in several contexts, such a notion of spontaneity must not be confused simplistically with Cartesian certainty or the mere assertion of will or human power. It emerges precisely as a criticism of such attempts at a transparent or immediate self-satisfaction, and as rejection of the possibility of any simple reliance on the passions, on any immediate self-willing, or on a "mythic wish" for security.

While it certainly may be the case that some particular modern version of human autonomy secretly or unconsciously reflects such mythic fears or subterranean passions, the idea of "exposing" such dependence and its unintended consequences itself already reflects the insistence on critical self-consciousness and so the ideal of genuine independence characteristic of philosophic modernism. Moreover, the Hegelian critique of Kant suggests in the clearest way why the emergence of the issue of a self-determining subjectivity brought with it the dialectical problem of reconciliation, or a notion of dependence that was in some way reached or attained as a result of the demand for independence. Autonomy "after Hegel," we might say, was never to be understood as kind of divine self-sufficiency, but, "dialectically," as a condition for the recognition of whatever dependence or finitude (on law, other subjects, or history) would ultimately come to count as decisive.[13] Autonomy, Hegel argued, needs to be understood as a possible human achievement, not a given condition of human agency, one wherein the terms in which such autonomy comes to be understood can be experienced as genuinely "self-imposed" (wherein one is "reconciled" with oneself) something that itself requires, Hegel thinks he can show, a reconciliation with others, or the achievement of genuinely "concrete" universality.

Of course, someone like Adorno would react to these suggestions by claiming that this attempt at a restoration of the original Idealist version of the dialectic of modernity represents nothing more than a kind of nostalgia for an earlier, far more dynamic, even if class-based, phase of capitalism. It may once have been the case that actual exercises of autonomy ecomically and socially did generate the problem of reconciliation and some initial, unstable, social, and especially

political forms of reconciliation. But, the story goes, eventually
genuine exercises of autonomy were eliminated in an ever more
efficient, integrating system, and the modern self came to be formed
through a struggle that ended only in submission. Such a view of the
historically out-dated character of the Idealist dialectic was often cast
in psychological terms, in the claim that authorities which could be
autonomously resisted as well as accepted (like the father in Freud's
account) were displaced by anonymous social authorities, in forma-
tions of character manipulated by the culture industry, leading to
such compensatory mechanisms as widespread narcissism and greater and greater illusions of idividual power (as, say, in Reagan's
appeal to the white middle class). The Idealist dialectic is thus
out-dated and cannot get off the ground; one pole in its account, the
autonomy which creates the need for reconciliation, has been manipulated out of existence.

   This account, like much else in Adorno, concedes too much to the
success of scuh integrating systems and is to some extent undermined
by Adorno's own work on "negative" activities, like modernist art,
successfully resistant to the imperatives of "identity thinking." Demands for autonomy may have become more diffuse and "micro-
scopic", and may often involve symbolic and subtle codes (from
forms of fashion to sexual politics) but, I think it is fair to suggest, it
would be a gross simplification to deny any contemporary relevance
to the problems generated once the insistence on autonomy is at all
possible or partly realized. Moreover, as those influenced by Habermas point out, this integration and pressure to conform does not just
"occur" as if the result of some self-producing machine. It occurs as
self-imposed, or within a collective "inter-subjective" context, a discourse situation that still appeals to norms, justification, legitimacy,
etc., in ways that can only partially succeed, given the often unequal
and power-based structure at issue. Indeed, modern institutions, in
Habermas's famous account of a "legitimacy" crisis, are less and less
able to achieve successful social integration without more and more
explicit appeals to rationality, argument, and consensus. These
appeals may often be "distorted" and ideological, but they generate
a "logic" of their own which insures there cannot be any final
co-option of the autonomous subject.[14]

   The general questions we have been discussing revolve around the
much larger issue of whether this "dialectic" can be said to be
inherently illusory, not just historically out-dated, to have issued an
original false promise, a claim that Horkheimer and Adorno some-

times come close to making themselves. And in this narrative, that issue was best raised by Nietzsche. Nietzsche can be said to represent a rejection not only of any dogmatism, but, in his claims for the ubiquity of interpretive activity, a rejection of any reliance on an originary, unified subject of such activity, or any required rules or constraints on such an activity, all coupled with a deep suspicion of any possible reconciliation with oneself (= constant "self-overcoming") or with others (no "pity" or herd morality).

In the account I presented, Nietzsche's view of such reconciliation as always and everywhere "slavish" is insufficiently sensitive to the historical dialectic which generates the concrete and unavoidable need for such reconciliation (as famously portrayed in Hegel's Master-Slave dialectic), or insensitive to the paradoxes created by the "absolutization" of spontaneity or the will to power. These paradoxes can, I argued, be detected erupting throughout his own texts, and define a class of problems inherent in much radical aesthetic and social modernism. The "post" in Nietzsche's postmodernism, in other words, can be said to be focused on a very specific accusative, a delineation of modern timidity and fear that cannot be said to "represent" the entirety of modern self-understanding.

On the other hand, Heidegger can be said to represent a rejection of the possibility and desirability of the modern goal of autonomy *tout court*, and so to resurrect some sort of reconciliation with dependence and finitude. And again the issue is the inclusiveness of Heidegger's historical category, "modern subjectivity." By, to a large degree, adopting Nietzsche's reading of the modern tradition as the apotheosis (in Nietzsche) of the will to power, Heidegger is able to suggest that many of the limitations or unquestioned assumptions in Nietzsche's project count as the limitations of "Western metaphysics" itself. But the limitations of Cartesian representationalism, Kantian transcendentalism, and the whole Enlightenment notion of subjectivity, power, and the rationality of "the understanding" were all lively topics within a still modern self-understanding long before Heidegger (especially in Hegel),and prompted attempted resolutions of the philosophical difficulties that do not raise the difficulties suggested by a mytho-poetic thought, or the (at least) non-modern sensibility intimated by Heidegger. Given the influence of Nietzsche and Heidegger on so many recent discussions, it might then be said that those discussions are based either on a Nietzschean misreading of the modern sensibility, or, as in Heidegger, on a misreading of that misreading. And such a "narrowing" of the whole notion of "modern subjectivity" is just as problematic an issue in the account given by Horkheimer and Adorno of what is supposed to be "the dialectic"of "the" Enlightenment.

3 Postmodernity?

After the Second World War, the British historian Arnold Toynbee anounced that we had probably the entered the fourth and last phase of western history, the "postmodern" phase, an era of irrationalism and anxiety and lost hope. Althought this classification appears to be the original coinage of the notion of postmodernity,[15] the historical issues introduced by Toynbee were not initially influential and the term was instead taken up (or simultaneously invented) in literary criticism, as in Randall Jarrell's characterization of Lowell's poetry as "post or anti-modernist."[16] Later the term became even more important for critics who used it not merely to group together the Black Mountain or Beat or San Francisco Renaissance or New York poets, or various novelists, who did not seem to fit any of the characteristics of the high modernism of, say T.S. Eliot, but to anounce a new agenda in literature and culture itself.[17] Initially, some of this agenda involved issue of non-modernist style, diction, and technique, a 1960s reaction to the academicism, elitism, and museum domination in arts and letters. In the work of Leslie Fiedler, it especially involved an attack on the standard distinction between "High" and "Low" or "Pop" culture, a distinction quite important in modernism and for its philosophic defenders (e.g., Benjamin and Adorno).[18]

But this more prophetic tone in the use of the term also began to involve a number of philosophic issues as critics like Ihab Hassan began to make use of Foucaultean terms, like *episteme* (post-modernism represents the *episteme* of "unmaking") to advance their positions. Although Hassan views literary postmodernism as a kind of continuous development of the modernist sensibility, his insistence on its differences introduced some very general philosophic issues, many of which we have already encountered. Whereas, in modernism, the typical modern experience that "all that is solid melts into the air," or "the center does not hold," had prompted the creation of a "subjective center," an autonomous, self-defining artist, for postmodernism there is no center at all, the subject itself is "de-centered," no longer an origin or source, but itself a result, a product of multiple social and psychological forces, all requiring a discourse much less tied to the interior monologues favored by modernist novelists.[19] And with such themes, we are obviously close to the large issue of "anti-humanism" prominent in the discussions of "structuralism" and "post-structuralism" in Continental thought, the displacement of the proud modern reflective subject, first by the autonomous, anonymous "structures" of Lévi-Strauss or Althusser, and later by the "play" of discontinuity and power and indeterminacy associated with "genealogy" and "deconstruction." Or, what modernism experienced as a great "loss" of meaning, tradition, coherence, etc., is experienced by postmodernism as merely a shift or change, a "loss" only under assumptions about High Culture, the primacy of the Western experience, or even the "metaphysics of presence" that ought not to have been accepted in the first place. Or the endless self-reflexive and essentially bourgeois discourse of the modernists is replaced by the literature of silence (especially, say, Beckett), of "fragments or fractures, and a corresponding ideological commitment to minorities in politics, sex and language."[20]

Later still, the term made its way into architecture, where it came to represent first a rejection of the formalism and aesthetic pretensions to purity and functionist efficiency characteristic of Bauhaus modernism, and second a challenge, similar to much else in the postmodern phenomenon, to basic modern ideas of a unified artistic vision, to the modernist de-historicized insistence on originality, and the inhuman, technical, contextless efficiency of much of the modern urban landscape. If the central modern *ethos*, embodied in modernist architecture, was the idea of a self-sufficiency best realized by a functional rationality and control, the postmodern *ethos* was to express an ironic suspicion of such a possibility and so its displacement in favor of historical finitude, multiples of order, and the rejection of a pretension to a unified, autonomous vision. Postmodern buildings were to be "duble" or even multiply "coded," borrowing from the past as well as the future, unpretentious and so everywhere ironic, playful, and implicitly suspicious of dominant canons of taste.[21]

As is already apparent, many of the more expansive philosophical claims made in behalf of a postmodern sensibility retrieve and reinterpret central Nietzschean and Heideggerean issues. As one commentator has noted, the "beyond" implied by the idea of the postmodern often replays the many Heideggerean "beyonds": beyond humanism, beyond metaphysics, beyond transcendentalism, beyond representational, calculative thinking, beyond phenomenology, beyond modern subjectivity.[22] The Heideggerean *Abbau* or destruction of Western metaphysics has become the Derridean "deconstruction," now with even greater emphasis on the concealed, the fragmentary, the "unthought," because always "written," the perpetual "deferral"on meaning from its configuration. And the great Nietzschean emphasis on the contingency of interpretive schemata, on power, the *agon* of competing interpretations, the attack on unity or the "violence" of ordering systems, all in favor of difference, the Other, the body, etc., is again visible in the work of Deleuze, Foucault, Lyotard, and Bataille.

Of couse, it is not possible to survey the details of such philosophic positions. Interest in postmodernism has itself generated a diversity of issues worthy of the postmodernist *ethos* itself: heterogeneous, fragmentcd, resistant to general discussion. The postmodern label, now used so widely and casually as to be virtually meaningless, has become in the minds of many representative of various, quite diverse enterprises – deconstruction, hermeneutics, Foucaultean genealogy, post-structuralism, Lacanean psychoanalysis, or of the work of often very different people, from Harold Bloom to Jean Baudrillard. And it has certainly attracted various polemical counters. These range from Literary critics like Gerald Graff and Charles Newman charging the postmodernists with irrationalism and anti-intellectualism, to architecture critics like Clement Greenberg or Hilton Kramer characterizing postmodernism as a retreat from the high, rigorous standards of modernism into the commercialized mass culture of kitsch,[23] to the political concerns (neither critical nor celebratory but "homeopathic") of Frederic Jameson, or, in different ways, of Eagleton, Habermas, and others.[24]

But it is possible, I shall suggest, to detect sufficiently representative themes (or "traces" of themes) in the general debate inspired by such radical hermeneutical styles.[25] And it is possible at least to suggest that, for all the unique attention now paid to language, text, gender, desire, psychoanalysis, etc., such new positions still do not represent a resolution of any of the problems encountered in the thinkers first responsible for a radical critique of modernity, or an advance beyond the dialectical program suggested by Hegel as a response. Since nothing interesting can be said without some relatively unfair generalization, let us generalize "styles" of postmodern thought this way.

There is, on the one hand, a continuing Nietzschean suspicion about the intractable resistance of the "other," difference, or becoming to any rule or function, any ordering principle. Such ordering, especially in the service of the modern ideal of autonomy or self-

sufficiency, is always a kind of violence or a will to power, a subjugation usually propelled by some interpretation of autonomy as control
or domination. We are, according to Lyotard, now to abandon such
attempts at organizing ourselves into some smoothly "functioning"
whole, and also to abandon the "critical" attempt to identify opposed
groups struggling to control the social agenda, and then through a
process of enlightenment or critique, to identify our common universal bond and become reconciled with each other.[26] Totality, or holistic (and so "terroristic") thinking of all forms is the enemy; a "pagan
polytheism" the new hero.[27] We must respect instead the absolute
(the new "absolute") primacy of difference, the heterogeneity of
language games, and so accept an "agonistics," a permanently unre-
conciled "play" of opposition.[28]

Or, if this is too fragmented a view (and potentially conservative,
culturally isolationist, respecting the Other by benevolently leaving
him or her to their own impoverished games), we might prefer, with
Rorty, simply a "de-theoreticized sense of community," one supremely respectful of the bruth contingencies that unite us when they do,
attentive only to the seizure and abuse of power, and indifferent to
the issue of the "foundational" basis for our stake in each other.[29]

Such a position raises immediately the basic problems we encountered in assessing Nietzsche's account of modernity. Lyotard suggests, like Nietzsche, that we shall have to get along without at least
the traditional "grand narratives," like the advancement of knowledge or the liberation of humanity (or the will to truth). We require,
in legitimating what we do, only the "local" narratives of heterogeneous language games. But, as far as I can see, we still don't know
what could count as the unity or success of such narratives, or what
Nietzsche called more honestly the "legislation" of values. We don't
know what counts as one game, as opposed to others, or why playing
it is any less hegemonistic or "terrorist" than a "grander" game. If
we just happan to be playing it, recognize that, and continue playing
it, then questions of power and validity have been grossly confused
without any motivation.[30] Fragmentation and anomie, the *Zerissung* of
culture long age identified by Hegel as the chief effect of modernization, are simply to be accepted as some sort of (ironically) "grand"
and final resolution of history, and the issue of a possible relation
between the "actual" and the "possible," the concrete need for, and
potentiality of, forms of reconciliation is, as it were, "transcendentally" ruled out of court.

Moreover, Nietzsche was at least consistent enough, or sensitive
enough to the idealist heritage, to doubt that it would ever be

possible to identify, much less to respect or be "open" to, "The Other In Itself" (not to mention the residue of Christian "pity" he would detect in such a sensibility).[31] Such an Other, or the Different, or the identification of "our" contingent community of interests, all would still be taken up within a perspective, and not one that could claim any ontological or post-historical authority.[32]

On the other hand, the extraordinarily influential enterprise proposed by Derrida, "deconstruction," does not mount a successful indictment of modernity either, however radically it might be said to correct the methodological *naïvete* of structuralism, Lyotard, or Foucaultean archeology. His problems, I want very briefly to suggest, return us to many of Heidegger's unresolved issues.

Derrida, like Heidegger, is best known for a critique of such things as the *naïveté* of Cartesianism, representational thinking, assumptions about referentiality, sources, origins, "sense," and the possibility of a secure, metaphysically grounded "method." But, like Heidegger, he denies that such a critique (even if in some sense "Kantian" in spirit) implies that he is heading towards some Kantian conclusion, some idealist hermeneutics, or textual fetishism, or existential solipsism, towards a radically skeptical denial of anything "outside" the text, a new form of "self-interiority" or a new idealism "of the text". Rather, for both the very terms within which this ancient dilemma is posed are to be undermined, shown to be historically contingent, a self-refuting metaphysical game, deconstructed. (There is no "inside" closed off to an "outside." If there is no possible contrast between an essentially "inside" versus an "outside," there is no new "nominalism"; because there is no way to identify the radically individual, the differing or the fragmented as such.) Especially in Derrida's case, once the shift is made from conceptual to linguistic or "writing" analysis, he denies that we could ever identify anything like "textuality" itself, or "rules," conditions for the possibility of a text that closes off the world to us. The text is itself a world referred to, and its rules would only themselves be inscribed within another specific text, with its own tropes, and "economies." The text cannot function as origin except as permanently "deferred" or displaced. Something like such a search for origins, or "the nature of writing" is inescapable, but it is always itself written "under erasure", or as a "double game," aware of its own fragility and specificity. (He echoes Heidegger's occasional remarks that, despite all the polemic against a metaphysics of presence, and so all metaphysics, there can be no "break" with such assumptions, no revealing that is not also a metaphysical concealing. Or they both share the same intimations of human finitude.)[33]

And, again like Heidegger, Derrida is especially resistant to the idea that the path to any such "non-principle" leads through an account of human subjectivity, as if texts (or "meanings," or the meaning of Being) can in any sense be viewed as products of self-reflexive subjects or communities, sustained by and meaningful only within the self-regulating practices of such communities. So, speaking very generally, like Heidegger, he is insisting on the original and fundamental dependence of what we have come to think of as self-defining subjects on something other than and prior to the possibility of reflection and self-determination, in this case, again very roughly, a dependence on text or writing.

And thereby the same Heideggerean problems emerge. On the one hand, Derrida might be read as simply encouraging us to think of all philosophy and critical reflection or deconstruction as "just another form of writing," as essentially rhetoric, and so as offering a practical suggestion, proposing that we live differently, more humbly in effect, tenuously, aware of such finitude and dependence, more suspicious, less inclined to believe anyone who appeals to any metaphysical presence, to a truth or spirit (*pneuma*) "behind" the word. (Rorty reads Derrida like this.)[34] But as Derrida himself is at pains to point out, such a suggestion is arbitrary and wholly unmotivated unless accompanied by some account of why we should look at things this way, an account that is necessarily tied to an ambiguously "transcendental" demonstration that we are in fact or in truth in some sense, as "dependent" as Derrida says we are.[35] This in turn cannot be done *ad hoc*, by showing that this or that text relies on figures of speech, strategies, tropes, images, that tend to undermine, let us say, any attempt at "transcendence" or an independent, unified "sense" within the text, independence from its own fragmentary, dispersed site, its own conditioning and contingency. But a more general Derridean analysis can only appeal to "the signifier," in general or universally, or "the" impossibility of reference, by some sort of a "formalization" of such principles, or of such an *arche*.[36]

But unless Derrida, like Heidegger, wants to invoke some notion of an autonomous *arche* like an ontological happening or appropriation (a dogmatic appeal which, he clearly realizes, raises its own problems) he, like Heidegger , thus lands us right back in Hegel's critique of Kantian original formalization, the orginal move or strategy in the critique by reason of itself. As in that archetypal debate about the philosophical implications of modernity, we would soon encounter the suspicion that Derrida cannot be engaged in some ultimate disclosure about the possibility of meaning, but a current historical self-construal in the history of that sense-making practice known as philosophy (or "metaphysics"). Precisely to the extent that "the activity of deconstruction is strictly inconceivable outside the tradition of enlightened rational critique whose classic formulations are still found in Kant,"[37] to that extent we are returned to the Kantian *aporiai* exposed first by Fichte and made so much of in Hegel's endless paradoxical play on being "outside" limits in order to set them.[38]

Now in Derrida's own reading of Hegel, this would return us to issues much deeper than the terms used above could express, to what he calls the "economic" strategy of Hegel, which, for Derrida, figures the economy of all philosophy. Hegelianism is the establishment or production of meaning, an attempt at a divine "sovereignty"that is not *sui generis*, or innate, but originates essentially in a particular economy of production and circulation (sovereignty is important because a certain sort of economic whole has already been assumed: the preservation and extension of "life," an orientation that pre-ordains a view of philosophy as a sort of productive work). It is this (as in Heidegger, vain, hubristic, now "comical") attempt at mastery that simultaneously insures a kind of submission or servitude, a fundamental submission to the imperatives of "life" in order to master them, and so to sense, order, integration and unity; an attempt which can face its "other," death, the absence of significance, only by a rhetorical and ultimately "violent" ruse, by categorizing it as "abstract negativity," to be postponed, deferred, defeated by "work." The Hegelian economy – what is produced, for what purpose – is thus "restricted" in ways that cannot be defended, and which ultimately undermine the attempt, insuring an oscillation between left (sovereign) and right (submissive) Hegelianism, or the whole history of post-Hegelian thought.

The counter to this would be a "risky" kind of writing, one which "risks making sense, risks agreeing to the reasonableness of reason, of philosophy, of Hegel, who is always right, as soon as one opens one's mouth in order to articulate meaning."[39] This would be a "general" economy, or one without "reserve," one that did not already and (necessarily) arbitrarily prescribe the bounds between a sovereign type of signification, and an excluded domain not allowed to circulate, of no "monetary" or exchange value in the economy. In speculating with and on Bataille's reading of Hegel, this "cashes out," though, in a familiar song:

> In order not to govern, that is to say, in order not to be subjugated, it
> [i.e., a new post-Hegelian sort of sovereignty] *must* subordinate nothing
> (direct object), that is to say, be subordinated to *nothing or no one*
> (servile mediation of the indirect object): it must expand itself without
> reserve, lose itself, lose consciousness, lose all memory of itself and all
> the interiority of itself; as opposed to *Erinnerung*, as opposed to the
> avarice that assimilates meaning, it must *practice forgetting, the aktive
> Vergesslichkeit* of which Nietzsche speaks; and, as the ultimate sub-
> version of lordship, it must no longer seek to be recognized.[40]

We have seen enough of Hegel's position to suspect that, originally, "The very metaphor of economy is the point of [Derrida's]
restriction,"[41] that he has subjugated Hegelian "speculation" with a
metaphorical advance which, in effect, constitutes an unfair fight for
recognition between them ("the avarice that assimilates meaning").
And we have also already expressed enough doubt about attempts to
"come out the other side" of the modern pursuit of self-consciousness
with a hyper-sophisticated, memory-less refusal of the struggle for
recognition, and those doubts need not be rehearsed again. There is,
though, an extremely serious point at issue in Derrida's engagement
with Hegel, one of almost unmanageable theoretical complexity and
profound practical consequences.

The theoretical issue involves what Hegelians would call the problem of "absolute negativity," or the problem of the *nihil absolutum*, a
problem which in different forms stretches back in Western rationalism through Plato to Parmenides. In the Hegelian context, among
other things, this problem involves Hegel's defense of any claim that
some practical situation or ethical claim, or the theoretical position,
turns out to be, experientially and "logically," impossible, that the
whole apparatus of speculative reflection is *called for* by such an
internal impossibility, that it is necessary, not "imposed"; that some
sort of "self-negation" determines a possible resolutive, succeeding
claim or position. Originally, or at the origin of any such analysis, this always raises the question of whether Hegel's anti-
foundationalist, supposedly "self-moving," or internally justifactory
logic ultimately so defines "for-itself" the conditions of its own success, that it simply defines internally what is impossible, that what
violates, or offends, or eludes "thought" has been originally referred

to in a way that insures its ultimate "absorption" or "reconciliation" with thought. (All of this is the "speculative" formulation of the "independence-dependence" dialectic we have been invoking throughout, re-stated formally in terms of an ideal "positing" and presupposed "negation".) This is the core issue in any Hegelianism or neo-Hegelianism (as well as, by the way, many currently fashionable views of historical rationality in the philosophy of science) and for all his problems, Derrida has his hands gripped tightly around this vulnerable area.[42]

But just stating the issue in these terms is already quite confusing enough, and it is certainly not an issue we can settle or even enter into here. The same problem, though, is involved at a more accessible level. If we assume for the moment that Derrida's characterization of modern philosophy in terms of "Hegelianism" has both underestimated the complexity and resources of Hegel's position, as argued in chapter 3, and, in effect by rejecting it, simply led us back to *aporiai* familiar since Nietzsche and Heidegger, as in chapters 4 and 5, how, especially concretely, might a more nuanced and powerful reading of the modern tradition sensitive to this outcome and these dilemmas, suggest an analysis that does not replay these *aporiai*? If, in attempts to end or overcome the modern project, we seem no further along in resolving difficulties or avoiding paradoxes than we were when the most radical and consistent versions of its philosophical assumptions were first conceived, what ought we to conclude from this?

4 Modernity as Dialectic

It has been pointed out to me that there is something unsatisfying and certainly undramatic in a narration of modernity in which the crucial events unfold in the middle, rather than at the end. This is especially the case when those important events result in still ambiguous and still unfulfilled promissory notes (to continue the economics metaphor one last time). However undramatic, though, there is something unavoidable, I have argued, about such a requirement, about the centrality of Hegel, "the first philosopher ... for whom modernity became a problem,"[43] and his arguments with Kant and the tradition, in any philosophic account of the problem of modernity. The difficulty has always been not only understanding what Hegel manages to render problematic in the modern experience, but his resolutions, his suggestions about what follows if his criticisms hold, attempts that seem confined within a nowadays almost inaccessible and implausible "system." Given that problem, and the context sketched throughout here, what would it mean to take seriously some version of the fate of modernist philosophy from a "Hegelian" orientation?

Consider the context first. While a decisive legitimation of modernity does not follow from anything that has been said, it seems impossible to deny the deep appeal of the modern insistence on a satisfying, self-conscious form of autonomy, together with the always corresponding suspicion of any traditionalist, historicist, "tragic," or religious appeal to human finitude. Since Kant, such appeals look less like discoveries or realizations, and more like how we come, at some moment in time, to construe ourselves or the cosmos. (And part of what the above discussion of postmodernism shows is that such a critical sensibility is as appropriate to any contemporary version of what we have supposedly "found out" about ourselves or about textuality or about desire as it was in early modernity.) The emergence of this sense of the unavoidable role of a spontaneous self-determination even in self-limiting or self-effacing activities is the great theme in much nineteenth-century reflection on the contingencies of religion, custom, and social life. It receives its most sophisticated treatment in Hegel's account of the emerging historical realization "for itself" of what had only been the "in itself" truth of such activities.

Read this way, modernity is thus not a hubristic, autochthonous "will" to autonomy and self-sufficiency, as Heidegger and others read it, but is itself irresistibly provoked by the growing, ever more plausible possibility that what had been taken to be absolute and transcendent was contingent and finite, since always "self-determined," a contingent product of a human positing. Or, the modern *ethos* is always as self-deflating as self-inflating, and is always both at the same time. Again as presented by Kant, this means that the central sensibility that results from such a reading of the modern revolution is not so much a need for some new positive realization of who or what we "truly" are, as it is a great, pervasive, eternal uneasiness with anyone pretending to speak in the name of such a truth.

What this all also means is that no exhibition of the various crises of failed community, anomie, consumerism, thoughtlessness, kitsch, moral nihilism, theoretical self-refutation, and so forth, characteristic, let us assume for the sake of argument, of much of modernity,

however justified such dissatisfactions might be, could ever legitimate
some sort of philosophic nostalgia, some language of loss and possible
retrieval. At least, such dissatisfactions alone could not do so. Kant
stands permamently at the door of such return trips.[44]

But, once such a context is granted, any advance inspired by Hegel
would seem foreclosed by the extreme ambition of his project. If what
is required for such an advance is what he seems to say is required
(speculative wisdom), then we have simply painted ourselves into a
corner. The perceived failure of Hegel's attempt at a complete, self-
justifying account by reason of itself (a "conceiving" of the concep-
tualizing subject) split apart into modernist and existentialist (or
non-conceptual, often aesthetic) accounts of such a subject, and more
modest, constrained technical pursuits and unself-conscious, simply
insistent, powerful methodologies. This failure or its perceived
failure, is the heart of all the familiar claims of the late Schelling,
Kierkegaard, Schopenhauer, Adorno, and most recently Habermas:[45]
that Hegel identified the problem in Kant correctly, but "overcorrected" in his logico-metaphysical, contingency devouring *Wissen-
schaft* machine.

By contrast, while admitting that there is no complete speculative
logic,[46] I have been trying to suggest that Hegel was not trying to
"transform the world into a concept," and so to offer a final substantive account. His attempt was to do justice to that process whereby
the world must be conceived to be intelligible, but must also always
be re-conceived, given the perpetual absence of any measure for such
conceiving, either in nature, the transcendental ego, the ideal speech
situation, or a sort of a practical wisdom (itself unintelligible except
when conceived).

It is in this sense, once the great uneasiness and uncertainty
provoked by such a self-consciousness originates, that it cannot be
forgotten or ended, that the very notion of epochality or the closure
and determining force implied by some epochal view of history, is
foreclosed, and "modernity" is indeed (ironically and paradoxically)
the "last" epoch, because the end of epochality itself. Once we give
up the idea of a radical, ahistorical self-grounding, either in a scientific or "phenomenological" method, or in a pure transcendentalism,
the philosophical problem of modernity in the European tradition
cannot be resolved or avoided by those convinced that all modern
attempts at an independent self-reflection, even when formulated
historically and concretely, are always naive historically, still reflect
"prejudices," interests, desires, the unconscious, other parts of an
inter-referential text, the voice of Being, the will to power; or that, as

one hears it put, everything is "interpretation all the way down."
(I include in this category both those who wish simply to "replace
theory by interpretation," or "seeing" with endless "talking," and
those who claim to "see," or to have a unique theory about, some
arche that requires such a replacement.)[47] To identify such depend-
encies is always to claim a renewed form of independence, and it is
a claim for independence or autonomy that now ("after Hegel") can
seek no re-assurance in self-certainty or foundations, and provokes
again the "groundless" search for reconciliation with other self-
conscious agents unavoidable in modernity.

Thus, in a way I think quite compatible with Hegel's own
intentions,[48] it was inevitable that this problem could not be "resolved" in Hegel's project or even in modern history, that thinking of
it as prompting a resolution is already a misreading of modernity's
perpetual dissatisfactions. There is also no Hegelian guarantee that
the kind of reconstruction and attempt at legitimation suggested here
can even be provisionally accomplished, even if Hegel is right that
only by attempting to accomplish it can we be said even to understand the institutions in question. He may have exaggerated the
potentiality for a rational "ethical life" inherent in contemporary
institutions like the bourgeois family, the market economy, the state,
or in modern science or philosophy. But on the reading defended
here, objections in principle to such an attempt inevitably re-raise
problems that prompted the "critical" turn in the first place, and
objections based on the usual fears of the usual, or "terroristic,"
totalizing Hegel grossly underestimate the radicality and consistency
of his modernism. And we shall only know how much we can "concretely" understand and "historically" justify by trying.

Notes

Notes to chapter 1

1 Lyotard (1984). The full title is *The Post-Modern Condition: A Report on Knowledge*, and it is described by its author as a "report on knowledge in the most highly developed societies" and was "presented to the Conseil des Universités of the government of Quebec at the request of its president" (p. xxv). See also Lyotard's account of post-modernism *expliqué aux enfants* (1986).

2 See, *inter alia*, Arac (1986), Benhabib (1984), M. Berman (1988), Calinescu (1987), Connolly (1988), Foster (1983), Habermas (1987), Hassan (1982), Hoffman et al. (1977), Huyssen (1986), Jameson (1988b), Jencks (1986), Lyotard (1984), Pippin (1990a), Ross (1988), Silverman and Welton (1988), Vattimo (1988), Warren (1988), Wellmer (1985a, 1985b), S. White (1990).

3 See Vattimo's essay "The Crisis of Humanism" (1988), pp. 31–47.

4 I note immediately something I discuss further below and in the next chapter: that this dissatisfaction with the bourgeois or Enlightenment version of modernity is often accompanied by a renewed, more radical sense of modernity, an attempt to avoid the "Christian" qualifications and conservative hesitations of modernity and, for the first time, to be "truly" modern. This complexity is especially visible in Nietzsche, who has nothing but contempt for the Cartesian, liberal-democratic, and post-Kantian modern projects, but who seems to retain some sort of modern insistence (now, as he sees it, radicalized) on "enlightenment," intellectual honesty, reflective self-consciousness, and so forth. See the discussion in chapter 4.

5 Hegel, especially, is often treated by Bataille, Deleuze, Lyotard, and, to a lesser extent, by Derrida, as a kind of *reductio ad absurdum* of all modernism, and so a mere foil by means of which to advance post-modernist ideas.

6 I agree with Toulmin (1990) that, "The phrase, 'The Enlightenment project', then, is sometimes used in ways that telescope ideas in Britain,

France, and Germany over three or four generations," (p. 142) and that there are significant differences between the grand projects of Descartes and the Cambridge Platonists, Newtonian cosmologists, and French Encyclopedists. But, for my purposes, for all their differences, their similarities, particularly on the issues of "autonomy" and "dependence," are much more important in understanding the reaction of Hegel, Nietzsche, Heidegger, and others.

7 One of the most famous cases of such complexity is Bacon, at once a partisan of the mastery of nature by natural science, and intensely aware of the limitations of such a program, an awareness connected with the classical political themes in his work. See the helpful study by Weinberger (1985). For a thorough and compelling study of the role played by theological themes (especially the problem of divine attributes) in early modern science, see Funkenstein (1986).

8 For a summary of this moment in European history, see Löwith (1966).

9 Since Nietzsche the central strategy in such accounts of finitude has been to focus attention on the whole problem of "saying" anything about it, to develop a form of discourse that would not simply assert claims about finitude in a proposition, something that of course reflects a kind of (ultimately inconsistent) hyper-Enlightenment, or implies a claim to complete wisdom. Hegel first formulated this problem in his critique of Kant's claims for a restriction of human knowledge to phenomena, and Nietzsche was one of the first to realize that the only way around such a problem was, in some sense, not to "do" philosophy at all; hence his attention to tragic drama, irony, aphorisms, etc. And hence too, Heidegger's onto-poetic language, Derrida's attempt to write *sous rature*, and so forth. Stanley Rosen has stated the general problem in his "A Modest Proposal to Rethink Enlightenment," in Rosen (1989), pp. 2–21.

10 This roughly is the spirit of Marshall Berman's adventurous book (1988). See especially his account of the various stages in the development of a modern culture in the "Introduction" to that book, pp. 15–36. For a discussion of the centrality of aesthetics in modernity, see Vattimo's essay on the "The Structure of Artistic Revolutions" (1988), pp. 90–109, and Eagleton's chapter on Kant (1990) pp. 70–101.

11 Weber (1930), pp. 181–3.

12 Steiner (1971), p. 30.

13 Ibid. Such a question evokes Adorno's even more pointed one: how there can be poetry at all after Auschwitz? Of course, the same sort of unease was created, in some ways even more intensely, by the Great War. Cf. Toulmin's discussion (1990) of the similarities between this reaction, much of it an intensification of the narrowest and most abstract aspects of Enlightenment rationalism, and the European unease after the Thirty Years' War in the seventeenth century.

14 For a brief summary of the social dimensions of the modernization

problem, see Peter Berger's essay, "Toward a Critique of Modernity" (1977), pp. 70–82. For a more detailed account see Berger et al. (1974).

15 While this issue (the connection between modernization and westerniza-tion) is mostly discussed in socioeconomic terms (see Enzensberger's witty essay "Eurozentrismus wider Willen" (1982), pp. 31ff), it can also be posed in a much more sweeping way, as Heidegger (in "A Dialogue on Language") does in his dialogue with a Japanese interlocutor, warn-ing about the "complete Europeanization of the earth and of man," *OL*, p. 15.

16 I mean here the familiar attempts by Marx himself, Lukacs in *History and Class Consciousness*, Horkheimer and Adorno in *The Dialectic of Enlightenment*, Benjamin's work, or to take a more recent example, Eagleton's attempt (1990) to understand the growing importance of "the aesthetic" in late modernity as an "ideological" phenomenon.

17 See especially Velkley's fine study (1989), and Yack's narrative (1986).

18 Again, I should stress, this is a short book, and I shall make no attempt to prove that the philosophical issues I explore alone "made possible" or alone undermined the decisive non-intellectual institutions of modernity. Such an issue would take us quickly into Hegelian com-plexities best discussed independently.

19 Aside from some general remarks in the last chapter, and occasional asides, I have also had to omit any treatment of the so-called "critical theory" discussion of modernity. For a few of the many discussions that would complement what I say here, see Feenberg's discussion of "cultu-ral Marxism" in Feenberg (1986), pp. 172–200; J. Bernstein's discus-sion of "Marxism and Modernism,"(1984), pp. 228–67; M. Berman (1988), pp. 87–129; the first chapter of Kellner (1989); Habermas on the "young Hegelians" and Horkheimer and Adorno in Habermas (1987), pp. 51–74, 106–30; R. Berman (1989), especially chapters 1 and 7; Held (1980); Rose (1981).

20 For a general discussion of the lines of historical influence and thematic links, (at least with Nietzsche), see Schwartz (1985), especially chapter 1. Eliot's link with the Idealist tradition is evident in his dissertation on Bradley: "We have the right to say that the world is a construction. Not to say that it is *my* construction, for in that way 'I' am as much 'my' construction as the world is." Quoted in Lachtermann (1989), p. ix.

21 This is the term used by Habermas (1987) to describe Hegel's attempt and the general problem of modernity's self-legitimation (p. 42). As will be apparent in the account I give of German Idealism in chapter 3, I do not share an essential premise in Habermas's account – that all of modern philosophy, including Kant and Hegel, can be correctly de-scribed as the 'philosophy of consciousness," and can be unfavorably con-trasted with a philosophy of "inter-subjectivity," or "communicative activity."

22 I am not of course denying than multitudes of "discoveries" are, within

certain assumptions, possible. The question at issue concerns their significance, what they tell us about what it is to be human, or responsible, or rational. The original notion of autonomy does not promise a kind of divine (or Sartrean) complete self-sufficiency. The issue of self-determination is relevant only at a certain "level" or within a certain "domain," generating all the problems about how to bring the "transcendental" and "empirical" back together again.

Notes to chapter 2

1 Cf. the discussions in Jauss (1964, 1965); Schabert (1978), pp. 42ff; Calinescu (1977), pp. 13–22; Curtius (1963), pp. 251ff.
2 Cf. the extensive discussion of the historical dimensions of this issue in Gössman (1974) and Steffen (1965), and Lachtermann's apposite remarks about the "finality" and "endlessness" implied by the notion of the modern (1989), p. 2.
3 Cf. the discussion in Calinescu (1977), p. 61, and the quotation there by Paz.
4 This is not to claim that what we now call the "Middle Ages" embraced without qualification the revolutionary potential of the Christian eschatology. De Rougement (1957) even characterizes the whole period, however "Christian," as deeply resistant to the implications of the "revolutionary ferment introduced into the world by the Gospel" (p. 90) as Western Europe's "Eastern" period.
5 John of Salisbury (1971), p. 167. See also Calinescu (1977), p. 15, and Schabert (1978), p. 45.
6 So, by the early sixteenth century, Rabelais in *Pantagruel*, would reject the dwarfs/giants image and explicitly assert the superiority of modernity to the time of Plato or Cicero. In 1566 Jean Bodin could assert what would become an ever more typical claim: that while we ought to thank the ancients for their discovery of so many useful arts and sciences, we must recognize that they solved very few problems and left much for us, us moderns, to resolve; which, Bodin insists, we are rapidly doing. And in 1584 Giordano Bruno could decisively reverse the usual contrast between ancients and moderns, arguing in an image that would be made more famous by Bacon that the so-called ancients were really children, beginners. *We* are the true ancients, beneficiaries of centuries of accumulated wisdom, and ready now to exercise that wisdom.
7 Toulmin (1990) has recently argued that we ought to view modernity as having a dual origin, in the sixteenth-century Renaissance, *and* in seventeenth-century rationalism; indeed that the latter represents a kind of "counter-Renaissance," and that its failure need not inaugurate any "post-modernity," as much as it can return us to the original humanistic insights of modernity's first founding (especially, say, in the thought

of Montaigne, the hero of Toulmin's book). This raises the questions: (a) in what sense can the Renaissance Christian humanists be said to be "modern"? (b) if the virtues they promoted depended essentially on a religious view of the whole (see p. 25), what chance could any attempt to "revive" such virtues stand in a post-religious age? (c) why shouldn't we regard these virtues – scepticism, tolerance, prudence, etc. – when translated into contemporary society, or a society without the social and cultural hegemony of sixteenth-century, small communities, as leading to the kind of anomie and cultural fragmentation described by Weber? (d) might there not have been good reasons, internal to the rather "theoretically superficial," if attractive, thought of Erasmus and Montaigne, for the historical collapse of the option they represented, when confronted with the powerful questions raised by Descartes or Hobbes? Can so much in the success of the projects of the latter be accounted for by reference to a kind of hysterical quest for certainty generated by social, economic and military crises? See also below, n. 13.

8   To put the matter in language a bit more reminiscent of Schiller and Hölderlin than Swift. See chapter 3.

9   Blumenberg (1983).

10 One of the reasons the modernity problem was experienced as such a problem in Germany has to do with the influence of this epochal and national mode of thought, a belief in some sort of historical "whole" or "spirit of the age." Herder was as responsible as anyone else for this, but is a complicated story. Yack (1986) does a good job of explaining the role of such a notion in the post-Kantian tradition, especially its role in what he calls "the longing for total revolution."

11 The last something greatly stressed, perhaps exaggerated, by Blumenberg. See my account in Pippin (1987b).

12 Such remarks skirt the edge of a vast issue: the historical "provocation" of modernity, or the claim that major components of the premodern social and intellectual tradition began to encounter a variety of paradoxes or even dead ends not resolvable by traditional means, thus provoking a revolutionary approach. The topic spans *aporiai* in the theological tradition, unforseen consequences in distinctions like that between natural and revealed theology, or between possibility *de potentia Dei absoluta* and *de potentia Dei ordinata*, alterations in the economic order that made possible a reconception of the notion of human individuality, and so on. Here I simply have to assume there was such a crisis, that some revolutionary approach was called for, and I shall try to suggest later that the German idealist approach, the suggestion that the center of that crisis concerned an unrepressable, emerging self-consciousness about the pervasive role of "subjective activity" in institutions and practices, is a plausible approach. More than that would require several volumes, or at least books the size and weight of Blumenberg's and Funkenstein's.

13 Lachtermann (1989) has recently shown convincingly the centrality of

the idea of construction, especially mathematical construction, in the very possibility of a theoretically consistent "modernity." His fine book deserves much more careful study than can be provided here, but I permit myself two remarks. First, his account raises the question of the historical influence of the modern attachment to a unique view of mathematical construction in other "wider" applications (eventually "the construction of reality," etc.). See pp. 6–7. I am not sure that there is as much "transmitted power" in the notion as he ascribes to it. The lines of force that attracted Kant, for example, to the idea of spontaneity are already saturated with moral and "meta-ethical" concerns stemming from Rousseau (see Velkley (1989)), and the intoxication with mathematical success had decreased markedly by the time we get to the everywhere influential Hegel. (Although a point in Lachtermann's favor is that this caesura in the influence of the mathematical tradition is the single greatest reason why Hegel himself plays no positive role in official philosophy within the Anglo-American academy, still Cartesian and Kantian as it is.) Secondly, the centrality of mathematical constructability in the scheme of modern mastery is not itself an "origin" but a manifestation, an image. The question of the original remains, even though the details of this study should make forever impossible the popular, all too causal categorization of modern metaphysics as beginning with the ancients. I note too that this book concerns mostly Descartes, and Lachtermann has promised us another on similar themes in the likes of Leibniz and Kant.

A somewhat different evaluation of the issue of "construction" can be found in chapter 5 of Funkenstein (1986).

14 Or perhaps, as already suggested, there is a third alternative: its legitimacy is best understood as a reaction to the internal insufficiencies of the prior intellectual tradition. Modernity would then best be seen as quite determinately provoked, as an unavoidable response, and not as simply inaugurated.

15 Löwith (1970), p. 2.

16 Blumenberg (1983), p. 126.

17 Blumenberg (1983), p. 138.

18 Blumenberg (1983), p. 139.

19 These last two criticisms of Blumenberg were advanced by Richard Kennington in an American Political Science Association panel discussion in September, 1988.

20 Blumenberg (1983), p. 336.

21 I develop these points in more detail in Pippin (1987b). For a discussion of the secularization issue and Blumenberg, see Yack (1986), pp. 14ff, and for comments on the relevance of Blumenberg's argument to contemporary issues, see Martin Jay's essay, "Blumenberg and Modernism: Reflections on *The Legitimacy of the Modern Age* in Jay (1988), pp. 149–64.

I need also to emphasize again the extremely introductory and so

simplified nature of this discussion. For one thing "secularization" can
mean any number of things other than an unwitting appropriation of
religious themes or the pursuit of essentially religious ends by new
means. Funkenstein (1986) for example has developed a notion of
secularization quite different from Blumenberg's. He notes simply that
one feature of a "secularized" theology is that theology in early modernity begins to be done more and more by laymen. These laymen were
impressed with the results of the new mathematization of physics, and
the possible application of physics to all modes of knowledge, and so
entertained the very non-Aristotelian, non-Scholastic hope for a unified
system of knowledge, a system that would include theology. Thus it is
possible to show that secularization, rather than always denoting a
"hidden" religious agenda in secular pursuits, can denote a hidden or
explicit secular motive in theological discourse, and even, because of
that interest, a "sacralization" of the world, or our knowledge. See
chapter 1. I hope it is obvious that I am not taking a position on "the
origin of modernity" and mean only to introduce and motivate the
problem of a philosophical "self-grounding."

22 Hegel, while a "continuity" proponent, is not a "secularization"
    theorist because religion is not for him a basic *explicans*; it is itself a
    "representation," or a "sacralization" of essentially "secular" themes.

23 See especially Toulmin's discussion (1990). For reasons I do not under-
    stand, Toulmin thinks a "modernity crisis" in the West developed only
    very recently ("after 1945," p. 160) and especially in the last twenty
    years. The thought of Hegel, Nietzsche, and Heidegger, or the novels of
    Flaubert, or Proust, or Dostoyevsky, or the painting of Cézanne, or
    Seurat, or the poetry of Baudelaire, or Rimbaud, play no role in his
    narrative.

24 For some, like Harry Levin, the "heyday of modernism" should be
    confined to the 1918–1939 period, but, as I shall try to show, there are
    several reasons for using the term more broadly. See his "What Was
    Modernism?" in Levin (1966), pp. 271–95, and compare the defense of
    the 1870–1945 time frame in Beebe (1972). For a brief run-down on the
    various uses of the "modernist," "post-modernist" and "contemporary"
    labels, see the article by Hoffman et al. (1977) and the special issue of
    the *New German Critique* (1981). Calinescu (1977) is especially good at
    pointing out the two "faces" of modernism, that literary modernism is
    both modern and anti-modern at the same time.

25 See Yack's account of Schiller's early and non-modernist, romantic
    argument for such a thesis (1986), pp. 133–84, Eagleton's Marxist
    account of why this occurred (1990), and Vattimo's discussion in chap-
    ter 6 (1988) of the "centrality of the aesthetic in modernity" (p. 95).
    (The romantic hope for "harmony" has evaporated by the time of
    modernism's advent, to be replaced by an ideal of self-making either
    restricted to an artistic elite, or celebrated as constitutive of all experi-

ence, as in surrealism). Vattimo follows Nietzsche and Heidegger in describing this modernist phenomenon as a kind of culmination or logical extension of modernity's self-understanding. As will be apparent in a moment, my own view of the historical origin of such a "centrality" is that the situation is much more complex, and that such a centrality depends on a contemporary reading of those origins that is hardly straightforward, and raises more questions than it solves. See the discussion in chapter 5 where these issues come to a head.

26 Cf. the discussion in Spender (1963), pp. 71–2, and Calinescu's helpful discussion of the emergence of the "culture of rupture" (1977), pp. 68–92. Lionel Trilling's account in "On the Teaching of Modern Literature" makes probably the best known use of this negative element to characterize modernism, which he calls "the disenchantment of our culture with culture itself" (1961), p. 30.

27 Steiner (1971), p. 20.

28 This is, in my view, the explanation for what Irving Howe has described as modernism's ambiguity about "culture," sometimes apparently violently against "culture" (as in the later Rimbaud) at the same time that it makes a quasi-religion out of high culture, as in Joyce and Pound. See his "The Culture of Modernism," in Howe (1970), pp. 3–33. This expresses the difference between bourgeois modernity, and its radical reformulation in modernism. The interesting question is whether the latter is an extension or true transformation of the former.

29 The architecture issue is quite interesting since there, the rejection of the classical notion of perfection, or ideal form, and so the Renaissance notions of harmony and symmetry, quickly produced both the most rigorously consistent modernist art and what was and still is perceived as an in- or even anti-human formalism. Hence the dilemma: how to express this feeling of "inhuman" sterility and cold functionalism without relying on views of "the human" or of beauty whose metaphysical or religious implications are long discredited in high culture. This, of course, does not bother "popular" critics like Prince Charles, but why should it? He is, after all, a prince, not the most rigorously modern of positions. See the remarks in Schabert (1978), pp. 249–62, in Gloag (1975), pp. 309–18, and in Toulmin (1990), pp. 155–6. See also the apposite remarks by M. Berman (1988), pp. 6–7, on the gleaming, up-to-date, and in many ways, scary architecture of Brasilia.

30 As in many other cases, such formulations are familiar and easy to invoke but hard to explain. On the role of "romanticism" in Germany in "institutionalizing" the autonomy and priority of literature, in establising the "literary absolute," see the important study by Lacoue-Labarthe and Nancy (1988).

31 Cf. Howe (1970), pp. 12ff.

32 Baudelaire (1964) pp. 296–7.

33 Baudelaire (1964), p. 43.

34 Cf. M. Berman (1988), pp. 142–71, and the "Onziéme Prélude" in Lefebvre (1962), pp. 169–234, especially his remarks on the role of Baudelaire in the development of the "autoexaltation" that is modernism. For an account of the political side of Baudelaire's modernism see Clark (1982), pp. 141–77.

35 Achieving this affirmation, though, is more difficult than proposing it. De Man has argued that Baudelaire's modernism, his attempt, like Nietzsche's, to insist on the present and deny or forget the past, all immediately turns back on itself, as the artist becomes history (something that is concretely visible in Baudelaire's strange linguistic turns: *représentation du présent, mémoire du présent, ébauche finie*). And, he claims, that "inability to escape a condition that is felt to be unbearable" (i.e., history) is in fact "the distinctive character of literature" itself, and is a problem of great general significance once we realize that all historical knowledge is about literary texts "even if those texts masquerade in the guise of wars or revolutions." See "Literary Histroy and Literary Modernity" in de Man (1971), pp. 162, 165.

36 As in the famous remark by Flaubert, "I myself am Madame Bovary," quoted by Sartre in "Flaubert and *Madame Bovary*: Outline of a New Method," in Flaubert (1965), p. 302.

37 Cf. Flaubert's famous ideal, "What I deem beautiful, what I would want to do, is a book about nothing, a book without reference outside itself . . . a book that would be almost without a subject, or in which the subject would be almost invisible, if such a thing is possible" (January 16, 1852) and even "it makes no difference what one writes about" (June 25/6, 1853), quoted in Jean Rousset's "*Madame Bovary*: Flaubert's Anti-Novel" in Flaubert (1965), p. 440.

38 See especially Girard's closing chapter, (1988), pp. 290–314, and such typical remarks as: "Proust and Dostoyevsky do not define our universe by an absence of the sacred, as do the philosophers, but by the perversion and corruption of the sacred, which gradually poisons the sources of life" (p. 203). For the sake of an economical discussion, I am ignoring a number of important elements of Girard's full position, particularly his general theory of "imitation" or "mimesis," and its application to classical tragedy, ritual, and Christianity. See also Girard (1977).

39 The premise of his remarkable book is: "If the novel is the source of the greatest existential and social truth in the nineteenth century, it is because only the novel has turned its attention to the regions of existence where spiritual energy has taken refuge," Girard (1988), p. 111. His conclusion involves the claim that, to understand this "spiritual energy," we must "at last realize that Christian symbolism is universal for it alone is able to give form to the experience of the novel" (Ibid., p. 310).

Because Girard is a religious or traditionally metaphysical thinker, he is a useful target for critics more influenced by Nietzsche or Heidegger.

Girard believes in the "originary," or in "presence" and so has a different theory of the insufficiencies of all representation than do those influenced by the Heideggerean account of *aletheia*. See the interesting criticism by Philippe Lacoue-Labarthe (1989), pp. 102–38. Lacoue-Labarthe is right to note that Girard never takes on Hegel (or Heidegger) with sufficient depth, but I do not accept his Derrida and Bataille inspired conclusions about an omnipresent but non-"subjective" representing. (See p. 117.) It is Lacoue-Labarthe, not to mention Heidegger, Derrida, and Bataille, who have yet to deal with the heart of Hegel's actual (as opposed to historically transmitted) position. See the discussion in the following and concluding chapter, and Pippin (1989).

40 Much of this is anticipated in Kierkegaard's account in *The Present Age*, especially his description of "envy" as the "negative unifying principle" of modernity (1962), p. 47.

41 Girard, especially in chapter IV, seems committed to a kind of Sartrean position on the utter impossibility of, eventually, in the right social setting, a genuinely mutual recognition, a mutual affirmation of desires, with on "Masters" or "Slaves." I discuss Hegel's view of this issue in the chapter 3.

42 This combination of a revolutionary, liberating, negative spirit in modernist art, and a reductive, eventually sterile, formal, self-absorbtion – the combination in Manet of an attack on all the traditional framing conventions, and the hints of the realization that the consequence of such an attack would leave us only with paint, and the mere game of painting – is a well known dualism in modernist art criticism. The revolutionary side was represented most famously by Harold Rosenberg, and the formal, *art pour l'art* side by Clement Greenberg. The dualism appears in literature as well (say, in Adorno on modernism versus Roland Barthes), and, in the view I will defend, reflects a philosophical problem: the possibility of a self-grounding, a radical negation of the past and original instauration.

43 Olympia was, apparently, a pseudonym favored by prostitutes. See Clark's discussion (1984), p. 86, and pp. 79–146 for a thorough discussion of the painting in terms of "class."

44 This issue figures in a way the fate of the great modernist claim for the autonomy of art itself. Cf. Eagleton's concise formulation, that art became autonomous, "curiously enough, by being *integrated* into the capitalist mode of production. When art becomes a commodity, it is released from its traditional social functions within church, court and state into the anonymous freedom of the market place. Now it exists, not for any specific audience, but just for anybody with the taste to appreciate it and the money to buy it. And in so far as it exists for nothing and nobody in particular, it can be said to exist for itself. It is "independent" because it has been swallowed up by commodity production" (1990), p. 368.

45 See Clark (1984), pp. 205–58. Perhaps the greatest visual example of
    the social consequences of the modern dream of autonomy, when inter-
    preted in the bourgeois terms of individualism, prudently pursued
    pleasures, commercialized entertainment, etc., is Georges Seurat's
    magnificent *Un Dimanche après-midi à l'île de La Grande Jatte* (1884–86).
    Somehow Seurat manages to show all at once both the great
    liberation achieved in the bourgeois epoch – the possibility of fashion,
    self-expression, simple leisure itself – even as he shows the effects of
    such "liberation" – the anomie, the almost palpable "distance" between
    people, their own lack of solidity; ironically, in their expressivism, their
    conformity and lifelessness.

46 This situation is doubly ironic and brilliantly executed by Conrad since
    Marlowe is attracted to Kurz, to the jungle, the wildness at the heart
    of darkness, partly because of the sterility and deadness of the
    culture of the "whited sepulchre," attracted that is by the same things
    in the "primitive-as-authentic" mentality characteristic of much of
    modernism.

47 Cf. Schorske's remark that "modern architecture, modern music, mod-
    ern philosophy, modern science – all these define themselves not *out* of
    the past, scarcely *against* the past, but in independence of the past," that
    all "broke, more or less deliberately, their ties to the historical outlook
    central to the nineteenth century liberal culture in which they had been
    reared" (1981) pp. xvii–xviii. The same point is made at length in
    de Man's famous essay "Literary History and Literary Modernity,"
    (1971), pp. 142–65, and is expanded, through a discussion of Nietzsche,
    into an apposite account of the "contradictory way" modernity and
    history relate to each other (p. 151). For a discussion of why the desire
    for "total revolution" became so important, see Yack's study (1986).

48 This instability is also reflected in the consequences of this Baudelairean
    self-consciousness about the radically fleeting character of modern exist-
    ence. See Foucault's remarks on the "attitude of modernity" in Baude-
    laire, an "exercise in which extreme attention to what is real is
    confronted with the practice of liberty that simultaneously respects
    this reality and violates it" (Foucault (1984), p. 41). See also Rosen's
    quotations from Pascal on similar themes, in Rosen (1987), p. 19.
       The larger problem at issue is more apparent when the insistence on
    an aestheticization of existence is partly realized, when banks buy and
    hang paintings, people travel about with music all around them, watch
    drama and comedy every night, when "fashion" becomes so important,
    and so forth; or when the aestheticization of existence becomes mass
    culture or "the culture industry." (See Enzensberger's seminal essay on
    the "Industrialization of the Mind" (1974)). The problem then becomes
    distinguishing high and low art, and so an emphasis on difficulty,
    opacity, or the "silence" and inaccessibility Adorno likes in, say, Bec-
    kett. This is only a temporary "solution" however, as is apparent in

the current lack of interest in and criticism of "high modernism." See Vattimo (1988), pp. 56ff.

49 Rorty (1989), p. 100.

50 This is a problem for Nehamas's Nietzsche interpretation, too, as I argue in chapter 4.

51 Similar issues are involved in the contrast between the worlds of Combray and of Paris, (between a basically pre-modern, traditional, organic social existence, with the "church spire" at its center, and the world of the salon), and in the nationalist issues at play in the Guermantes/ Verdurin, Germany/France conflicts. See Girard (1988), pp. 193–228.

52 Put more simply, Proust's novel is a story of failed love, organized around three focal episodes, Swann and Odette, Marcel and Albertine, and Charlus and Morel. The failure of love in each case has, in some sense, to do with the failure of successful "narration," and so the failure of aesthetic "autonomy." As Sussman (1982) has shown, this can be connected to a wide variety of other "Hegelian metaphors" (general and particular, inside/outside, immediacy/mediation, etc.) and their re-appearance in literary modernism, that "the lines of force revealed in the modernist current derive from the Hegelian physics" see pp. 209, 212–30.

Notes to chapter 3

1 See especially Beiser's summary of Jacobi's hopes for Kant as an ally in the "Pantheismus" controversy, (1987), pp. 114 and 122.

2 This is not of course to imply that Kant's project was driven wholly by such transcendental concerns. Rousseau's argument that all Enlightenment appeals to the "nature of man" were always appealing to an already contingently socialized man; Rousseau's insistence that there could be no dignity or nobility apart from our own self-directed deeds, apart from what was due "to us"; and his general attack on the self-contradictory implications of the Enlightenment appeals to utility or "instrumental reason," all played important roles in Kant's case against any reliance on a metaphysics of nature, and his creation of a new "parctical" metaphysics. See the demonstration of these points by Velkley (1989), and the account in Gillespie (1984), pp. 27–33.

3 It was a criticism and a problem that was noticed and commented on almost immediately, as in Hamann's 1784 *Metakritik über den Purismus der reinen Vernunft*. See Beiser's account of Hamann in chapter 1 (1987) and of Herder in chapter 5.

4 Foucault (1984), p. 38.

5 Ibid., p. 39.

6 For two compelling accounts of the "moral" or practical origins of Kant's theoretical enterprise, see Krüger (1967) and Velkley (1989).

7   And, again, for some, this alone might seem to locate the whole broad
    issue of the origin and legitimacy of a modern attitude back again in
    "the will" or in a kind of bold resolution, and so return us to rhetoric or
    the issue of courage. See Stanley Rosen's account of "Transcendental
    Ambiguity: The Rhetoric of Enlightenments in (1987), chapter 1. Much
    of Rosen's interpretation of this problem in Kant can be summarized as
    an attempt to show that Kant's "comprehensive philosophy is equiva-
    lent to a hermeneutics of human nature," and so that "postmodernism
    is essentially Kantian," p. 24. My own view is that showing this
    connection depends on showing that and why Kant failed in his attempt
    to argue that human spontaneity, Kant's supreme principle, is realized
    as (and only as) universal law, that true spontaneity is self-legislating.
    As I shall try to show, depending on how one understands the nature of
    this failure, one ends up either with Hegel's historical and social view of
    rationality (which I favor) or with Nietzsche's *dichtende Vernunft*.
8   See my discussion of this connection in Pippin (1982).
9   As Velkley (1989), p. 20 shows, there are other, let us say "practical"
    ways in which Kant most certainly is a "Cartesian." Given that the
    ends of reason are self-legislated for Kant, that so much is now seen to
    be a result of human activity, the typical, distinctly modern (Cartesian)
    anxiety about scepticism and subjectivism could be said to be greater
    in Kant than Descartes. The task of philosophy is still a kind of
    self-reassurance and self-satisfaction, even if the means for such reassur-
    ance are no longer, I am claiming, themselves Cartesian.
10 Beck (1978), p. 30.
11 *F*, p. 80.
12 See chapter 3 of Pippin (1989).
13 This problem is connected with another, much more famous one in the
    post-Kantian tradition. Schiller again was one of the first to ask whether
    the notion of acting freely could be confined to an individual's attempt
    to obey the moral law purely for the sake of the moral law. Wouldn't I
    have to have some interest in seeing to it that the institutions within
    which I live do not impede, or somehow even "reflect" or help make
    possible such a free life? With such a question, the problem of an
    "alienation" between one's basic humanity (moral freedom) and the
    secular institutions of modernity is greatly sharpened, and the search for
    a "realization" of human freedom in modernity begins. See the useful
    discussion of the "left Kantians" by Yack (1986), pp. 89–184.
14 Kant of course, always claimed that he was not maintaining that there
    must be an opposition between duty and inclination, and that it would
    be a generally good thing if there weren't. But there need not be.
15 See the accounts of the relation between the "nihilism" issue and
    idealism in Pöggeler (1970) and Müller-Lauter (1975).
16 For a very helpful discussion of the manifold ways in which this prob-
    lem resurfaces, see Dews (1987), especially his discussion of "Derrida
    and German Idealism," pp. 19ff.

17 Cf. the following quotation from Ihab Hassan: "But the main point is this: art in process of "de-definition" as Harold Rosenberg says, is becoming, like the personality of the artist himself, an occurrence without clear boundaries: at worst a kind of social hallucination, at best an opening or inauguration" Hassan (1977), p. 57.
18 This issue, and the general picture of modern doctrines of freedom, is discussed very clearly in Taylor's "Legitimation Crisis" in Taylor (1985b), pp. 248–88.
19 See Taylor (1989).
20 For a full discussion of this issue and its role in the development of German idealism, see Henrich (1963).
21 *ET*, p. 85.
22 *FK*, p. 55.
23 *FK*, p. 56.
24 *FK*, p. 56.
25 *Diff*, p. 130.
26 See Pippin (1989). With respect to the issue of modernity, the problem has been formulated very well by Kolb, that "Hegel's criticisms of modernity involve the claim that the categories by which modern subjectivity understands itself are not ultimate in the logical sequence" (1986), pp. 49–50. For me the central category (and "logic") at issue is that of a self-determining subjectivity; Kolb concentrates mostly on the relation among the notions of universal, particular and individual in civil society; see chapter 4. Moreover, I disagree with Yack's claim (1986) that the mature Hegel somehow resigned himself to a permanent opposition between human freedom and nature in human social life, one that prevented any hope for a "longing for total revolution" characteristic of, say, Marx and Nietzsche. See pp. 185–226. It is hard to understand how such an opposition could be "sublated" in Absolute Knowledge (as Yack admits) if such a medication were not also somehow a "moment" of Objective Spirit. Spirit's permanent dissatisfactions in modernity are, in the account I am presenting, dissatisfactions with itself, not with its own finitude, or the eternal "otherness" of nature.
27 *EL*, p. 52.
28 *Diff*, p. 91.
29 This approach to Hegel obviously places a very great emphasis on Hegel's theory of sociality, an issue as relevant to his doctrine of "Absolute Knowledge" as to his more familiar discussions of morality, the state, etc. Other than Michael Theunissen (see references to his work in my 1989 Hegel book), one of the few commentators on Hegel to have discussed his account of knowledge as, in effect, a social institution, and so to have interpreted his intimidating theory of "the Absolute" in terms of social reconciliation (and to have connected his position with many of the *aporiai* of the modern social science tradition), is Gillian Rose in her original and persuasive book (1981). See especially her claims about the relation between the Kantian themes of intuition/

concept and the young Hegel's doctrine of "recognition." There is a parallel between her claim about the way the social science tradition replays so many of the original issues in Hegel's critique of Kant (structural sociology is "empty," liberal, individualist political theory is "blind, p. 214) and the claim I am making about the history of the modernity problem.

30   Rorty (1989), p. 78.

31   Ibid., p. 68.

32   Ibid., p. 6; see also pp. 9, 14, 16.

33   Ibid., p. 29.

34   Gillespie (1984) has suggested that the central question that must be posed to Hegel is whether he has defended a claim to have provided the "ground" of history, and he argues that this question should be approached in the light of Hegel's appropriation and transformation of Kant's Third Antinomy. See especially pp. 103–116. This means coming to grips with Hegel's claim that "consciousness" itself is antinomial, or in Hegel's language "dialectical" and so necessarily historical, even progressive. In the account I provide here, Hegel's "transcendental" attention to history flows much more directly from Kant's idealism, his accompanying account of spontaneity, and the paradoxes in his account of pure intuition first noticed by Fichte. This also leads to a different, less traditional reading of Hegel. I defend such views in Pippin (1989).

35   *Lec*, p. 217.

36   Cf. Rosen (1969), pp. 89–93, especially his discussion of the consequences in European philosophy of the rejection of Hegel's historical synthesis.

37   Sussman (1982) is thus right to stress with such insistence the importance of this Hegelian "trope" of the "play" of inside/outside for understanding the issues at stake in literary modernism and its philosophical implications. I have presented the issue somewhat differently, however, as concerning a self-determining idealism, and its various possible conditions, and will suggest throughout an interpretation more sympathetic to Hegel.

38   See Bubner's discussion of "norms" in his essay, "Norm and History," (1988), pp. 195–212. I disagree with his claim that Hegel, for all his attention to the historicity of such norms, attempts to rationalize such norms by "eliminating" contingency; see p. 207.

39   The presuppositions for such claims about action obviously involve a view of human activity very different from the "psychological-causal" approach so favored today. In Hegel's treatment, our own view of why are doing what we are doing (or an objective account of the neurophysiological event that causes the body movement) is not privileged and cannot tell us what we are doing. Such self-understanding must be achieved, and depends essentially on understanding the social context within which we come to understand ourselves a certain way. See the lucid account by Taylor (1985a), pp. 77–96.

40 This issue is an especially important one in the French reception of Hegel. See Butler's useful study (1987) and my review of the book, Pippin (1990d).

41 Cf. the account of "The Question of History" in the European tradition in chapter 1 of Gillespie (1984).

42 I am in agreement here with the insightful treatment of Hegel in Rose (1984). Cf. p. 3: "Hegelian and Marxist dialectic does not seek to legitimize the phantasy of historical completion with the imprimatur of supra-historical, absolute method, but focuses relentlessly on the historical production and reproduction of those illusory contraries which other systems of scientific thought naturalize, absolutize or deny. Dialectical history is multiple and complex, not as its critics would have it, unitary and simply progressive; it suspends the history of philosophy within the philosophy of history, and the philosophy of history within the history of philosophy."

43 *SL*, p. 759.

44 Bubner paints a particularly illuminating portrait of this antinomy between hermeneutical and critical thought in his essay "Philosophy is its Time Comprehended in Thought" (1988), pp. 37–62. See especially his comments (p. 52) on the centrality of Hegel in setting up these alternatives.

45 "Spuren der Vernunft," in Bubner (1984).

Notes to chapter 4

1 Itself of course a manifestation of "the will to power," the kind of simple "claim" made by Nietzsche that requires volumes of commentary and qualification, as we shall see.

2 *BGE*, #210. Cf. Hamacher's justifiable remark (1990), pp. 29–30: "It is uncertain how far Nietzsche's knowledge of Kant extended beyond the distortions of Schopenhauer and Kuno Fischer or beyond his study of the second part of the *Critique of Judgment*, which he subjected to a precise analysis in 1868, in connection with a planned dissertation to be entitled *Teleology Since Kant*."

3 For a survey and analysis of Nietzsche's views towards Kant, see Ansell-Pearson (1987), especially his contrast between Kant's critique of dogmatic metaphysics and Nietzsche's revaluation of all values, and the remarks on pp. 326, 330, and 333. I think Kant's "Christian dualism" is much less the standard version that Nietzsche works with, but there is no denying that Kant is a paradigmatically Christian philosopher. It's just that the "dualism" in question is the kind best articulated by Hegel: that between the "independence and dependence" of consciousness, or the "unhappy consciousness." See also p. 327.

4 *WP*, p. 7.

5 *WP*, p. 9.

6 *TI*, p. 95.
7 Habermas (1987), pp. 85 and 86.
8 In this and the following chapter, I shall defend the claim that Nietzsche and Heidegger failed to "break free" of modernity philosophically,
   and that the possibility of a dialectical continuation (though not completion) of modernity can be understood and partly defended by com-
   prehending this failure. I disagree, however, in two central respects with
   Habermas's version of a similar claim. First, I think his attention to
   self-referential paradoxes, typical of many attacks on relativism, is far
   too abstract to avoid the counter-charge that he is begging the very
   questions at issue. It also leads him to characterize Nietzsche's and
   Heidegger's position with little attention to how they want to say what
   they do, as if they were simply advancing positions. Secondly, I do
   not agree that Habermas's fallibilist, quasi-empirical reconstruction of
   normative presuppositions in communication is an effective counter to
   the problems he raises. See Pippin (1990c).
9 Taylor (1987), pp. 482ff.
10 Rosen (1989), p. 189.
11 Strauss (1953), p. 253.
12 MacIntyre (1984), p. 114.
13 *BGE*, p. 227.
14 "An Interview with Paul de Man," in de Man (1986), p. 121.
15 "Reading Unreadability," p. 58 in Miller (1987). I found both these
   references in Richard Rorty's lecture "On Bloom's Nietzsche," (pp. 14,
   15) published in *Nietzscheana*, no. 1 (May, 1989), by the North American
   Nietzsche Society, Urbana, Illinois.
16 *GS*, p. 308.
17 *OGM*, p. 77.
18 This epigram for the Third Essay of *OGM* is taken from "On Reading
   and Writing' in *TSZ*.
19 *WP*, p. 7.
20 *WP*, p. 9.
21 *WP*, p. 13.
22 *WP*, p. 51. See Kaufmann's note no. 45 for a complete explanation of
   the Magny reference.
23 *WP*, p. 7.
24 *TSZ*, p. 13.
25 *TSZ*, p. 17.
26 *TSZ*, p. 60.
27 *TSZ*, p. 18.
28 *TSZ*, p. 17.
29 Ibid.
30 See the use of this image in "On the Teachers of Virtue," *TSZ*, pp. 28ff,
   and the remark, "Blessed are the sleepy ones; for they shall soon drop
   off'", p. 30.

31 *TI*, p. 94.
32 *GS*, p. 304.
33 *WP*, p. 20.
34 *TI*, p. 95.
35 He does not completely neglect such affinities, especially with Spinoza. See his letter to Overbeck, July 30, 1881 in *W*, 3, pp. 117ff.
36 *BGE*, p. 115.
37 See especially, the First Essay, section 2 or *GM*, p. 26.
38 In Nietzsche's account, this "creation" of the "value" of rationality is due originally to Socrates, and his "plebeian" reaction to such things as the "tragic" view of existence embodied in Greek drama, and the crisis in Greek political life provoked by the Sophists. See Pippin (1983).
39 *BGE*, p. 30.
40 *OGM*, p. 17.
41 I shall not deal here with such claims for the 'self-devaluation' of values. See Pippin (1990a).
42 Although this raises a familiar problem, it remains an unavoidable one for the kind of line pushed, say, by Rorty. It is one thing to note the contingency or even irrelevancy of major philosophic positions; it is another to make something of that contingency, to elevate the realization of such contingency to epochal ("post-philosophical") status, and to appeal to others in support of such an "insight" into contingency.
43 *OGM*, p. 26.
44 *OGM*, p. 117. For a fuller discussion of the subtleties raised by this account of asceticism (which I am admittedly racing by to get to the larger point), see Nehamas (1985), chapter 4.
45 *OGM*, p. 117.
46 *TSZ*, pp. 137–42 ("On Redemption").
47 *TSZ*, p. 99.
48 *OGM*, pp. 149–50.
49 *OGM*, p. 150.
50 *OGM*, p. 161.
51 *BGE*, p. 21.
52 *BGE*, p. 85. See also the reference to "infinite" interpretations in *GS*, p. 336.
53 *WP*, p. 267.
54 *WP*, p. 280.
55 See Nehamas (1985), pp. 52–6 for a denial of the pragmatic reading of Nietzsche.
56 *BGE*, p. 48. See also *OGM*, p. 78.
57 *WP*, p. 290.
58 Cf. Michel Haar's discussion of these issues in Haar (1997), especially p. 15.
59 *WP*, p. 342. Cf. the discussion by Hamacher (1990) on the "promise of interpretation" in Kant and Nietzsche, especially pp. 38–43.

60   *WP*, p. 330.
61   None of which is to deny that Nietzsche's use and abuse of the notions
     of will to power and eternal recurrence are extremely complicated, or
     that there might not be much to be gained from reading such pro-
     nouncements more straightforwardly, let us say, once we distinguish
     between what Günther Abel in an imposing, huge study of these notions
     (1984), calls a *Gedanke* and a *wissenschaftliche Theorie*, p. 377.
62   Indeed, in some of Nietzsche's accounts, the former strategy results in
     much greater or more effective power, at least originally if not in the
     long run.
63   Nehamas (1985), pp. 34–7.
64   Ibid., p. 137.
65   Shapiro (1989) has recently argued that Nietzsche's own "critical narra-
     tology," his suspicion about various kinds of narratives, is compatible
     with other types of narratives Nietzsche means to affirm, narratives
     that do not assume the suspected "values." The question this raises is
     whether an open-ended or deconstructed narrative can qualify as narra-
     tive, given what we originally think a narrative is supposed to do. That
     is obviously too involved an issue to deal with in a note.
66   Nehamas (1985), p. 163.
67   Ibid., p. 227.
68   The problem here is similar to the issue of Proustean interpretation
     discussed in chapter 2.
69   *OGM*, Third Essay, #5. The context here (further fulminations against
     Wagner) might be argued to qualify these remarks, but nothing in the
     text shows that Nietzsche means his remarks to be addressed to some,
     or only contemporary artists. His remarks on poets in, say, *TSZ* are
     equally unqualified.
70   Whether Nietzsche might be understood as advancing some more soph-
     isticated, even "historical" materialism, I leave here an open question.
     See Eagleton's remarks (1990), pp. 234–61, especially about Nietzsche's
     exposing the contradiction within bourgeois society between the de-
     mands for autonomy and legality, and material occasion for such a
     contradiction, the historical condition of late bourgeois society, and
     Nietzsche's prescription; that "society should renounce such meta-
     physical pieties and live daringly, groundlessly, in the eternal truth of
     its material activity (p. 258). The last phrase introduces all the familiar
     problems.
71   Blanchot (1969), p. 244.
72   See Strong (1988c), pp. 284ff for suggestions about how to think about
     this problem, and Yack's brief rejoinder (1986), p. 352, with which I am
     in agreement.
73   Stanley Rosen, in the essay, "Poetic Reason in Nietzsche," (1989), has
     put this point in another way, one of great significance for most of his
     own work. In brief it is: "The mathematical element of Platonism

cannot be reduced to the poetical element of Nietzsche's own teaching" (or that Nietzsche's own poeticizing depends on some sort of successful, and not wholly illusory, structure and unity) and this essentially because, "A world, like an individual subject or object, is said by Nietzsche to be an illusion. But on Nietzschean grounds, a stronger statement is required: a world would seem to be impossible. An illusion of unity must itself be unified to function as an illusion, as *this* illusion" (p. 214). Part of what this means is that Nietzsche's view that nature is accessible only through or as art also means that "art is nature," (p. 221), that constant self-creation is not *itself* freely determined but a manifestation of what there is, nature, the will to power. Nietzsche, Rosen argues, vacillates between trying to provide some sort of ontological basis for his claims, and admitting there can be no such basis, that "his claims" are essentially political or rhetorical, and so quite dangerous. In a recent essay, he has stated very clearly his view of Nietzsche's esotericism, his need to attribute to himself a "quasi-divine standpoint beyond the relativity of human perspectives" (1990), p. 17. See also Rosen's compelling discussion of the need for a "rational interpretation of reason" in modernity, a way of understanding the "point to our success" in mastering nature (1969), pp. 56ff.

74 *WP*, p. 23.
75 *WP*, p. 69.
76 This is Nietzsche's advice in *BGE* to those who are "repelled" by "modern reality," p. 17.
77 And again, there is a great difference between "creating an unforgettable character," and knowing why one is bothering at all.
78 Nehamas (1985), p. 186. The claim that one can advance a literary view of Nietzschean interpretation without any commitment to a "new critical" view of organic unity (but rather a "deconstructive" or "dispersive" view) has recently been advanced by Gary Shapiro (1989). See his account of Nehamas, pp. 86–96.
79 Ibid., p. 186.
80 I pass over here another version of this issue I have discussed eleswhere, the difference between the "tragic point of view" and the Socratic. See Pippin (1983).
81 *BGE*, p. 209.
82 *OGM*, p. 26.
83 Ibid., p. 38. In general, this means that Deleuze is right to emphasize the link between *ressentiment* and philosophy, or traditional notions of justification, but wrong to think that Nietzsche's hostility to justification is so intense that he is uninterested in distinguishing his own position from those which merely "ape" it, or in arguing that only a certain, nuanced version of his affirmative stance is "justified." *TSZ* is all about such justification, especially in the relation between Zarathustra and his dwart, and between him and his disciples. Moreover, Nietzsche is quite

explicite abou this "contempt" for those who live "without questioning"
in *GS*, pp. 76–7. See Deleuze (1983), especially his sweeping claims
about Nietzsche's success in "breaking free of Kantianism," pp. 88–9.
See also Pippin (1988).

84   *BGE*, p. 201.

85   I stress again that I realize that Nietzsche very often sounds like
     Deleuze's Nietzsche, contemptuous of all issues of justification, or any
     defense of the "superiority" of the Master. I only point out that even as
     he expresses such contempt in the name of the Master he appeals to
     that contempt as justification for the Master's position and his superior-
     ity. The best general account of the tensions in Nietzsche's affirmation
     of a Master or "Overman" morality is Müller-Lauter's (1971). For a
     similar, briefer version of the problem, see Yack (1986). The best
     concise discussion of Deleuze's misreading of Nietzsche, and especially
     of his tendentious and hopelessly misinformed views of Hegel, is
     Breazeale's excellent piece (1975).

86   *OGM*, p. 39.

87   To add to the complexity, Nietzsche also takes pains to point out that,
     however laudatory, the noble type *does* "sin and blunder against real-
     ity," especially in misunderstanding those who are ruled. See *OGM*,
     37.

88   Ibid.

89   As is almost always the case with any criticism or qualification of
     something Nietzsche says, there are plenty of passages where he makes
     virtually the same criticism or qualification. In *OGM*, section II, #18
     undermining any abstract separation between active and reactive forces,
     he calls active form-creating a "self-rape," [*Selbst-Vergewaltigung*, politely
     translated by Kauffmann as "self-ravishment"] and insists on the
     dependence of the beautiful on the ugly.

90   Part of the reason for this ambiguity in Nietzsche's position is that,
     while he wants to encourage some sort of resurrection of the classical
     Master type, he fully realizes the "the conditions of our social orders
     and activities" are "utterly different from those of the ancients" and
     thus that "their pride" is "alien and impossible for us" *GS*, p. 91. His
     honesty in admitting this problem is admirable, but it has made it very
     unclear for his readers what *is* possible "for us."

91   Nietzsche himself seems to doubt it too, or at least often also balances
     his position with conflicting claims, as in his famous account of the
     social (or "communicative") nature of consciousness itself in *GS* #354.
     See Breazeale's summary of what he terms the "*rapprochement*" literature
     on the Hegel-Nietzsche relation (1975), pp. 147–52.

92   Strong (1988a).

93   Ibid., p. 162.

94   See Pippin (1989), chapter 6.

95 See Stanley Rosen's remarks at the conclusion of "Nietzsche's Revolution," (1989), p. 207. See also the discussion below of Zarathustra and irony.
96 Cf. Pippin (1988).
97 *TSZ*, p. 142.
98 *WPKM*, p. 178.

Notes to chapter 5

1 All of this, yet again, by way of introducing a difficulty, rather than demonstrating any fatal *lacuna*. Nietzsche is clearly introducing Zarathustra as a wholly different voice, legislating while beyond the usual assumptions concerning law, and what makes law possible, prophetic, and revelatory, while neither a judge nor a revolutionary. See Rose (1984), pp. 87–91. For me, this issue can only be addressed by raising the crucial problem of the deliberate pathos and irony of the work, issues which Heidegger, for example, completely misses. See Pippin (1988).

2 We reach again, in a simple formulation, a monumental issue. That this whole development has much to do with the antinomies inherent in the appeal to "law" itself has recently been argued pursuasuvely in a complex book by Gillian Rose (1984). We simply cannot *be*, at the same time, judge, witness, and clerk in the tribunal of reason; p. 87. Or: "There is heteronomy at the heart of autonomy: the *hetero-nomos* – the other, unknowable, law – is precisely the *auto nomos* – the law of the person," p. 23. On how the very posing of the Kantian question as a *quaestio quid iuris* will require a reformulation of the question as fundamentally historical, a shift from the judge of consciousness, to the judge of history, to, finally in Heidegger, "the court of the voice – of the judge, unbearable to behold, on Mount Sinai," p. 52, see chapters 3, 4, and 5.

That the issue has much to do with the "bourgeois" formulation of the notion of "law," or "order" in general, and the antinomies inherent in the bourgeois organization of production and consumption, has been argued, with respect to "aesthetic" problems, by Eagleton (1990).

3 *AWP*, p. 116.
4 Ibid., p. 134.
5 *WPKM*, p. 220.
6 *NW*, p. 107.
7 *WPKM*, p. 178.
8 *NW*, p. 54.
9 Ibid., p. 105.

10 Ibid., p. 88.

11 See *WPKN*, p. 8, and the additional comment there that "The age whose consummation unfolds in his [Nietzsche's] thought, the modern age, is a final age."

12 This double emphasis in the Nietzsche lectures, alternating between an affirmation of Nietzsche's achievement in revealing that Western metaphysics was nihilistic, and claims that Nietzsche himself did not break free of nihilism, and far from being a new sort of, or radical thinker, is in fact a kind of paradigm of the spirit of "technological" thinking, is reflected in the course of the lecture series. After the 1936 and 1937 lectures, which were generally very "pro"-Nietzsche, Heidegger, in 1939, with the series titled "The Will to Power as Knowledge," shifts tone noticeably in associating Nietzsche with modern subjectivism. See D. White (1988) pp. 110–20, for an account of how Heidegger shifts from construing Nietzsche's account of the Will to Power in terms of Master Morality, to an interpretation that associates the meaning of the expression much more closely with resentment and slavish attitudes. Since the later lectures also reflect more of an emphasis on Being as somehow independent of human decision and interpretation, this has all given rise to a good deal of speculation about the "turn" (*Kehre*) in Heidegger's thought and the role of his experience with National Socialism in this emphasis on passivity and fate. See Arendt (1978), pp. 172–85; Lacoue-Labarthe (1986), pp. 113–31; Habermas (1987), pp. 148–60.

13 Heidegger, of course, is well aware that Nietzsche presents himself as an anti-metaphysical thinker, and that, thus, Heidegger's classification will be controversial. Cf. *inter alia*, the beginning of the 1939 series in *WPKM*, p. 161.

14 A typical example of such a claim can be found in *QT*, p. 18, where Heidegger claims that "man does not have control over unconcealment itself, in which at any time the real shows itself or withdraws. The fact that the real has been showing itself in the light of Ideas ever since the time of Plato, Plato did not bring about. The thinker only responded to what addressed itself to him." See also *EN*, p. 181.

15 *NW*, p. 191.

16 *WPA*, pp. 4–5.

17 Vattimo, with his notion of a postmodern "weak thinking" (*il pensiero debole*) has done the most to emphasize and develop this aspect of Heidegger's thought. See (1988), especially the essay, "Nihilism and the Post-Modern in Philosophy," pp. 164–80.

18 For the relevant texts and secondary sources for these controversies, see Pippin (1990b).

19 *WPA* p. 4.

20 Ibid., p. 5.

21 Ibid., p. 4. To facilitate reference, I have tried to use Krell's transla-

tions of the lectures without much emendation, but there is one feature of his rendering that cannot be accepted. For reasons we shall see in a moment, it is extremely important to know when Heidegger is referring to a theory or account of the "beings" or entities, which he consistently refers to as *Seinde* (as in this passage, where the question is "Was ist das Seinde?") and when he means to refer to an account of the "meaning" or "essence" of Being, of *Sein*. This is a difficult problem (especially since, as just noted, Heidegger often refers to *das Seinde* as such, and it would be grossly inaccurate to translate that as "the entity") but an English-speaking reader needs more of an indication of Heidegger's variation in the cognates of "to be" than are provided by Krell's use of capitalization and plurals. Translating *das Seinde* as "Being" so frequently, as Krell does, makes a good deal of the text simply unintelligible.

22 Ibid., p. 3.
23 For criticisms of Heidegger's use of the notion of metaphysics in reading Nietzsche, see Magnus (1970), pp. 153, 131, and for a more qualified criticism, see Müller-Lauter (1974). One of the most interesting attacks on Heidegger's "totalistic" or unified reading of Nietzsche is Derrida's (1978a), where Derrida claims that the 'totality of Nietzsche's text, in some monstrous way, might be of the type "I have forgotten my umbrella",'(p. 133) one of the many entries in the notebooks that Heidegger ignores.
24 *NW*, p. 108.
25 *ERS*, p. 188.
26 Ibid., p. 188 (my emphasis). Clearly the implication of this passage is that avoiding this prior and distorting "determination" would be to avoid thinking of Being as an *arche*, as a principle or as intelligible by appeal to principles. As Schürmann (1987) has pointed out, in a book that develops this thought in a thoroughly Heideggerean way, this leaves us with *an-archy*, and so with a deconstruction of the dominant Western view of the theory-praxis relation.
27 See the discussion of *Entscheidung* in the first lecture of *WPKM*, pp. 3–9.
28 See the discussion in *WPKN*, pp. 28–31.
29 Admittedly this is said in a way too "Hegelian" for Heidegger's taste. He would prefer some language about the way the destiny of Being has unfolded, and would avoid talk about what we have made of ourselves. As I explain in section 4 below, I am suspicious that there is not much to be gained by this way of talking, or by the vaguely positivist references to "text" or "power" or "structure," etc., in much "postmodernism. See chapters 8 and 9 in Rose (1984).
30 *WPA*, p. 330.
31 See my discussion in the concluding section of Pippin (1983).
32 Schürmann (1987), pp. 1–21.

33 There are numerous examples in the *Nachlass* of passages that can be
   read this way. The clearest are from 1888: "all driving force is will to
   power ... there is no other physical, dynamic, or psychic force except
   this" (*WP*, #688); life itself "is merely a special case of the will to
   power" (*WP*, #692); or "the innermost essence of being is will to
   power" (*WP*, #693). The question is how Nietzsche means us to
   understand the authority of these claims, on what they are based,
   given his famous denials not just of "other worldly" but all "*true*
   worldly" metaphysics. In *BGE*, he more cautiously notes that the
   world "defined and determined according to its intelligible character is
   'will to power' and nothing else" (#36). That qualification will be
   important in answering such a question, as are his numerous claims in
   the *Nachlass*, such as those form #556–560, "that 'The origin of things
   is the work of that which imagines, thinks, wills, feels;'" that "thingness
   has been invented by us owing to the requirements of logic;" and
   especially "That things possess a constitution in themselves quite
   apart from interpretation and subjectivity, is a quite idle hypothesis."
   See Heidegger's discussion of the period 1879–91, during which
   "Nietzsche went through a period of extreme positivism," (*WPA*, p.
   154) and Heidegger's suggestions throughout these lectures that Nietzsche's "inversion" of the Platonic supersensuous in favor of the sen-
   suous is better understood by appeal to his understanding of art's
   sensuality than any epistemological appeal to sensation or sensibility.
   Later in the lecture series, Heidegger is so much more concerned with
   Nietzsche's general failure to overcome nihilism that he pays much less
   attention to the subtleties of Nietzsche's position on art.
34 See especially lectures 9 and 10 in *WPA* (pp. 54–68) for Heidegger's
   clear association of Nietzsche with the German Idealist tradition, and
   thereby his denial that Nietzsche's account of the dependence of the
   intelligibility of Being on "will" should be understood voluntaristical-
   ly, as having anything to do with decisions, or the desire for power.
35 *WPA*, pp. 34–5.
36 See especially lecture 13, "Suspicions Concerning the 'Humanization'
   of Beings," in *ERS*, pp. 98–105. The clearest discussion of this delicate
   issue ("balanced" as it were between Heidegger's criticisms of Western
   subjectivism and his own insistence on the centrality of *Dasein* in the
   "occurrence" of Being) can be found in his Kant interpretation. See
   KM, sections #36–45, and the last two-thirds of *WT*.
37 *WPA*, p. 41.
38 Ibid., p. 51.
39 Ibid., p. 61.
40 This co-dependence has recently been made much of in an excep-
   tionally clear treatment by Olafson (1987).
41 In the Nietzsche lectures, the co-originality of man and Being is
   stressed, especially in the late (1944–6) series, "Nihilism as Deter-

mined by the History of Being." There is much elusive talk there about how Being "needs" an abode, and "uses" man, and sentences like, "Being lightens as the advent of the keeping-to-itself of the refusal of its unconcealment." See *EN*, pp. 243–4.

42 *WPKM*, p. 189.

43 This is most clearly expressed in *ERS*, pp. 198–208, where Heidegger argues that "Will to power, in its essence and according to its inner possibility, is eternal recurrence of the same," (p. 203) and where he begins to suggest that because Nietzsche requires what we might call the "metaphysical perspective" on interpretation that the eternal return thought creates, he can be understood to be, as he himself once said "stamping" becoming with the "character of Being," (p. 203) and so to be still under the sway of the Western notion of presence. In other words, even the radical flux implied by the will to power must be conceived as a kind of "standing" permanent flux.

44 See the 1953 essay, "Who is Nietzsche's Zarathustra?" where the overman is said to express Nietzsche's hope for a teaching "free from revenge' against time (or for the eternal return of the same teaching) p. 228, *ERS*. Again here this hope is said to be futile, that "Zarathustra's doctrine does not bring redemption from revenge" (p. 229), again because of its origins in the will to power.

45 *WPKM*, p. 126: 'When Nietzsche rejects the concept of truth in the sense of copying adequation, and rightly so, he need not thus already reject truth in the sense of harmony with the actual. In no way does he reject this traditional ... determination of truth." See also pp. 137–49, and for the typical charge against Nietzsche, that he has still "anthropomorphized" the beings, see p. 154.

46 *WPKM*, pp. 3ff.

47 Ibid., p. 6.

48 Ibid., p. 6.

49 See Ibid., pp. 32–7; and *WN*, pp. 71–81.

50 *PDT*, p. 269.

51 *WPKM*, p. 96.

52 See Schürmann (1987) p. 7, "Presencing is one, but simply as the unity of the *formal* traits that link the epochs," (my emphasis). See also p. 13 on "the directionality of the orderings by which constellations of presencing produce themselves."

53 At bottom, Heidegger is trying to suggest that the temporality of presencing, or Being itself, is fundamentally "ecstatic," not linear, continuous or progressive. He clearly believes that learning to "think" in this ecstatic way will require enormous efforts, since all "ontic" or metaphysical thought is dominated by a conception of time as a continuous series of "now's." On the originary time sought by Heidegger, see Rose (1984), pp. 50–67. See also her summary of the temporal dimensions of Heidegger's "magical nihilism," p. 76.

54 Ibid., p. 155.
55 Ibid., p. 21. See my discussion of this remark (the last half of which in brackets is a 1961 emendation) in Pippin (1990b), note 26.
56 *EN*, pp. 96–7.
57 Ibid., p. 99.
58 Ibid., p. 110. This is perhaps the place to note that Heidegger makes extremely wide-ranging use of the notion of representation, often even in interpreting philosophers who consider themselves critics of the modern notion of representation. This is especially true of Heidegger's account of Hegel (See *HCE*, p. 39). For the (correct, I think) Hegelian response, see Chaffin (1988), pp. 85ff.
59 Ibid., p. 116.
60 Heidegger puts this in his own way by saying that "representation, which is essentially represented to itself, posits Being as represented-ness and truth as certitude. That to which everything is referred back as to an unshakeable ground is the *full essence of representation itself*, insofar as the essence of Being and truth is determined by it, as well as the essence of man, as the one representing, and the nature of the definitive standard as such." Ibid., p. 114.
61 Ibid., p. 103.
62 Ibid., p. 137.
63 Ibid., p. 148.
64 Ibid., p. 149.
65 *WPKM*, p. 174.
66 Ibid., p. 175.
67 Ibid.
68 Ibid., p. 179.
69 Ibid., p. 180.
70 *NW*, p. 95.
71 *EN*, p. 22.
72 Ibid.
73 For a summary discussion of the translation problems posed by this term, see Kolb (1986), pp. 144–6.
74 Cf. this typical passage in *T* (p. 41): "The coming to presence of Enframing is the danger. As the danger, Being turns about into the oblivion of its coming to presence, turns away from this coming to presence, and in that way simultaneously turns counter to the truth of its coming to presence."
75 See *WPKM*, p. 173 for Heidegger's formulations about the Nietzschean confusions about the "essence" of Being as "its consummate non-essence."
76 Cf. Schürmann (1987), pp. 17–8.
77 On the manifold translation problems for *Ereignis*, see Rose (1984), pp. 58–67, and Kolb's brief summary (1986), p. 159.
78 Ibid., p. 35.

79 A dangerous term, too. While it is always roughly accurate to say that Heidegger wants to revive attention to the mythic or achaic, his own re-writings of *arche* and *mythos* are so extensive as to make the characterization misleading. See, for example, the much contested criticism by Habermas (1983), p. 59.

80 Heidegger's famous "turn," his criticism of his own reliance on phenomenology as too "subjectivistic," and his increasing insistence on what has been characterized as the "passivity" of human being in relation to historical presencing, began to emerge in the 1930 *The Essence of Truth*, and was given its most accessible formulation in the *Letter on Humanism*. See Olafson (1987), pp. 161–93.

81 See the very useful Nietzschean riposte by Michel Haar (1983), pp. 86ff, and my discussion in Pippin (1990b), section V.

82 See Schürmann's discussion (1987), pp. 53–62. He argues that while Marx and Nietzsche "had a foreboding of the closure," they "did not think 'the turning'" (p. 53). Schürmann means to point to what he calls the genuine "an-archy" in the event, the end of metaphysics, not yet fully appreciated by Marx or Nietzsche, but in my view Nietzsche, at least, was simply more careful about the tensions and ambiguities.

83 Perhaps the clearest example of this yoking of Nietzsche and Heidegger together, despite Heidegger's Nietzsche lectures, is Vattimo's interpretation. See his use of the purportedly common attack on "exchange value" in both, in "an Apology for Nihilism," (1988), pp. 19–30.

84 See Apel (1973), pp. 259, 273–4. I don't agree that Heidegger reintroduces against his will *eine gegenständliche Vorstellung*, as Apel claims. The deeper problem is that Heidegger's attempt at postmodernism, is, in Lachtermann's phrase, like war viz-a-viz diplomacy, a continuation of modernity by other means," (1989), p. x. Perhaps the most famous, though now relatively discredited, version of the critique that Heidegger resurrects a pre-critical objectivism or realism is Adorno's discussion of "The Ontological Need" in chapter 1 of *Negative Dialectics*, Adorno (1973), pp. 61–96. See also (1978), pp. 70–75.

85 For the differences between Hegel on "recognition" versus Heidegger on "repetition" induced by this difference, see Rose (1984), pp. 80–1.

86 *ID*, pp. 100–01.

87 No matter how carefully Heidegger formulates his position about the "line" dividing us from or including us within, nihilism, this appeal to an epochal ending or beginning is unavoidable. See Rose's quotations and discussion, (1984), pp. 68–9.

88 I should stress here that I mean the term "positivity" in the Hegelian sense introduced in chapter 3. I am not accusing Heidegger of any naive claim to know some "fact" about "how history works." The *Ereignis* in question is precisely not a fact (a word that already carries the modern connotation of *factum*, a thing made) for consciousness. But it is appealed to as a "condition" on which all knowing and thinking

and acting are said to depend, without there being any account of how
such a condition, whatever it is, could itself be said to be known, or
thought, or glimpsed, or "heard," or, certainly, most famously, how it
might be judged.

89   Vattimo (1988), p. 12.
90   They occur mostly in *Holzwege*, *Vorträge und Aufsätze*, and *Identität und Differenz*.
91   Vattimo (1988), p. 172.
92   See especially the comments on the relation between this issue and humanism, ibid., p. 41. On the issue of hermeneutics as recollection, or Kierkegaardean repetition, see Spanos (1976), p. 462.
93   Vattimo (1988), p. 2.
94   Ibid., p. 27 (my emphasis).
95   Ibid., p. 28.
96   Schürmann (1987), p. 19.
97   Ibid., p. 41.
98   Ibid., p. 294.
99   Ibid.
100 For more on the "transcendental" issue, see Kolb (1986), pp. 172–7.
101 Eagleton has coined an interesting oxymoron to characterize post-Heideggereans who have inherited this problem (struggling against "identity thinking" or the "violence" of metaphysics, but sceptical that any "escape" from law, metaphysics, meaning, or power is possible): "libertarian pessimists" (1990), p. 387. My own view is that the problem designated by the expressions runs deeper in the very idea of a modern project than can be captured by examining its social manifestations/origins. See the last section of chapter 6 below.
102 There are various "deconstructions" of individual philosophers, para-digmatically Nietzsche, designed to show the *aporiai* and forgetfulness reached when Being's "originary" presencing is denied or obscured by the assertion of human subjectivity, but these alone cannot establish anything about any ontological condition. Nietzsche and Heidegger, for example, agree about many of the details of the failures of such projects, but disagree about whether this is because the "highest values have devalued themselves" and so require a "transvaluation," or whether it is because Being itself has been rendered a "value" in the first place. The deconstruction alone can only establish the conditions Heidegger requires by presupposing them at the outset.
103 Schürmann (1987), p. 316.
104 *EN*, p. 96.
105 Ibid., p. 89.
106 Ibid., p. 99.
107 See especially *EN*, pp. 199–250. I should also mention that this talk of the historical *Gestell* of technology, of "destiny," "fate", and so forth, is not meant to be a historical relativism, as if individuals are "locked" within some historical perspective. "Presencing" is not a "view" or

attitude or *Weltanschauung* people can be said to "have," and Heidegger frequently entertains the possibility of the modern en-framing occurring within a "larger" space to which we have some access. See *ID*, pp. 36–9, *WCT*, p. 33, and Kolb (1986), pp. 156ff. For a good general discussion of the basic "Heideggerean" response to the issue of relativism and historicism (phrased in terms of Gadamer's hermeneutics), see Hoy (1982), pp. 41–72.

108 Cf. Kolb's criticisms of Heidegger's account (1986), pp. 118–50, especially p. 140.

109 See again the account by Toulmin (1990); on this issue particularly, a useful and detailed corrective to "perennialist" or "secularization" theorists.

110 *SG*, p. 73.

111 Ibid., p. 188. See also the discussion by Schürmann, pp. 38–43.

112 Admittedly, this just scratches the surface. The basic issue between Hegel and Heidegger concerns Heidegger's charge that Hegel is the supreme philosopher or "identity," and that Heidegger alone has formulated the true "matter of thinking," "difference as difference." The Hegelian response would involve an interpretation of Hegel's central principle: "being a self" *in* another. Both charge and counter are matters for future discussion. The issues themselves come up often and are explored in depth in Rose (1984).

Notes to chapter 6

1 It is this sense that it would be *roughly* correct to say, as has so often been said, that so much of European intellectual (and perhaps concrete, social) history was and is a debate between "left" and "right" wing Hegelianism.

2 Again, admittedly, the Nietzschean point about such self-interrogation is that its authority as a question already depends on a complex historical experience and social distribution of power, the Christain or "slave" experience. I have already tried to indicate why I think that claim to be tendentious and unsatisfying.

3 I am thinking of Rorty's pragmatism here. See (1985), p. 174.

4 For many, as noted earlier, such a position is already "Habermasean." My own view is that Habermas is not anything like "Hegelian" enough for that to be true, and I defend that claim in Pippin (1990c). Habermas's attempt at an "empirically reconstructive," fallibilist methodology, used to identify the teleological presuppositions inherent in everyday communicative practices, insures, I claim, a return of the Hegelian, "historical" critique of Kant (e.g., what he identifies are not "conditions," but what we have come to regard as required in social practices), as does his restricting his own account to issues of "justice" (or procedural problems) and not the substantive issue of "the good life."

The nineteenth-century wheel is re-invented, and turns now no a linguistic, rather than a *geistige*, axis. For very interesting "Hegelian" criticisms and reconstructions of Habermas, see Honneth (1985), the sympathetic Habermasean account of post-structuralism in Dews (1987), and also the criticisms advanced by Benhabib in her (1986) book.

5 Unusual given the sketchy, often chaotic organization of the book. See Habermas's account of its composition (1987), pp. 106–7, and its "special influence upon the intellectual development of the Federal Republic of Germany."

6 Horkheimer and Adorno (1972), p. xii.

7 The original version of the claim that the "Enlightenment struggle with superstition" is itself a sectarian *religious* struggle can be found in Hegel's *PhS*, pp. 328ff. For what could be called a parallel narrative of the Enlightenment as an "inexorable journey into postmodern decadence," from which very different conclusions are drawn, see Rosen (1987), pp. 175ff, especially such claims as: "Precisely if the founders of modernity are correct and ignorance is superstition, the unleashing of passion and desire gurantees the triumph, not the conquest, of superstition. For passion and desire cannot tolerate *any* restrictions, least of all those of the intellect" (p. 181). See also his comments on Horkheimer and Adorno, p. 10.

8 See the idiosyncratic association of Kant with de Sade on "the organization of life as a whole which is deprived of any substantial goal," ibid., p. 88.

9 See especially the account in the "excursus," on "Juliette or Enlightenment Morality," Ibid., pp. 81–119.

10 Ibid., p. 4.

11 Ibid., p. 11.

12 I am agreeing here with Habermas's claim that the *Dialectic of Enlightenment* "has to oversimplify its image of modernity so astoundingly," and especially that it fails to recognize genuinely modern forms of resistance to the totalization of instrumental reason. See (1987), pp. 112–13. I do not agree, though, that the proper response to this simplification is an abstract "differentiation of validity spheres" finally realized by modernity and clarified by Habermas's "empirical reconstruction" of the various conditions of these spheres. See the discussion below, and in Pippin (1990c).

13 Hegel in other words is certainly not denying that, "all human beings are frail, mortal and needy, vulnerable to suffering and death. The fact that these transhistorical truths are always culturally specific, always variably instantiated, is no argument against their transhistoricality." Eagleton (1990), pp. 410.

14 See the discussion in Dews (1987), pp. 224–42.

15 For an economical and very useful history and appraisal, see the section

"On Postmodernism" in Calinescu's 1987 version of his book, and especially his references on p. 357 to more extensive histories. See also Hoffman et al. (1977).

16 See Calinescu, p. 267, and his reference to Jerome Mazzaro's book, *Postmodern American Poetry*, on p. 357.

17 For a finer grained account of the emergence of the postmodern idea, especially in American poetry, see Antin (1972), and for a good discussion of some of the philosophical issues at stake, see Wellmer (1985b). A fuller description would also have to account for the emergence of other forms of art at odds with and often directly directed against, the seriousness and high culture pretensions of modernist art, by the beginning of the sixties canonized in universities, museums, etc. These would include pop art, performance art, the oral poetry movement, John Cage, etc.

18 Cf. Fiedler (1971).

19 But see Antin (1972) on the 'collage' techniques of many modernists.

20 Hassan (1977), p. 55.

21 The general relation between assumptions inherent in architecture of all historical epochs and broad philosophical issues is not limited to the modernism/postmodernism controversy. The relation between the idea of self-sufficiency and architecture goes back at least to the Tower of Babel story. The best discussion known to me of that issue and its relation to contemporary discussions occurs in an article by Gillian Rose (1988).

22 Palmer (1976), pp. 413–14.

23 For a summary of "Critiques of Postmodernism," see Calinescu (1987), pp. 288–302.

24 Jameson interprets postmodernity as essentially tied to the developments of late capitalism, or as something to be accounted for, its potentials assessed, rather than appealed to or castigated. See his interview, Stephanson (1988b), pp. 3–30, and Jameson's piece, "The Politics of Theory: Ideological Positions in the Postmodernism Debate," (1988b), pp. 103–13. In general, the idea of a "postmodern politics," as in Warren's book on Nietzsche (1988) or Connolly's book (1988), or the essays in Ross (1988) has not yet, it seems to me, resolved the political antinomies created by Nietzsche's thought and discussed above in chapter 4 (roughly: no understanding of any concrete *reconciliation* with others emerges from some radical *recognition* of their otherness, and so no politics, other than war, emerges), but that is a separate issue and one I do not have the space to discuss here. For interesting criticisms, see Ansell-Pearson's (1990) and S. White (1990).

25 To mention one point I shall not have space to discuss: the self-congratulatory, potentially dogmatic language of "epochal" self-consciousness is not foreign to these discussions. See the prophetic language with which Derrida begins *Of Grammatology*, his "glimpse" of the "closure" of the "historico-metaphysical" epoch, his hope for a

"way of thinking that is faithful and attentive to the ineluctable world of the future which proclaims itself at present, beyond the closure of knowledge;" (1974), p. 4; and Foucault's chiliastic remarks at the end of *The Order of Things*, his description of the "drawing to a close" of the idea of "man," his "sensing the possibility" that in the future, man will be "erased," "like a face drawn in sand at the edge of the sea" (1970), p. 387.

26 Lyotard (1984), pp. 11–14.

27 Descombes (1980), p. 184. See also Benhabib (1984), p. 121.

28 Lyotard (1984), p. 10.

29 Rorty (1985).

30 For a number of other problems in Lyotard's account, see the critcisms by Dews in his (1986) "Introduction." See also his account in (1987), especially on the debate about "naive naturalism," pp. 132ff.

31 Such problems would be relevant to the interesting reconciliationist suggestions made by S. White (1990).

32 The same suspicions about methodological *naïveté*, the failure of Nietzsche's second innocence, etc., could be argued to be relevant to Foucault's attempt to "speak for" those marginalized and excluded by the modern notion of reason, the mad or the criminal, as his student Derrida pointed out convincingly long ago. See the "Preface" to Foucault (1975), and Derrida's "Cogito and the History of Madness," (1978b), pp. 31–63. In this case, as in all such cases, "intuitions without concepts" are still blind.

   This, to be sure, at first involves only the so-called early Foucault, but the general question at issue is the value of what Foucault later called an attempt at "eventalization," an attempt like Nietzsche's to unmask the historical contingency or "singularity" of a version of rationality or knowledge or order (Foucault (1987), p. 104), his attempt to inject "a little anxiety or uncertainty into forms of action, thought or expertise that operate unquestionably with routine self-evidence"; Rajchman (1989), p. 172. The problem is the assumption, after Kant-Hegel, that it is possible, in some quasi-empirical or methodologically innocent way, to identify *events* at all, especially as brute "singularities."

33 A claim taken up and elaborately expanded by Vattimo (1988).

34 See the essay, "Philosophy as a Kind of Writing: An Essay on Derrida" in Rorty (1982), pp. 90–109.

35 On Derrida's "strange affair with transcendental philosophy which he woos and disdains, coaxing it into and repelling it fom his embrace," see Rose's compelling chapter 8 in (1984).

36 On the difference between Derrida and Hegel on such a "formalization" see Rose (1984), pp. 147–9.

37 Norris (1987), p. 162.

38 A different but related criticism of Derrida, one that reveals the "metaphysical" or "identity thinking" tendencies in his own thought,

when viewed from Adorno's perspective, can be found in Dews (1987), pp. 38–44. Gasché (1986) has written an interpretation of Derrida that motivates his enterprise from the *aporiai* of the doctrines of reflection in the classical German tradition. In presenting his version of that tradition, however, Gasché relies heavily on an interpretation of reflection which I dispute in Pippin (1989) chapter 3.

39 Derrida (1978b), p. 263.

40 Ibid., p. 265.

41 Rose (1984), p. 162. Cf. p. 163, Derrida "produces not a reactionary or a revolutionary reading of Hegel but a naive one."

42 Many of Rose's formulations in her (1984) book counter Derrida's reading with a genuinely speculative and so not "economical" Hegel, and by revealing the poverty of Derrida's "unknowable absolute" (p. 163) when contrasted with such a subtler reading. I agree with much of what she says but would argue that Derrida's position cannot be fully countered without engaging directly this *nihil absolutum* issue.

43 Habermas (1987), p. 43. Rousseauans will no doubt be offended by such claims, but Habermas means that Hegel was the first to see that modernity *itself* was a "philosophical problem."

44 Or, in other words, there just cannot be a "neo-Aristoteleanism" in ethics without a neo-Aristotelean theory of nature, one that does far more than merely borrow modern biology's non-Aristotelean concepts of species and function. There cannot be a revival of interest in communitarianism without some acount of the metaphysical status of the claim for the priority of or even the equality of community over individual. We cannot just insist that contemporary students appeciate the Platonic theories of virtue, and the call for a "rank ordering" of human types, by hoping that modern confusions will make the picture look attractive. Of course it will look attractive. The philosophical issue comes down to dealing with the now centuries-old scepticism, criticism, and various deflationary strategies long directed against such enterprises.

45 Cf. Rosen's apposite formulation (1980), p. 219.

46 See Pippin (1989), chapter 10. As I try to suggest there, the failure of such a logic, and the many difficulties Hegel creates for himself by proposing an encyclopedic system, do not undermine many aspects of Hegelian speculation, nor do they foreclose important suggestions in Hegel's *Realphilosophie*.

47 These are the terms used in Rosen's "Hyperborean Hermeneutics," (1990), p. 1, summarizing the claims of his (1987) book.

48 See again the quotation for *SL* cited in chapter 3, n. 34, and my discussion in Pippin (1989), chapter 10.

Bibliography

Abbreviations of Primary Texts

Kant

A/B *Critique of Pure Reason*, trans. Norman Kemp Smith. New York: St Martin's Preis, 1965.

E   "An Answer to the Question: "What is Enlightenment" in *Kant's Political Writings*, ed. trans. Hans Reiss. Cambridge and Cambridge University Press, 1970, pp. 54–60.

F   *Foundations of the Metaphysics of Morals*, trans. L.W. Beck. New York: Bobbs-Merrill, 1969.

Hegel

Diff *The Difference between Fichte's and Schelling's System of Philosophy*, trans. H.S. Harris and W. Cerf. Albany: SUNY Press, 1977.

EL   *Hegel's Logic: Part One of the Encyclopedia of the Philosophical Sciences.* trans. W. Wallace. Oxford: Clarendon Press, 1975.

ET   *Early Theological Writings*, trans. T.M. Knox. Philadelphia: University of Pennsylvania Press, 1971.

FK   *Faith and Knowledge*, trans. W. Cerf and H.S. Harris. Albany: SUNY Press, 1977.

Lec   *Lectures on the History of Philosophy*, trans. E.S. Haldane and F.H. Simson, vol. III. New York: Humanities Press, 1974.

PhS *Phenomenology of Spirit*, trans. A. Miller. Oxford: Clarendon Press, 1977.

SL   *Hegel's Science of Logic*, trans. A.V. Miller. London: George Allen & Unwin, 1969.

Heidegger

AWP   "The Age of the World Picture," in *QT*, pp. 115–54.

BT   *Being and Time*, transl. J. Macquarrie and E. Robinson. New York: Harper and Row, 1962.

EN   *Nietzsche. Volume IV. Nihilism*, trans. David Krell. San Francisco: Harper and Row, 1982.

ERS   *Nietzsche. Volume II. The Eternal Recurrence of the Same*, trans. David Krell. San Francisco: Harper and Row, 1984.

HCE   *Hegel's Concept of Experience*. New York: Harper and Row, 1970.

ID   *Identity and Difference*, trans. J. Stambough. New York: Harper and Row, 1969.

IM   *An Introduction to Metaphysics*, trans. R. Mannheim. Garden City: Anchor.

KM   *Kant and the Problem of Metaphysics*, trans. James C. Churchill. Bloomington: Indiana University Press, 1968.

NW   "The Word of Nietzsche: 'God is Dead' ", in *QT*, pp. 53–112.

OL   *On the Way to Language*, trans. P. Hertz. New York: Harper and Row, 1971.

PDT   "Plato's Doctrine of Truth," trans. J. Barlow, in *Philosophy in the Twentieth Century*, ed. W. Barrett and H. Aiken, vol. III, pp. 251–70.

QT   *The Question Concerning technology and Other Essays*. New York: Harper and Row, 1977.

SG   *Der Satz Vom Grund*. Pfullingen: Neske, 1957.

T   "The Turning," in *QT*, pp. 36–49.

WCT   *What is Called Thinking*, trans. F. Wieck and J. Glen Gray. New York: Harper and Row, 1968.

WPA   *Nietzsche. Volume I. The Will to Power as Art*, trans. David Krell. San Francisco: Harper and Row, 1979.

WPKM   *Nietzsche. Volume III. The Will to Power as Knowledge and Metaphysics*, trans. David Krell. San Francisco: Harper and Row, 1987.

WT   *What is a Thing?* trans. W.B. Barton, Jr., and Vera Deutsch. South Bend: Regnery, 1967.

Nietzsche

AC   *The Anti-Christ*, trans. R.J. Hollingdale. Baltimore: Penguin, 1968.

AD   *On the Advantage and Disadvantage of History for Life*, trans. Peter Preuss. Indianapolis: Hackett, 1980.

BGE   *Beyond Good and Evil*, trans. Walter Kaufmann. New York: Vintage, 1966.

BT   *The Birth of Tragedy*, trans. W. Kaufmann. New York: Modern Lib-
        rary, 1968.
D   *Daybreak*, trans. R.J. Hollingdale. Cambridge: Cambridge University
        Press, 1982.
GS   *The Gay Science*, trans. Walter Kaufmann. New York: Vintage, 1974.
OGM   *On the Genealogy of Morals*, trans. Walter Kaufmann and R.J. Holling-
        dale. New York: Vintage, 1969.
TI   *Twilight of the Idols*, trans. R.J. Hollingdale. Baltimore: Penguin,
        1968.
TSZ   *Thus Spoke Zarathustra*, trans. Walter Kaufmann. New York: Viking,
        1966.
W   *Werke in qrei Bänden*, ed. K. Schlechta. Munich: Carl Hanser, 1966.
WP   *The Will to Power*, trans. Walter Kaufmann. New York: Vintage,
        1967.

                                *   *   *

Aaron, P. (1968) *Progress and Disillusion: The Dialectics of Modern Society*. New
    York: Praeger.
Abel, G. (1984) *Nietzsche: Die Dynamik der Willen zur Macht and die ewige
    Wiederkehr*. Berlin: de Gruyter.
Adorno, T. (1973) *Negative Dialectics*, trans. E.B. Ashton. London: Routledge
    & Kegan Paul.
Allison, D., ed. (1977) *The New Nietzsche*. New York: Delta.
Ansell-Pearson, K. (1987) "Nietzsche's Overcoming of Kant and Metaphy-
    sics: From Tragedy to Nihilism," *Nietzsche-Studien*, 16, pp. 310–39.
    (1990) "Nietzsche: a Radical Challenge to Political Theory?" *Radical
    Philosophy*, 54, pp. 10–18.
Antin, D. (1972) "Modernism and Postmodernism: Approaching the Present
    in American Poetry," *boundary 2*, pp. 98–146.
Apel, K.-O. (1973) *Transformation der Philosophie*. Bd. I. Frankfurt: Suhrkamp.
Arac, J., ed. (1986) *Postmodernism and Politics*. Minneapolis: University of
    Minnesota Press.
Arendt, H. (1958) *The Human Condition*. Chicago: University of Chicago
    Press.
    (1978) *The Life of the Mind*. San Diego: Harcourt, Brace, Jovanovich.
Baudelaire, P.C. (1964) *Baudelaire as a Literary Critic: Selected Essays*, introd.
    and trans. by Lois Boe Hyslop and Francis E. Hyslop, Jr. University Park,
    Pa.: Penn State Press.
Baynes, K. et al., eds. (1987) *After Philosophy: End or Transformation*. Cam-
    bridge, Mass.: MIT Press.
Beck, L. (1978) "Towards a Meta-Critique of Pure Reason" in *Essays on
    Kant and Hume*. New Haven, Yale University Press.

Beebe, M. (1972) "*Ulysses* and the Age of Modernism," *James Joyce Quarterly*, 10, pp. 172–88.

Beiser, F. (1987) *The Fate of Reason: German Philosophy from Kant to Fichte*. Cambridge, Mass.: Harvard University Press.

Benhabib, S. (1984) "Epistemologies of Postmodernism: A Rejoinder to Jean-Francois Lyotard," *New German Critique*, no. 33, pp. 103–26.

(1986) *Critique, Norm, and Utopia*. New York: Columbia University Press.

Berger, P. (1977) *Facing up to Modernity*. New York, Basic Books.

Berger, P., Berger, B., and Kellner, H. (1974) *The Homeless Mind*. New York: Vintage Books.

Berman, M. (1988) *All That is Solid Melts in the Air: The Experience of Modernity*. New York: Penguin Books.

Berman, R. (1989) *Modern Culture and Critical Theory: Art, Politics, and the Legacy of the Frankfurt School*. Madison: University of Wisconsin Press.

Bernstein, J. (1984) *The Philosophy of the Novel: Lukacs, Marxism and the Dialectic of Form*. Minneapolis, University of Minnesota Press.

Bernstein, R., ed. (1985) *Habermas and Modernity*. Cambridge, Mass.: MIT Press.

Blanchot, M. (1969) *L'entretien infini*. Paris, Gallimard.

Blumenberg, H. (1983) *The Legitimacy of the Modern Age*, trans. Robert Wallace. Cambridge, Mass.: MIT Press.

Breazeale, D. (1975) "The Hegel-Nietzsche Problem," *Nietzsche-Studien*, 4, pp. 146–64.

Bubner, R. (1984) "Rationalität, Lebensform, und Geschichte," in Schnädelbach (1984), pp. 198–217.

(1988) *Essays in Hermeneutics and Critical Theory*, trans. E. Matthews. New York: Columbia University Press.

Butler, J. (1987) *Subjects of Desire: Hegelian Reflections in Twentieth Century France*. New York: Columbia University Press.

Calinescu, M. (1977) *Faces of Modernity: Avant-Garde, Decadence, Kitsch*. Bloomington: Indiana University Press.

(1987) *Five Faces of Modernity: Modernism, Avant-Garde, Decadence, Kitsch, Postmodernism*. Second edition of (1977), with new concluding chapter on Postmodernism. Bloomington: Indiana University Press.

Chaffin, D. (1988) "Hegelian Dialectic and the Limits of Representation," in Silverman and Welton (1988), pp. 85–95.

Clark, T. (1973) *The Absolute Bourgeois: Artists and Politics in France, 1848–1851*. Princeton: Princeton University Press.

(1982) *Image of the People: Gustave Courbet and the 1848 Revolution*. Princeton: Princeton University Press.

(1984) *The Painting of Modern Life: Paris in the Art of Monet and his Followers*. Princeton: Princeton University Press.

Connolly, W. (1988) *Political Theory and Modernity*. Oxford: Basil Blackwell.

Curtius, E.R. (1963) *European Literature and the Latin Middle Ages*, trans. W.R. Trask. New York: Harper and Row.

Deleuze, G. (1977) "Nomad Thought," in Allison (1977), pp. 142–9.
    (1983) *Nietzsche and Philosophy*, trans. H. Tomlinson. New York: Columbia University Press.
de Man, P. (1971) *Blindness and Insight: Essays in the Rhetoric of Contemporary Criticism*. Minneapolis, University of Minnesota Press.
    (1986) *The Resistance to Theory*. Minneapolis: University of Minnesota Press.
de Rougement, D. (1957) *Man's Western Quest*, trans. Montgomery Belgion. New York: Harper.
Derrida, J. (1974) *Of Grammatology*, trans. G. Spivak. Baltimore: Johns Hopkins Press.
    (1978a) *Spurs: Nietzsche's Styles*, trans. B Harlow. Chicago: University of Chicago Press.
    (1978b) *Writing and Difference*, trans. A. Bass. Chicago: University of Chicago Press.
    (1983) *Margins of Philosophy*, trans. A. Bass. Chicago: University of Chicago Press.
Descombes, V. (1980) *Modern French Philosophy*, trans. L. Scott-Fox and J.M. Harding. Cambridge: Cambridge University Press.
Dews, P., ed. (1986) *Habermas: Autonomy and Solidarity. Interviews with Jürgen Habermas*. London, Verso.
    (1987) *Logics of Disintegration: Post-Structuralist Thought and the Claims of Critical Theory*. London: Verso.
Eagleton, Terry. (1990) *The Ideology of the Aesthetic*. Oxford, Basil Blackwell.
Eco, U. (1985) "Innovation and Repetition: Between Modern and Postmodern Aesthetics," *Daedalus*, 114, pp. 161–84.
Enzensberger, H.M. (1974) *The Consciousness Industry*. New York: Seabury.
    (1982) *Politische Brosamen*. Frankfurt: Suhrkamp.
Feenberg, A. (1986) *Lukacs, Marx and the Sources of Critical Theory*. Oxford, Oxford University Press.
Fiedler, L. (1971) *The Collected Essays of Leslie Fiedler*. New York: Stein and Day.
Flaubert, G. (1965) *Madame Bovary*, ed. and trans. Paul de Man. Norton Critical Edition. New York: Norton.
Foster, H., ed. (1983) *The Anti-Aesthetic: Essays on Post-Modern Culture*. Port Townsend, May Press.
    (1984) "(Post) Modern Polemics," *New German Critique*, no. 33, pp. 67–78.
Foucault, M. (1970) *The Order of Things*. New York: Vintage.
    (1973) *Madness and Civilization*. New York: Vintage.
    (1984) *The Foucault Reader*, ed. Paul Rabinow. Pantheon: New York.
    (1987) "Questions of Method: An Interview with Michel Foucault," in Baynes, et al. (1987), pp. 100–24.

Fraser, N. (1984) "The French Derrideans: Politicizing Deconstruction or Deconstructing Politics," *New German Critique*, no. 33, pp. 127–54.

Funkenstein, A. (1986) *Theology and the Scientific Imagination from the Middle Ages to the Seventeenth Century*. Princeton: Princeton University Press.

Gasché, R. (1986) *The Tain of the Mirror: Derrida and the Philosophy of Reflection*. Cambridge, Mass.: Harvard University Press.

(1988) "Postmodernism and Rationality," *Journal of Philosophy*, 85, pp. 528–38.

Gehlen, A. (1957) *Man in the Age of Technology*, trans. P. Lipscomb. New York: Columbia University Press.

(1967) "Die Säkularisierung des Fortschrittess," in *Einblicke*, Bd. VII, ed. K. Rehberg. Frankfurt: Klostermann, 1978.

Gillespie, M. (1984) *Hegel, Heidegger, and the Ground of History*. Chicago: University of Chicago Press.

Girard, R. (1977) *Violence and the Sacred*, trans. Patrick Gregory. Baltimore: Johns Hopkins University Press.

(1988) *Deceit, Desire and the Novel: Self and Other in Literary Structure*, trans. Yvonne Freccero. Baltimore: Johns Hopkins University Press.

Gloag, J. (1975) *The Architectural Interpretation of History*. London: Adam and Charles Black.

Gössman, E. (1974) *Antiqui und Moderni im Mittelalter: Eine geschichtliche Standortbestimmung*. Munich: F. Schoningh.

Haar, M. (1977) "Nietzsche and Metaphysical Language,' in Allison (1977), pp. 5–36.

(1983) "La Critique nietzschéenne de la subjectivité," *Nietzsche-Studien*, 12, pp. 80–110.

Habermas, J. (1981) "Modernity versus Postmodernity," *New German Critique*, no. 22, pp. 3–14.

(1982) "A Reply to My Critics," in Thompson and Held (1982), pp. 219–83.

(1983) *Philosophical-Political Profiles*, trans. F. Lawrence. Cambridge, Mass.: MIT Press.

(1984a) "The French Path to Postmodernity," *New German Critique*, no. 33, pp. 79–102.

(1984b) *The Theory of Communicative Action. Volume One. Reason and Rationalization of Society*, trans. T. McCarthy. Boston: Beacon Press.

(1984c) Über Moralität und Sittlichkeit. Was macht eine Lebensform "rational"? in Schnädelbach (1984), pp. 218–35.

(1985) "Questions and Counterquestions," in Bernstein (1985), pp. 192–216.

(1987) *The Philosophical Discourse of Modernity*, trans. F. Lawrence. Cambridge, Mass.: MIT Press.

Hamacher, W. (1990) "The Promise of Interpretation: Reflections on the Hermeneutical Imperative in Kant and Nietzsche," in Rickels (1990), pp. 19–47.

Hassan, I. (1977) "The Critic as Innovator: The Tutzing Statement in X Frames," *Amerikastudien*, 22, no. 1.

(1982) *The Dismemberment of Orpheus: Toward a Postmodern Literature.* Madison, University of Wisconsin Press.

Hazard, P. (1953) *The European Mind (1680–1715)*, trans. J. Lewis May. London: Hollis and Carter.

Held, D. (1980) *Introduction to Critical Theory: Horkheimer to Habermas.* Berkeley: University of California Press.

and Thompson, J. (1982) *Habermas: Critical Debates.* Cambridge, Mass.: MIT Press.

Henrich, D. (1963) "Das Problem der Grundlegung der Ethik und im spekulativen Idealismus," in Engelhardt, P., ed., *Sein und Ethos*, pp. 350–86. Mainz: Matthias-Grünewald.

Hoffman, G., Hornung, A., and Kunow, R. (1977) "Modern," "Post-Modern," and "Contemporary" as Criteria for the Analysis of 20th Century Literature." *Amerikastudien*, 1, pp. 19–46.

Honneth, A. (1985) *Kritik der Macht: Reflexionsstufen einer kritischen Gesellschaftstheorie.* Frankfurt: Suhrkamp.

Horkheimer, M., and Adorno, T. (1972) *The Dialectic of Enlightenment.* New York: Seabury.

Howe, I. (1970) *Decline of the New.* New York: Harcourt, Brace, and World.

Hoy, D. (1976) "The Owl and the Poet: Heidegger's Critique of Hegel," in *boundary 2*, IV, pp. 393–410.

(1982) *The Critical Circle: Literature, History, and Philosophical Hermeneutics.* Berkeley: University of California Press.

Huyssen, A. (1984) "Mapping the Postmodern," *New German Critique*, no. 33, pp. 5–52.

(1986) *After the Great Divide: Modernism, Mass Culture, Postmodernism.* Bloomingtom: Indiana University Press.

Hyppolite, J. (1969) *Studies on Marx and Hegel*, trans. J. O'Neill. New York: Basic Books.

Jameson, F. (1979) *Fables of Aggression: Wyndham Lewis, the Modernist as Fascist*, Berkeley: University of California Press.

(1984) "The Politics of Theory," *New German Critique*, no. 33, pp. 53–66.

(1988a) "Beyond the Cave: Demystifying the Ideology of Modernism," in Jameson (1988c), pp. 115–32.

(1988b) "The Politics of Theory: Ideological Positions in the Postmodernism Debate," in Jameson (1988c), pp. 133–47.

(1988c) *The Ideologies of Theory. Volume Two: Syntax of History.* Minneapolis: University of Minnesota Press.

Jauss, H.-R. (1964) "Introduction" to Charles Perrault *Parallèle des anciens et des modernes en ce qui regarde les arts et les sciences.* Munich: Eidos.

(1965) "Literarische Tradition und gegenwärtiges Bewusstsein der Modernität," in Steffen (1965), pp. 150–97.

Jay, M. (1984) *Marxism and Totality: The Adventures of a Concept from Lukacs to Habermas*. Berkeley: University of California Press.
    (1988) *Fin de Siècle Socialism and Other Essays*. New York: Routledge.
Jencks, C. (1986) *What is Post-Modernism?* New York: St Martin's.
John of Salsibury (1971) *The Metalogicon*, trans. with introduction and notes by Daniel D. McGary. Gloucester, Mass.: Peter Smith.
Kellner, D. (1989) *Critical Theory, Marxism and Modernity*. Baltimore: Johns Hopkins University Press.
Kierkegaard, S. (1962) *The Present Age*, trans. A. Dru. New York: Harper and Row.
Kockelmans, J. (1984) *On the Truth of Being: Reflections on Heidegger's Later Philosophy*. Bloomingtom: Indiana University Press.
Kolb, D. (1986) *The Critique of Pure Modernity: Hegel, Heidegger and After*. Chicago: University of Chicago Press.
Krüger, G. (1967) *Philosophie und Moral in der kantischen Kritik*. Second edition. Tübingen: J.C.B. Mohr.
Lachtermann, D. (1989) *The Ethics of Geometry: A Genealogy of Modernity*. London: Routledge.
Lacoue-Labarthe, P. (1986) *L'imitation des modernes*. Paris: Galileé.
    and Nancy, Jean-Luc. (1988) *The Literary Absolute: The Theory of Literature in German Romanticism*, trans. P. Barnard and C. Lester. Albany: SUNY Press.
    (1989) *Typography. Mimesis, Philosophy, Politics*, ed. Christopher Fynsk. Cambridge, Mass.: Harvard University Press.
Lefebvre, H. (1962) *Introduction à la Modernité*. Paris: Editions de Minuit.
Levin, Harry. (1966) *Refractions: Essays in Compartive Literature*. New York: Oxford University Press.
Löwith, K. (1966) "The Historical Background of European Nihilism," in *Nature, History and Existentialism*. Evanston: Northwestern University Press.
    (1970) *Meaning in History*. Chicago: University of Chicago Press.
Lyotard, J.-F. (1984) *The Post-Modern Condition: A Report on Knowledge*, trans. G. Bennington and B. Massumi. Minneapolis, University of Minnesota Press.
    (1986) *Le postmoderne expliqué aux enfants*. Paris: Editions Galilée.
McCormick, P. (1976) *Heidegger and the Language of the World*. Ottawa: University of Ottawa Press.
MacIntyre, A. (1984) *After Virtue*. Notre Dame: University of Notre Dame Press.
Magnus, B. (1970) *Heidegger's Meta-History of Philosophy: Amor Fati, Being and Truth*. The Hague: Nijhoff.
Megill, A. (1985) *Prophets of Extremity: Nietzsche, Heidegger, Foucault, Derrida*. Berkeley: University of California Press.
Miller, J.H. (1975) "Deconstructing the Deconstructers," *Diacritics*, 5, pp. 24–31.
    (1987) *The Ethics of Reading*. New York: Columbia University Press.

Müller-Lauter, W. (1971) *Nietzsche: seine Philosophe der Gegensätze und die Gegensätze seiner Philosophie.* Berlin: De Gruyter.

(1974) "Nietzsches Lehre vom Willen zur Macht," *Nietzsche-Studien,* Bd 3, pp. 1–60.

(1975) "Nihilismus als Konsequenz des Idealismus: F.H. Jacobi's Kritik an der Transzendental-philosophie und ihre philosophiegeschichtlichen Folge," in *Denken im Schatten des Nihilismus,* ed. A. Schwan, pp. 113–63. Darmstadt: Wissenscahftliche Buchgesellshaft.

Nancy, J.-L. and Lacoue-Labarthe, P. (1988) *The Literary Absolute: The Theory of Literature in German Romanticism,* trans. P. Barnard and C. Lester. Albany: SUNY Press.

Nehamas, A. (1985) *Nietzsche: Life as Literature.* Cambridge, Mass.: Harvard University Press.

Norris, C. (1987) *Derrida.* Cambridge, Mass.: Harvard University Press.

Olafson, F. (1987) *Heidegger and the Philosophy of Mind.* New Haven: Yale University Press.

Palmer, R. (1976) "The Postmodernity of Heidegger," *boundary 2,* IV, pp. 411–88.

Pippin, R. (1982) *Kant's Theory of Form: An Essay on the Critique of Pure Reason.* New Haven: Yale University Press.

(1983) "Nietzsche and the Origin of the Idea of Modernism," *Inquiry,* 26, pp. 151–80.

(1987a) "Kant on the Spontaneity of Mind," *Canadian Journal of Philosophy,* 17, pp. 449–76.

(1987b) "Blumenberg and the Modernity Problem," *Review of Metaphysics,* 40, pp. 535–57.

(1988) "Irony and Affirmation in Nietzsche's *Thus Spoke Zarathustra* in *Nietzsche's New Seas,*" ed. M. Gillespie and Tracy Strong, pp. 45–71. Chicago: University of Chicago Press.

(1989) *Hegel's Idealism: The Satisfactions of Self-Consciousness.* New York: Cambridge University Press.

(1990a) "Nietzsche's Farewell: Modernity, Pre-Modernity, Post-Modernity," in *Nietzsche,* ed. B. Magnus. New York: Cambridge University Press, (forthcoming).

(1990b) "Nietzsche, Heidegger, and the Metaphysics of Modernity," in *Nietzsche and Modern German Thought,* ed. Keith Ansell Pearson. New York: Routledge, (forthcoming).

(1990c) "Hegel, Habermas, and Modernism," *Monist* (forthcoming).

(1990d) Review of Judith Butler, *Subjects of Desire. Philosophical Review,* XCIX. pp. 129–31.

Pöggeler, O. (1970) "Hegel und die Anfänge der Nihilismus-Diskussion," *Man and World,* 3, pp. 143–99.

Rajchman, J. (1989) "Habermas's Complaint," *New German Critique,* pp. 46–8.

Raulet, G. (1984) "From Modernity as One-Way Street to Postmodernity as Dead End," *New German Critique,* no. 33, pp. 155–78.

Rickels, L., ed. (1990) *Looking after Nietzsche*. Albany: SUNY Press.
Rorty, R. (1982) *Consequences of Pragmatism*. Minneapolis: University of Minnesota Press.
    (1985) "Habermas and Lyotard on Postmodernity," in Bernstein (1985), pp. 161–75.
    (1987) "Posties," *London Review of Books*, 3 September, pp. 11–13.
    (1989) *Contingency, Irony, and Solidarity*. Cambridge: Cambridge University Press.
Rose, G. (1978) *The Melancholy Science: An Introduction to the Thought of Theolon W. Adorno*. New York: Columbia University Press.
    (1981) *Hegel Contra Sociology*. London: Athlone.
    (1984) *Dialectic of Nihilism*. Oxford: Basil Blackwell.
    (1988) "Architecture to Philosophy – The Postmodern Complicity." Unpublished manuscript.
Rosen, S. (1969) *Nihilism*. New Haven: Yale University Press.
    (1974) *G.W.F. Hegel: An Introduction to the Science of Wisdom*. New Haven: Yale University Press.
    (1980) *The Limits of Analysis*. New York: Basic Books.
    (1987) *Hermeneutics as Politics*. Oxford: Oxford University Press.
    (1988) *The Quarrel between Philosophy and Poetry*. New York: Routledge.
    (1989) *The Ancients and the Moderns*. New Haven: Yale University Press.
    (1990) "Hyperborean Hermeneutics." Unpublished manuscript.
Rosenberg, H. (1959) *The Traditon of the New*. New York: Horizon Press.
Ross, A., ed. (1988) *Universal Abandon? The Politics of Postmodernism*. Minneapolis: University of Minnesota Press.
Schabert, T. (1978) *Gewalt und Humanität: Ueber philosophische und politische Manifestationen von Modernität*. Munich: Karl Alber.
Schnädelbach, H., ed. (1984) *Rationalität: Philosophische Beiträge*. Frankfurt: Suhrkamp.
Schorske, C. (1981) *Fin-de-Siècle Vienna: Politics and Culture*. New York: Random House.
Schürmann, R. (1979) "Anti-Hummanism: Reflections on the Turn Towards the Post-Modern Epoch," in *Man and World*, 12, pp. 160–77.
    (1987) *Heidegger on Being and Acting: From Principles to Anarchy*, trans. Christine-Marie Gros and the author. Bloomington: Indiana University Press.
Schwartz, S. (1985) *The Matrix of Modernism: Pound, Eliot and Early Twentieth Century Thought*. Princeton: Princeton University Press.
Shapiro, G. (1989) *Nietzschean Narratives*. Bloomington: Indiana University Press.
Silverman, H. and Welton, D. (1988) *Postmodernism and Continental Philosophy*. Albany: SUNY Press.
Spanos, W. (1976) "Heidegger, Kierkegaard, and the Hermeneutic Circle: Towards a Postmodern Theory of Interpretation as Dis-closure," *boundary 2*, 4, pp. 455–88.
Spender, S. (1963) *The Struggle of the Modern*. London: Hamilton.

Steffen, H. ed. (1965) *Aspekte der Modernität.* Göttingen: Vandenhoeck and Ruprecht.
Steiner, G. (1971) *In Bluebeard's Castle: Some Notes Towards the Redefinition of Culture.* New Haven: Yale University Press.
Stephanson, A. (1988) "Regarding Postmodernism: A Conversation with Frederic Jameson," in Ross (1988), pp. 3–30.
Strauss, L. (1953) *Natural Right and History.* Chicago: University of Chicago Press.
Strong, T. and Gillespie, M. (1988a) *Nietzsche's New Seas: Explorations in Philosophy, Aesthetics and Politics.* Chicago: University of Chicago Press.
Strong, T. (1988b) "Nietzsche's Political Aesthetics," in Strong and Gillespie (1988a), pp. 153–74.
 (1988c) *Friederich Nietzsche and the Politics of Transfiguration.* Expanded version. Berkeley: University of California Press.
Sussman, H. (1982) *The Hegelian Aftermath: Readings in Hegel, Kierkegaard, Freud, Proust and James.* Baltimore: Johns Hopkins University Press.
Taylor, C. (1985a) *Human Agency and Language. Philosophical Papers, Volume One.* Cambridge: Cambridge University Press.
 (1985b) *Philosophy and the Human Sciences. Philosophical Papers, Volume Two.* Cambridge: Cambridge University Press.
 (1987) "Overcoming Epistemology," in Baynes, et al. (1987), pp. 464–88.
 (1989) *Sources of the Self.* Cambridge, Mass.: Harvard University Press.
Thompson, J., and Held, D. (1982) *Habermas: Critical Debates.* Cambridge, Mass.: MIT Press.
Toulmin, S. (1990) *Cosmopolis: The Hidden Agenda of Modernity.* New York: Free Press.
Trilling, L. (1961) *Beyond Culture.* New York: Viking Press.
Vattimo, G. (1988) *The End of Modernity: Nihilism and Hermeneutics in Post-modern Culture,* trans. Jon R. Snyder. Baltimore: Johns Hopkins University Press.
Velkley, R. (1989) *Freedom and the End of Reason: On the Moral Foundations of Kant's Critical Philosophy.* Chicago: University of Chicago Press.
Warren, M. (1988) *Nietzsche and Political Thought.* Cambridge, Mass.: MIT Press.
Weber, M. (1930) *The Protestant Ethic and the Sprit of Capitalism,* trans. Talcott Parsons. New York, Scribver's.
Weinberger, J. (1985) *Science, Faith and Politics. Francis Bacon and the Utopian Roots of the Modern Age. A Commentary on Bacon's "Advancement of Learning."* Ithaca: Cornell University Press.
Wellmer, A. (1985a) "On the Dialectic of Modernism and Postmodernism," *Praxis International,* 4, pp. 337–61.
 (1985b) *Zur Dialektik von Moderne und Postmoderne.* Frankfurt: Suhrkamp.
White, D. (1988) "Heidegger on Nietzsche: The Question of Value," in Silverman and Welton (1988), pp. 110–20.

White, H. (1973) *Metahistory: The Historical Imagination in Nineteenth Century Europe*. Baltimore: Johns Hopkins Press.

White, S. (1990) "Heidegger and the Difficulties of a Postmodern Ethics and Politics," *Political Theory*, 18, pp. 80–103.

Yack, B. (1986) *The Longing for Total Revolution: Philosophical Sources of Social Discontent from Rousseau to Marx and Nietzsche*. Princeton: Princeton University Press.

Index